# Decoding Your Cat

# Decoding Your Cat

THE ULTIMATE EXPERTS
EXPLAIN COMMON CAT BEHAVIORS
AND REVEAL HOW TO PREVENT
OR CHANGE UNWANTED ONES

*American College of Veterinary Behaviorists*
Edited by

## Meghan E. Herron, DVM, DACVB,

## Debra F. Horwitz, DVM, DACVB, and

## Carlo Siracusa, DVM, PhD, DACVB, DECAWBM

Introduction by STEVE DALE

HARVEST
*An Imprint of* WILLIAM MORROW

BOSTON   NEW YORK

www.harpercollins.com

*Library of Congress Cataloging-in-Publication Data*
Names: Herron, Meghan E., editor.
Title: Decoding your cat : the ultimate experts explain common cat behaviors and reveal how to prevent or change unwanted ones / edited by Meghan E. Herron, DVM, DACVB, Debra F. Horwitz, DVM, DACVB, and Carlo Siracusa, DVM, PhD, DACVB, DECAWBM ; introduction by Steve Dale.
Description: Boston : HarperCollins Publishers, 2020. | Includes index.
Identifiers: LCCN 2019038031 (print) | LCCN 2019038032 (ebook) |
ISBN 9781328489906 (hardcover) | ISBN 9780358310273 | ISBN 9780358310358 |
ISBN 9781328489852 (ebook) | ISBN 9780358566045 (pbk.)
Subjects: LCSH: Cats—Behavior. | Cats—Training.
Classification: LCC SF446.5 .D43 2020 (print) | LCC SF446.5 (ebook) | DDC 636.8/0835—dc23
LC record available at https://lccn.loc.gov/2019038031
LC ebook record available at https://lccn.loc.gov/2019038032

Printed in the United States of America
22 23 24 25 26 LBC 8 7 6 5 4

AUTHORS' NOTE: We, the editors and authors, believe that cats are sentient beings and should not be referred to as "it." In anecdotes about specific cats, we use whatever gender pronoun applies. When talking about cats in general, we alternate between "she" and "he" (the same pronoun throughout the entire chapter), because we believe cats have a special place in all our hearts and minds.

In order to highlight members of the American College of Veterinary Behaviorists as the collective author of this book we have listed "DACVB" behind their names when mentioned in the text.

We dedicate *Decoding Your Cat* to Dr. Bonnie Beaver, a founding member of the American College of Veterinary Behaviorists (ACVB) and its executive director for over twenty-five years. An accomplished author and educator, she wrote one of the most foundational books on feline behavior, *Feline Behavior: A Guide for Veterinarians*. Additionally, she served decades as faculty in Behavioral Medicine at Texas A&M's College of Veterinary Medicine and Biomedical Sciences. She is a pioneer in the veterinary behavior world as well as in the veterinary profession in general. We owe her a great debt of gratitude for her leadership and guidance as the ACVB grew from the eight original founding members to nearly one hundred today. Her vision and accomplishments inspire all of us.

# CONTENTS

# FOREWORD

The problem with cat behavior is that it's hilarious. But it's more serious than it sounds.

Let me give you a hypothetical example. (Okay, okay! I admit it! It's not hypothetical. It's happened to me on multiple occasions.) My family and I go on vacation, leaving our cats, Lucy and Squeezie, in the care of a pet-sitter. When we return, Lucy is ecstatic. She runs up to greet me and collect a week's worth of chin scratches, and as I head upstairs, she trots alongside me, purring loudly. Just as I'm getting into bed, she squats down, stares me dead in the eye, and poops on my pillow.

This is undoubtedly a serious behavior issue, and also a serious mess issue. I should be reading books, probably this one, to figure out how to deal with it. But, instead, my reaction is *That's hilarious!* Because it is.

"Did you see that?" I say, eager to share the news with any disgusted family members who might be nearby. "She missed me so much . . . but she was so angry at me for leaving that she pooped on the pillow! She loves me, and that's the only way she knows how to say it!" That's not very helpful.

If it seems like I know a huge amount about cat behavior, it's because I've studied under some of the most prominent names in the field: Cinnamon, Pepper, Baby Beast, Lisa and Cy, Lucy and Squeezie. Sometimes I was studying math, sometimes physics. They didn't care. They just wanted something warm to sit on. As long as I was paying full attention to something other than them, they wanted in.

The same thing happens when I'm doing a jigsaw puzzle. Lucy jumps up on the table and stands on top of the loose pieces, because that's what I'm paying attention to instead of her. They stick to her paws, so she shakes them off violently, flinging them around the room. Sometimes they go down a heating vent in the floor. *It's hilarious!* I can always get another puzzle, and I don't like doing puzzles anyway. I'd rather watch Lucy hurl the pieces down a heating vent.

Why do cats do these things? I have no idea! I'm just writing the foreword to this book, which is kind of an honorary deal. If I knew anything, I would have written the "book" part of the book. So please believe me when I say that you're not going to get any quality answers from me, just idle speculation on my part. When we're done here, we can both read the "book" part of the book and see what, if anything, I got right.

Now, I know what you're thinking: "Can cats be trained?" First of all, don't ask me. I feel I've been more than forthright about the fact that I don't know what I'm talking about. And second of all, yes.

I've trained both of my current cats. With Lucy, I run around the room tapping on different pieces of furniture, and she chases after me, leaping majestically from one shredded sofa to the next. It's a one-ring circus of feline acrobatics, plus a guy running around. It is truly one of the greatest sights you will ever see — if you are permanently confined to my living room.

But Squeezie! She is my ultimate triumph as a cat trainer. I've trained her to lie on my shoulders, indifferent, wrapped limply around my neck like a fuzzy scarf with chicken breath. I walk around the house like that, up and down the stairs, out to the yard . . . and the whole time, she does nothing whatsoever.

Here's how I achieved these wonders.

In Lucy's case, I observed that she liked to leap from one piece of furniture to another, so I went with that, running around and taking credit from anyone who was watching. And I rewarded her with scratches under the chin, the most valuable currency in her economy.

But with Squeezie, it took more effort. The key insight was when I noticed that she liked to lie down and not move very much. I thought I could work that into my act by having her do something similar on my shoulders, but it turned out she preferred sitting just about anywhere else. Still, I stuck with it, picking her up and hanging her around my neck over a period of months, and feeding her "oven-roasted chicken" treats, her personal favorite. (I'm not sure what kind of oven roasts a chicken into a green pellet, but that's probably a subject for a book about ovens.)

Anyway, after a few months of this, Squeezie grew bored and decided sitting on my shoulders was the same as sitting in any other place. And thus an act was born!

I frequently say that when I'm looking at cats, I'm never not entertained. (I know it's a double negative, but writers are allowed to break the rules, so please, don't not continue reading.) I find it unbearably entertaining when cats spread their toes and chew furiously on their toenails. I love it when they jump on the table and lick my salad, because any human food is better than all cat food. I squeal with joy when I feed them something they don't like and they get offended, turn around, and kick imaginary sand on it like they're burying it in the litter box.

Why do cats make us so happy? Here's what I think: I think it's because they don't care about making us happy. Not the slightest bit. They only care about themselves, with absolute honesty and innocence. If they pile on us and snuggle up and purr, it's not to make *us* happy; it's because we make *them* happy. And, really, isn't that what makes us happier than anything? Isn't that, for lack of a more understated conclusion, what gives meaning to our very lives?

Maybe! Like I said, I have no idea. But you know who does? The experts from the American College of Veterinary Behaviorists, that's who. And, conveniently, they've written this excellent book to help with any behavior issue you may be hypothetically having with *your* cat, possibly involving a pillow, and sometimes, I'm sorry to say, all of the sheets and blankets as well. So let's read on. Quickly. Quickly!

DAVID X. COHEN, May 2019

# PREFACE

The role our feline friends play in society has changed considerably over the past few decades. We recognize that cats should no longer be classified as "low-maintenance pets" for owners who are gone from home for long periods of time, or for those who wish to own a pet who doesn't require much attention. We now see that cats have individual personalities that endear them to us and allow them to be loved members of our family, deserving of the same time, attention, dedication, and respect we give our canine family members — and sometimes our children.

New research tells us that being around cats is just plain good for us. Exposure to cats in childhood can help reduce the risk of developing asthma. Owning, or even just petting, cats can reduce our stress, lower our heart rate and blood pressure, and make us generally happier. Cats are unique and comedic. Who can't laugh at a cat trying to shove herself into a tiny box?

Cats have important jobs that benefit us as well. They help control rodent populations in agricultural situations. Research into their afflictions often gives us enlightening information about similar human diseases. They entertain us in movies, commercials, and stage shows. They come visit us in hospitals and nursing homes to provide comfort with their soft fur and soothing purring.

In recompense, the scientific community is delving into the true nature of cats. Cats deserve their own reality, rather than having us extrapolate that of another species onto them. Cats are not children, or rabbits, or small dogs. They are cats, and we should understand and treat them as such.

This is the goal of *Decoding Your Cat:* To bring the most current and scientifically accurate information regarding cat behavior to the public. To allow everyone the opportunity to climb into the minds of our cats — to the degree that such a thing is even possible.

The diplomates of the American College of Veterinary Behaviorists have hundreds of years of collective knowledge and experience about animal behavior and veterinary medicine. Our members include rabbit enthusiasts, dog trainers, obedience competitors, equestrians, herpetologists, cat fanciers, police officers, soldiers, professors, pharmaceutical professionals, and many others. While our backgrounds are diverse, we all have a deeply rooted passion for animal behavior and an equally strong drive to share this passion and knowledge with others. We are emotionally bonded and committed to our pets and our patients, but we also understand that emotion isn't enough. Facts matter, and for this reason, the science of animal behavior is crucial to allow us to live well and honorably among our feline friends.

This book is written by humans who love and admire cats, but it is written on a foundation of objective, factual knowledge. *Decoding Your Cat* is our homage to cats and our opportunity to help dispel common myths about cat behavior.

In this book, you will learn about cat behavior from kittenhood to the geriatric years. We discuss normal feline behaviors and body language, as well as behaviors that are abnormal due to various medical or environmental problems. *Decoding Your Cat* includes information on doing the best for feral and shelter cats, and also how to create a harmonious multicat household and avoid fighting cats — topics the reader will be hard-pressed to find in other feline behavior books. The book also enlightens readers on the science of learning and training (yes, cats really can be trained!), which will empower caregivers and enable them to cope with common behavior problems. Most important, each chapter informs readers about ways to enrich cats' lives so they can reach their full potential as companions and live relatively free from fear, distress, and potentially harmful assumptions.

We hope you enjoy reading this book as much as we enjoyed writing it. We also hope reading this book inspires you to learn even more about cats and find ways to deepen your relationship with the cats around you.

LORE I. HAUG, DVM, MS, DACVB
Past President, American College of Veterinary Behaviorists

# ACKNOWLEDGMENTS

## Meghan E. Herron

This book is a dream come true, long in the making, and I have many to thank for its remarkable content and organization. I first want to thank my colleagues Drs. Debra Horwitz and John Ciribassi for paving the way with their stellar editing and presentation of *Decoding Your Dog*. Without its success, *Decoding Your Cat* may not have ever seen a bookshelf.

I am ever grateful for the mentorship and encouragement from Debra as she stayed on to help us bring this book to fruition. Thank you, Debra, for being a friend, mentor, and "mom" as we have made this journey. I'd also like to thank our fellow editor, Dr. Carlo Siracusa. Carlo and I spent many a long afternoon muddling over the content, organization, and appeal of each and every chapter. Carlo, your unique perspective and depth of experience have given this book an edge that wouldn't have been there without you. The three of us live impossibly busy lives, yet we all made time to come together and complete this book.

Thanks also to Jeff Kleinman of Folio Literary Management for keeping our best interests at heart and continually helping us navigate the publishing and marketing world. I can always count on Jeff for a quick and accurate answer, without any hint of annoyance at my ignorance or pestering.

A book has no future without a publisher that believes in it. Houghton Mifflin Harcourt has supported our mission from the time the first pages of *Decoding Your Dog* were written, and welcomed the proposal for *Decoding Your Cat* with open arms. The editorial staff, led by Sarah Kwak, brought charisma and captivation to each page, turning the book into a true work of art. Thank you, Steve Dale, for being the lead cheerleader for veterinary behaviorists and for pushing us all to make both these books a reality. I am humbled by your endless support for what we do and for your devotion to improving the lives of pets everywhere.

Personally, I want to thank the late Dr. Linda Lord for inspiring me to go to veterinary school in the first place and helping me see and interact with the world in a way that is meaningful and fulfilling. This little grasshopper has come a long way thanks to Linda. Thank also to Dr. Ilana Reisner, DACVB, for teaching me proper English and shaping me into the veterinary behaviorist I am today.

I am ever grateful for the unrelenting support and encouragement from my husband, Josh Black. You put the skip in my step and the smile on my face, and I look forward to watching our smart, strong, beautiful girls, Rowan and Amelia, grow into smart, strong, beautiful women. Finally, a special thanks to the feline friends in my life who have helped give this book its personal perspective. You were (are) all special in your own, very different ways: Bo-Bo, Sassy, Katie, Cammie, Lepanto, Moco, Primo, Junebug, and, the most unique of all, Mr. Girard Bigglesworth.

## Debra F. Horwitz

Our first book, *Decoding Your Dog,* was a wonderful educational experience for me as an editor and for the entire American College of Veterinary Behaviorists. Within a short period of time, the public began clamoring for another book, this one about cats. And, thanks to the ACVB, I am so excited to have been involved in the creation of this new book, *Decoding Your Cat.* My coeditors, friends, and fellow diplomates Meghan Herron and Carlo Siracusa led the team, and together we have created another masterpiece. All of us brought not only our scientific knowledge and practice experience but also our love of cats as wonderful family companions. Furthermore, my talented colleagues who contributed to this book were all devoted to creating the best educational treatise for cat owners. I also want to add my thanks to Jeff Kleinman and Houghton Mifflin Harcourt for helping us bring another book to fruition.

My life with cats goes back a long way. My father was a cat lover, and the first pet I remember as a child was a cat named Mao (meaning "cat" in Chinese), a beloved family pet and my good buddy. Many other cats followed and captured my heart. Each one taught me how special cats are, and each one was an individual to be cherished. Sharing my love of cats and my memories with other cat owners has been a heartwarming experience.

My husband, Eugene, loved all our cats. I am sure he would have found this book engaging and would have wholeheartedly supported its publication. Thank you, Eugene, for your unwavering support in all my endeavors. You are missed. Thank you also to my children, Jeff, Laura, and Ben, who are also pet lovers. Veterinary medicine and educating pet owners and veterinarians have been my passions. I am grateful for the opportunity to continue to practice what I love.

Enjoy the book!

## Carlo Siracusa

As a child, I desperately wanted to have a cat. I used to buy cat magazines and leave them around the house to send a clear message to my parents. They thought that if they resisted for a few months, I would forget about the cat and shift my attention to something else. But this did not happen, and soon my obsession became a nightmare for my parents, who were not thrilled by the idea of having one more living being to take care of in addition to their three demanding children.

As often happens with me, I found a way to get what I wanted and brought home my first cat, a beautiful domestic longhair named Pelouche. It did not take long for Pelouche to prove me right and steal the heart of the whole family. Then I got two cats . . . then three . . . then four . . . and at twenty years old, I was a registered breeder of Persians, British Short-hairs, and Scottish Folds.

At that time, though, I could never have imagined that, many years later, my passion for cats would bring me to work on a cat book. And not just one of many books on cat behavior, but the official cat book of the American College of Veterinary Behaviorists! I am one of the lucky ones who can live their childhood dream every day of their adult life. Now I have a chance to share this dream with the readers of this book. Thank you, dear reader, for your time and attention.

Most important, I want to thank the American College of Veterinary Behaviorists for giving me this opportunity. I am very proud to represent this organization. I also need to acknowledge my coeditors and friends, Dr. Debra Horwitz and Dr. Meghan Herron, for sharing this experience with me. Meghan was the first to believe that I could make a contribution to the project and proposed that I join. Since then, Debra has been the best mentor for a junior editor like me. It has been an absolute pleasure to work with both of them.

Jeff Kleinman, our agent from Folio Literary Management, assisted us throughout the project and believed in it from the very beginning. Without his knowledge and professionalism, this book would have not seen the light of day. Thank you, Jeff.

My biggest gratitude goes to our publisher, Houghton Mifflin Harcourt, for investing in our vision and understanding why *Decoding Your Cat* is not just another book on cat behavior, but a gate to the knowledge and unique expertise of board-certified veterinary behaviorists.

On a more personal level, I am extremely grateful to my family for supporting me and my passion for so many years. All of them have loved and accepted the cats I've wanted to live with, including my beloved calico, Elsa, who is my feline companion now. Certainly, I would not have achieved many of my professional goals without the mentors who taught me: Maria Grazia Pennisi, Jaume Fatjo, Xavier Manteca, Josep Pastor, Patrick Pageat, Daniel Mills, James Serpell, Ilana Reisner, and everyone else who has shared knowledge, thoughts, and ideas with me.

# INTRODUCTION

Veterinary behaviorists are last responders. When no one else can help, they swoop in and save the day. It's a small army, as there are fewer than one hundred veterinarians who are board-certified in animal behavior in North America. Lives saved by their expertise are incalculable.

Here's what often transpires: The cat's been urinating on the carpet or scratching the sofa for months or even years, and finally the desperate cat owner takes him to a behaviorist and says, "It's up to you to fix the problem, or the cat goes." Not only are behaviorists required to "fix" the problem, but their goal is also to maintain the human-animal bond.

The Internet can be a source of accurate information. However, going to a website can't tell you why *your* cat is thinking outside the box or yowling at three a.m. Veterinary behaviorist Dr. Meghan Herron (who coedited this book) told me that when she was in private practice, about half of all her presumed feline behavior problems were, in reality, a result of a medical problem — or at least it was a contributing factor. This is why whenever your cat's behavior changes, I want you to think, "Why *now?*" Don't assume the problem is solely behavioral. Consult your veterinarian, not a website.

When it comes to cats, there are so many misconceptions. For example, many people think cats — even their own beloved cats — may be sinister or spiteful, or that they don't really bond to humans. That's simply untrue.

I myself was once guilty of not understanding how intensely cats can bond with people.

Ricky was a handsome, stark-white Devon Rex who loved people. From the start, he demonstrated affection even toward strangers. Ricky loved when people visited. He often smothered our unsuspecting guests with love by hopping on their shoulder and purring into their ear. In part it was because of his breed, but arguably the real secret to his affection was breeder Leslie Spiller, who did a great job of socialization. We continued that process.

One day my wife, Robin, returned from an animal-assisted therapy session with our miniature Australian Shepherd, Lucy. She suggested I teach Lucy a new trick. Lucy knew lots of tricks, even singing to children on cue at the Rehabilitation Institute of Chicago. I don't recall why, but I thought I'd teach her to play a little kid's piano.

I closed the door of our "training room" (a second bedroom) and began the process of clicker training Lucy. I started by shaping her behavior. As her paw came closer to the keyboard, I would click the clicker and offer a treat. Gradually, she began to learn and would lift her paw toward the keyboard.

But I hadn't closed the door to the room all the way, and in walked Ricky. He looked at me, looked at the lesser species (the dog), and proceeded to play the piano. No clicker. No treat. (Though I quickly began to reinforce his playing with cat treats.)

It wasn't long before Ricky was literally jumping through hoops and over dogs on a down-stay, offering high fives, and coming when called. People were amazed.

How could a cat do all that?

Most people assume that cats can't be trained. In fact, they can — or they train us to continue to work with them, which is exactly what Ricky did.

Ricky began giving recitals at local pet stores and on TV, including the Animal Planet channel and National Geographic Channel. Ricky taught me and millions of others what cats are capable of, and our bond was palpable. Video crews couldn't help but capture it.

At Ricky's next checkup, at my veterinarian's request, he performed a few of his improvisational jazz tunes for the staff and the clients who happened to be there with their dogs — all crowded into a little exam room. After the applause (a standing ovation — there were no seats in the room), Dr. Donna Solomon began the exam by listening to Ricky's heart.

Her face told the story. She heard a murmur. Veterinary cardiologist Dr. Michael Luethy confirmed that Ricky had feline hypertrophic cardiomyopathy (HCM), an abnormal thickening of the heart wall. While medication may slow the disease progress, nothing can stop it. Some cats diagnosed with HCM live out a normal life span; most do not.

Happily, Ricky never read the diagnosis and probably felt well until his final months. As his celebrity grew, I even turned down an appearance on David Letterman's Stupid Pet Tricks because I wouldn't fly with Ricky to New York City or drive there from Chicago.

Ricky was only four and a half years old when he suddenly succumbed to HCM in 2002. He just collapsed. I still remember that moment as if it were yesterday.

I was determined to honor Ricky by making a difference. HCM might be the most common cause of death of cats from about three to ten years old. How could such a widespread disease have no effective treatment?

I partnered with the Winn Feline Foundation — a nonprofit funder of cat health and behavior studies — and created the Ricky Fund to raise money for HCM research. Today, we've raised well over $250,000. The good news is that with that money a genetic test was developed to detect a gene defect related to HCM in Maine Coon and Ragdoll cats. Breeders using the simple and inexpensive test in their breeding programs have saved lives. Still, my heart breaks, because in the time it has taken you to read this story, a cat somewhere has succumbed to HCM.

Like Ricky did in his short life, *Decoding Your Cat* busts antiquated myths. Ricky not only stole my heart, he stole the show. He also taught me all that cats can be. And this book does the same.

Cats must no longer be the Rodney Dangerfield of pets; they deserve respect for what they are. If we love cats, it's only right that we make the effort to better understand what really makes them tick. It's not quite as mysterious as some people might have us believe.

I was honored to be a coeditor of the companion volume to this book, *Decoding Your Dog*. That book, also written by members of the American College of Veterinary Behaviorists, was in part motivated by the work of a legendary veterinary behaviorist, the late Dr. R. K. Anderson. An icon in the world of positive reinforcement dog training, Dr. Anderson once told me, "Don't just do a dog book and be done with it. I leave it to you to follow up with a cat book. People don't know it, but I'm really more a cat guy. People may tend not to get help as readily for cat behavior problems — or assume they know the answer, which may not be quite right. Please, climb the highest mountain and then holler out that veterinary behaviorists can help cats, too."

Veterinary behaviorists preach the gospel of science, and everything they do is based on it. Everything you read in this book is based on science as well. Often, it's veterinary behaviorists who conduct that science to better understand cats in the first place.

It wasn't too long ago that cats were mostly outdoor pets. Today, most cats in America are indoors only. Cats are more popular than dogs, and most homes with a cat have, on average, just over two cats. Yet we're still learning about cat behavior. The best teachers have written this book. I know my friend Dr. Anderson would have been yowling with joy — as am I.

STEVE DALE, CABC

# Decoding Your Cat

# The Language of Meow
*Feline Phonics from Nose to Tail*

Rachel Malamed, DVM, DACVB, and
Karen Lynn Chieko Sueda, DVM, DACVB

Misty slowly walked into the living room. Amy was happy to see her out and about. Though she had been part of the family for fifteen years, Misty had recently been spending most of her time alone in the guest bedroom. But who could blame her? Between Amy's work schedule and the kids' activities, the house had become chaotic.

Amy watched as Misty jumped up on the couch next to her. Taking advantage of the momentary peace in the house, Amy picked Misty up to snuggle. Misty gave a rusty meow before settling on Amy's lap. As Amy stroked Misty's back, Misty's ears turned to the side, and the tip of her tail began twitching. Amy recognized that Misty was upset but couldn't imagine why. "What's the matter, kiddo?" Misty began licking her hand in response. "Aww," Amy thought, "she's grooming me," and she gave Misty an affectionate pat on the back. All of a sudden, Misty hissed, swatted Amy's hand, jumped off her lap, and ran out of the room. Amy looked at her hand and saw she was bleeding from the scratch.

Amy was distraught. What had happened? She had just been petting Misty. What if the cat had done this to one of her children? Amy wondered whether Misty could be trusted around the kids.

This exchange was very different from Misty's point of view. She hadn't been feeling well recently. Her knees and back hurt, and it was hard to stay out of the children's way as they ran around the house. It was easier to stay put on the guest bed. But now it was quiet, and there was a patch of sun on the living room couch. Jumping up would be uncomfortable, but the allure of the sunbeam made it worth the effort.

When Amy picked her up, Misty winced as she felt a twinge in her back. Ow! But it was over in a second, and Amy's lap was warm. Although she enjoyed Amy's company, Misty couldn't understand why Amy kept touching her aching back. Misty pinned her ears back and twitched her tail as a warning sign. She tried to move away, but her knees were sore.

Amy stopped stroking her back and rubbed her cheek instead. Misty licked Amy's hand to let her know she was confused: *I like the warmth of your lap, but I don't like you touching my back.* All of a sudden Amy hit her on the back. That hurt! Misty swatted Amy's hand away and ran out of the room.

Misty was distraught. What had happened? Amy had been hurting her, and she had defended herself. Misty wondered if Amy was safe and doubted whether she could trust Amy to pet her again.

As this story illustrates, cats and people find it difficult to communicate, because the two species don't speak the same language. However, once we learn how (and why) cats send us messages, we can become better at receiving and correctly interpreting them. This will enable us to respond appropriately and prevent any miscommunication between our feline friends and us.

## Facts, Not Fiction

The Egyptian feline goddess Bastet, familiars of witches, Garfield, Grumpy Cat: throughout history, humans have viewed cats as mysterious, self-centered creatures to be either worshipped or vilified. This reputation may be due in part to cats' mercurial nature — friendly one second and aloof or defensive the next. What cat owner hasn't wondered what their cat was thinking behind those beautiful eyes?

Humans are accustomed to dealing with demonstrative beings, whether it's our dog ecstatically licking our face or our friend extolling the brilliance of the tweet she wrote. If communication had a volume control, humans would shout, dogs would talk, and cats would whisper. Cats use much subtler forms of communication than we are used to receiving. But once we recognize what to look and listen for, we can easily decipher the cryptic language of cats.

## What Does That Mean?

**Affiliative behaviors:** These "come closer" behaviors indicate friendly intent, reduce tension, and communicate a desire to approach. They include:

- **Allogrooming:** Mutual grooming between two friendly cats.
- **Allorubbing:** A cat rubbing her body against another cat or a person.
- **Bunting:** A cat rubbing her cheek on objects. Cats have scent glands in their cheeks, and this action is used to mark objects and people with pheromones when a cat finds them to be safe and comforting.

**Aggression:** The range of "go away" behaviors a cat uses to frighten or threaten harm to another individual. The goal is to increase the distance between the cat and the perceived threat. Although people regard the word "aggression" as being offensive, it is most often used for self-defense, and at times is a normal and necessary behavior. Motivations for aggressive responses include fear, self-defense, protecting a resource or territory, and defending offspring. Aggressive behaviors range from subtle body language used to intimidate or scare (such as staring) to severe attacks resulting in injury or death.

**Piloerection:** The involuntary reflex of raised hair along the body and tail, commonly seen when a cat is in an emotionally aroused or fearful state.

**Displacement behaviors:** Normal behaviors displayed outside the context in which they typically occur. Animals usually exhibit displacement behaviors when they are anxious, confused, or frustrated. Common displacement behaviors in cats include grooming and scratching, and may be thought of as the kitty equivalent of people bouncing their leg or biting their nails when they are nervous.

**Caterwaul:** A loud, harsh vocalization usually emitted by cats as a mating call.

**Trill:** A vocalization used by a mother cat communicating with her kittens. It is also a positive vocalization heard during friendly interactions with people and other cats. A trill sounds like a ringtone meow or a question.

**Pheromones:** Species-specific chemical signals that animals use to communicate with others of the same species. Pheromones differ from scents or odors because only individuals of the same species can detect them. Cats use several types of pheromones to send messages to other cats, including the feline facial pheromone, the maternal appeasing pheromone (along the mammary chain of nursing females), the feline interdigital pheromone (in the paws), and pheromones in urine.

**Social spacing:** The distribution of cats in space and time in the area where they live. Social spacing is used to maintain distance between individuals, even within the home. Visual communication and marking may be helpful to establish space and "zoning" for individual cats. For free-ranging cats, social spacing is largely influenced by the availability and distribution of resources such as food. The density of cats is higher in areas where there is more plentiful and uniformly distributed food (for example, where many small rodents are equally scattered across an area).

**Brachycephalic:** Having a short nose and flat face. Cat breeds with this feature include the Exotic Shorthair and Persian.

Cats' behavior seems inscrutable because they rely on different forms of communication than humans. Humans are a verbal species — we communicate primarily through spoken and written language. Though cats communicate using vocalizations, they also depend heavily on visual, olfactory (smell), and tactile (touch) signals — forms of communication humans are not very attuned to (see "Feline Communication Methods" opposite).

It's easy for us to recognize a purr or a hiss, but much harder to determine a cat's emotions based on facial expression, pupil size, or ear position. Don't feel bad; even animal experts find it difficult to assess how a cat is feeling using only visual signs. In a study by Dr. E. Holden of the University of Glasgow, veterinarians and veterinary staff found that it is difficult to determine whether a cat is in pain based on facial expression alone.

## Feline Communication Methods

| | Forms | Examples | Distance Requirements |
|---|---|---|---|
| **Olfactory (scent)** | Waste odors | Urine and feces marking | Communication over longer distance and duration |
| | Pheromones | Feline facial pheromone | |
| | | Feline interdigital pheromone in paw pads | Sender is able to deposit the signal and leave the area |
| **Visual (sight)** | Body language | Ears pinned back (fearful) | Sender and recipient must be able to see each other (except for visual marks left behind) |
| | Behavior | Hiding | |
| | Visual marks (prompts closer investigation) | Scratch marks left on a tree or chair | |
| | | Upright flagpole tail | |
| | | Outstretched paw (soliciting play) | |
| **Auditory (sound)** | Vocalizations | Meow | Intermediate range |
| | | Purr | Sender may remain hidden |
| | | Hiss | |
| | | Yowl | |
| **Tactile (touch)** | Touching | Friendly touch (allorub, allogroom) | Immediate proximity is necessary |
| | | Aggressive touch (swat, bite) | |

We can train ourselves to be better observers of feline body language and behavior, but there are some forms of feline communication we are physically incapable of detecting. These include pheromones — species-specific chemicals cats leave behind when, for example, they rub their cheek against us or scratch the couch. We can never fully comprehend this valuable scent information, but other cats can.

Cats detect and process information contained in pheromones using a specialized sensory structure called the vomeronasal organ. The vomeronasal organ has a microscopic opening just behind cats' upper incisors, which acts like a specialized tiny nose. When a cat inhales an interesting odor or pheromone, she opens her mouth and brings a small amount of the scent into the opening of the vomeronasal organ. This open-mouth expression, called a gape or flehmen, enables cats to interpret species-specific information that is inaccessible to humans.

Seymour gapes to take in pheromone information from a new kitten being fostered in his home.
*Sara Bennett*

Why do cats need so many ways to communicate? Each form of communication is best suited to certain types of messages. For example, when a cat sprays urine, pheromones in her urine let other cats know that she was there and provide some personal information, such as her sex and relationship status. Think of it as "Kitty Facebook." The ability to post information and walk away enables cats to multitask: while their message is displayed in one location, they are free to engage in activities elsewhere, such as finding food, shelter, or a mate. Similarly, the ability to leave "pee mail" in one location before moving to another enables cats to post messages over a large area but still avoid predators or competitors. These olfactory messages help maintain social spacing between cats who would rather avoid a confrontation.

On the opposite end of the spectrum, cats must be in relatively close proximity for visual signals (such as body language) to be effective. When they are farther apart, cats use larger gestures, such as signaling friendly intent by raising their tail like a flagpole. They reserve smaller gestures, such as ear movements and tail twitches, for closer interactions.

This stray cat approached with his tail raised like a flagpole and followed Dr. Karen Sueda through the small German village where he lived. *Karen Lynn Chieko Sueda*

Cats can quickly adjust their body language to respond to changing interactions. If the mood goes from friendly to tense, for example, cats will let you know by altering their ear position, eyes, tail carriage, or body posture in a flash. Maintaining an open dialogue with your cat involves constantly observing how her body language changes in reaction to your behavior.

Even though these two cats are playing, the calico on top of the cat tree is probably defending her perch from her brown tabby sister below. The tabby's ears are slightly pinned back and to the side, indicating concern and apprehension, while the calico's are alert and forward, indicating excitement and arousal. *Karen Lynn Chieko Sueda*

Cats reserve tactile communication for close friends — or aggressive encounters. Tactile communication includes mutual grooming (allogrooming) and rubbing against each other to exchange pheromones (allorubbing). Cats appreciate having plenty of personal space, so choosing to be in close contact with another cat or a human signifies a close bond.

Though not littermates, these two girls were adopted together from the shelter and have been inseparable ever since. They often lie in physical contact and allogroom. *Amy C. Sturlini*

Like people, cats tend to form friendships with related or familiar individuals, and frequent or prolonged physical contact occurs only between friends and family. You might be willing to hold a loved one's hand, but stop at a brief handshake with a stranger. Similarly, a cat may rub against an unfamiliar person's leg to mark him with her scent, but only choose to sleep on the lap of a person she knows well.

## Body Postures

In general, body postures can be grouped into two categories: those that encourage others to come closer and those that say "go away." We briefly discussed one "come closer" posture — a cat approaching with an upright flagpole tail — earlier in this chapter. Cats use this signal to invite interaction. Similarly, a relaxed body accompanied by a cheek rub or an outstretched paw (with sheathed claws) indicates a cat's desire to make a connection.

"Go away" body postures serve one of two purposes: to make a cat seem smaller in order to help her hide, or to make her appear larger and more formidable in order to ward off an attacker. Fearful cats create a smaller silhouette by pinning back their ears, tucking their legs underneath their body, and wrapping their tail under or around themselves. These cats hope to avoid detection by crouching and remaining hidden — out of sight, out of mind.

However, if an attacker (sometimes a perceived threat, not a real one) finds and confronts the cat, her fight-or-flight response will take over. If she cannot flee, she may display another "go away" body posture — that of a Halloween cat. To intimidate her attacker, a terrified cat will contract special muscles in her skin, causing her fur to stand on end, or piloerect. Piloerection, combined with the cat standing straight up and arching her back, makes her appear larger and more intimidating than she actually is. Add a soundtrack of hissing and spitting, and the cat has an impressive defensive strategy to drive off a would-be attacker.

The Halloween cat: this kitty's arched back, piloerect fur, flattened ears, open-mouth hissing, and dilated pupils are a display of profound fear.
*Sharon Crowell-Davis*

## Feline Body Language

*Observe all body parts, overall carriage, and behavior when reading your cat's signals.*

| Body Part | Position | What It Can Mean |
|---|---|---|
| Eyes | Closed | Sleeping, relaxed |
| | | May be in pain or uncomfortable if accompanied by tense facial features |
| | Casual gaze | Calm |
| | Blinking slowly | Calm, relaxed |
| | Averted gaze | Nervous |
| | Pupils dilated (big, wide) | Fearful, aroused |
| | Fixed stare | Tense, possibly aggressive |
| Ears | Relaxed, neutral position | Calm |
| | Forward | Alert, attentive, aggressive |
| | Semi-rotated outward | Fearful |
| | Flattened against the head, either to the side (airplane wings) or backward (earless appearance) | Very fearful, fearfully aggressive |
| Mouth | Tight | Tense, fearful |
| | Open | Vocalizing, often aggressive (for example, hissing when fearfully aggressive) |
| | Gape (also called flehmen) | Assessing pheromones |
| | Pant | Difficulty breathing |
| Tail | Neutral, relaxed, tail tip may move slightly | Calm |
| | Upright (called flagpole) | Friendly |
| | Curled tightly around body or hidden | Fear, uncertainty |
| | Twitching or lashing | Aroused, agitated |
| Body carriage | Hunched/crouched, body tense or curled, appears small | Fear, uncertainty |
| | Stretched out, loose | Relaxed |
| | Halloween cat (arched back with bottle-brush tail, ears may be back) | Very fearfully aggressive |
| | Rolled on back, stretching, loose body | Relaxed, greeting behavior |
| | Rolled on back, tense body | Fearfully aggressive |
| | Tense | Alert, aroused |

## Vocalizations

Like body postures, feline vocalizations may be divided roughly into "come closer" and "go away" meanings. "Go away" messages include hissing, spitting, growling, and yowling. Cats hiss or spit when they are scared and protecting themselves (defensive aggression). Cats may growl or yowl when they are defending themselves or when they are offensively aggressive (a more confident, proactive type of aggression), such as when they are fighting with other cats over resources like territory or access to food or mates.

### The Cat's Meow

Cats communicate with us using the same language they use to speak to other cats. Meows are the exception. Adult cats don't often meow to other cats, but they do commonly meow at humans. Why do cats reserve this vocalization for people?

Meowing is actually a kitten vocalization that cats adapt to communicate with human caregivers. Kittens begin crying and meowing at birth, even before their eyes and ears are open. Kittens' meows stimulate adult cats to pay attention to them.

The ability to meow remains in adult cats and is applied to the next caregiver — cat owners. Adult cats learn to meow at humans for the same reason they meowed at their mom — to get attention. Humans are a vocal species, and we tend to pay more attention to vocalizations than to visual cues. When our cat meows, we pay attention to her, which reinforces the cat's meowing — a positive feedback loop.

Cat owners can identify specific meanings for different meows. One meow may mean "Feed me," while another means "Pet me." When Dr. Sarah Ellis at the University of Lincoln in England played recordings of meows to cat owners, the owners could identify why their own cat was meowing (hungry vs. waiting for food vs. confined behind a barrier vs. wanting attention), but they had more trouble determining why unfamiliar cats were vocalizing. It seems that rather than there being a universal "meow code," each individual cat and owner develop their own "meow language" that's unique to them.

Cats say "come closer" using several vocalizations, including the trill, purr, and meow. Cats trill or chirp when they are greeting friends — another cat or a person. Cats purr around other cats as well as people. Purring appears to signal a cat's request for comforting, since purring occurs both when a cat is content and when she is uncomfortable or in pain (see "Purring: Nature and Nurture" later in this chapter). Meowing, however, appears to be a unique vocalization reserved primarily for people, as cats meow at other cats infrequently (see "The Cat's Meow" opposite).

## Feline Vocalizations

| Intent | Vocalization | Situation |
|---|---|---|
| Affiliative/friendly | Trill/chirp | Greeting |
| | Purr | Soliciting care in either pleasurable social situations or when ill |
| | Meow | Seeking attention from people |
| Aggressive | Growl | Offensive or defensive aggression |
| | Hiss | Defensive aggression |
| | Spit | Defensive aggression |
| | Yowl | Offensive or defensive aggression |
| | Shriek | Pain or fear |
| Sexual | Caterwaul | Mating call |
| Hunting | Chatter | Predatory/feeding behavior |

## Redundant and Mixed Signals

Cats combine visual and vocal signals, often sending redundant messages to make sure their intention is clear. This is similar to a person saying yes while nodding their head. For example, a friendly cat may approach with a raised flagpole tail and trill a greeting. A fearful, defensive cat may turn her ears back, lean away, and lash her tail while growling.

Occasionally, cats send mixed signals. For example, a cat may appear to be relaxed, because she is lying on her side with her eyes half-closed, but her ears are slightly turned back and her tail is twitching. Which part of her body do we believe? When cats display varied or even conflicting body language, they are expressing ambivalence or uncertainty about a situation. The cat in this example may be happy and content lying in the sun, but not want you or another cat to come too close.

People send mixed signals in many situations. For example, you bump into an acquaintance while out running errands on your lunch break, and you want to show her a dozen pictures of your new grandchild. She may smile politely, a friendly gesture, but also lean away and raise her hand in front of her to decline, unconsciously saying "stay away." As with people, when cats send mixed signals, it's best to play it safe and heed the "stay away" part of the message. You can always reevaluate the situation later to see if the message has changed.

Careful cat observers read the entire cat. If you're uncertain what your cat is saying, consider all her signals to determine whether they are all saying the same thing.

## Predators and Prey

Hidden from view, she waited, crouched and taut, with only the tip of her tail moving. Ears perked, she watched her prey, eyes wide to take in the light. At the last moment, she drew her paws under her and pounced. The paper ball was hers at last!

Nature molded cats to be formidable hunters. Possessing good night vision, independently swiveling ears, and the ability to hear ultrasonic rodent squeaks, cats can locate prey that's invisible to humans. Despite being predators themselves, though, cats are also preyed upon by larger animals. Cougars, bobcats, coyotes, dogs, and even eagles and owls attack and kill cats. Being solitary rather than pack hunters, cats are usually alone when they encounter enemies. Therefore, their best strategy when faced with a threat is to run and hide.

This has caused cats to adopt a "run first, ask questions later" policy. Cats typically cope with stressful situations through avoidance rather than confrontation. Whether threatened by another cat, a dog, or a trip to the veterinarian, cats tend to flee to either hidden (under the bed) or elevated (top of the bookcase) safe areas where they can evade the threat.

This tuxedo cat has just seen an unfamiliar dog and jumped up on a stool to escape. His crouched posture and lowered tail are signs of fear. The hair along his spine is also standing on end (piloerection), and he has a bottle-brush tail, which makes him appear larger—a defensive strategy. *Karen Lynn Chieko Sueda*

For lesser threats, cats practice more subtle avoidance strategies and choose just to stay away. This avoidance is also a kind of communication. In the story at the start of this chapter, Misty chose to stay out of the living room when the children were home.

Similarly, if two cats aren't getting along, they may actively avoid encounters as a way to prevent direct confrontations or fights. For example, one cat may turn and walk away if she notices the other cat lying in the hallway. Or she may use the cat tree only in the morning, when the other cat is sleeping in another room. The two cats arrange things so they are never in the same place at the same time.

Because cats apply similar maneuvers if they are afraid of the family dog, visitors, or even some family members, noticing their evasion tactics helps us detect and address early signs of tension and fear before they get worse.

Yet another result of cats being prey animals is that they are very good at hiding illness. While this is an excellent self-protection strategy in the wild (predators can't target them as easy prey), it makes it exceptionally difficult for owners to recognize when to take their cats to the veterinarian. In addition to obvious physical signs (such as vomiting or loss of appetite), cat owners should interpret any change in behavior as a possible sign of illness. (See avoiding Catastrophe: How to Recognize Signs of Pain and Illness in Your Cat" later in this chapter to learn more about identifying signs of illness in cats.)

## Is That Really True?

*Do cats like belly rubs?* Kate grew up with dogs, but Nala was her first cat. As Kate gazed down at Nala lying in the sunbeam, Nala yawned, stretched out her paw, and rolled onto her back. "Aww . . . she wants her tummy rubbed," Kate thought. As soon as Kate touched Nala's belly, the cat grabbed Kate's arm, bit her hand, and kicked her with her back claws. Kate was shocked. "Why would she ask for a belly rub and then attack me?" she wondered.

Cats do not want a belly rub when they expose their belly. Some cats may roll on their back and expose their tummy when they greet you or when they are content and relaxed. This is the ultimate compliment. Your cat is demonstrating her trust in you by exposing a vulnerable body part. However, it is usually not an invitation to pet her. Though there are exceptions, most cats do not enjoy having their belly rubbed, and doing so is intrusive — like someone tickling you while you're stretching.

This brown tabby has voluntarily rolled onto her back but does not want a belly rub. She would likely grab and bite your hand if you reached for her.

*Karen Lynn Chieko Sueda*

Cats also may lie on their back when they're frightened. To drive the point home, they may exhibit multiple signs of fear, such as pinning their ears back while growling and hissing at their assailant. Lying on their back puts all four sets of claws between them and their attacker. Cats in this position are ready to defend themselves and will likely interpret your approaching hand as a threat.

Another sometimes confusing signal is that cats wag their tail when they are upset, not happy. It's best not to approach a cat with a rapidly moving tail. In general, the more a cat's tail thrashes or twitches, the more aroused the cat is. Cats show mild to moderate annoyance by flicking the tip of their tail — similar to people drumming their fingers in an irritated manner. As the frustration builds, more of the cat's tail may become involved. You may notice this angry, lashing tail right before a cat fight or when your cat sees an unfamiliar cat through the window.

Licking can be a sign of confusion or annoyance. We all know that cats groom themselves by licking their fur. In fact, cats have special barbs on their tongue that help them do this (which is why cats' tongues feel rough when they lick us). However, cats also lick themselves when they are anxious or confused. Think of the last time you saw your cat attempt a jump but miss. To cover up her "embarrassment," she probably stopped and groomed herself for a few seconds. This is similar to a nervous person playing with their hair. These normal behaviors, displayed in unusual situations, are called displacement behaviors and indicate that a cat is worried or unsure.

Cats may lick themselves excessively, resulting in fur loss or even bald patches. While this overgrooming may be due to anxiety or stress in some cats (see chapter 10 for a discussion of compulsive behaviors), a study by Dr. Gary Landsberg, DACVB, and his colleagues found that it is more often the result of a physical illness that is causing pain and discomfort, such as an allergy or a gastrointestinal disorder.

Cats may also lick us for attention. Between two friendly cats, allogrooming helps them bond. Similarly, when your cat licks you while being petted, this may be a form of allogrooming, although not all licking is a sign of friendliness. Sometimes cats lick us not for attention, but as a displacement behavior if they are feeling anxious. In the story at the start of this chapter, Misty licked Amy because she was confused; she liked Amy's petting, but it was also painful. Amy did not realize that Misty was nervous about the interaction and continued to pet her, which later caused Misty to swat Amy's hand.

How do you determine whether licking is friendly allogrooming or a nervous displacement behavior? Observe the rest of your cat's body language. Are her ears and tail telling you she's relaxed or worried? Rather than focusing on one body part or behavior, read your cat's entire body and overall behavior to determine how she is feeling.

## How Do We Begin?

Whether you are interacting with a person or a cat, communication is straightforward if you follow some simple guidelines: observe the individual's behavior, interpret her body language, make sure all her body parts are congruent (they all say the same thing), interact, and then reevaluate. Better communication with our feline companions comes down to six simple steps.

1. Learn their language.
2. Listen with all your senses.
3. Use cues that work for cats.
4. Avoid miscommunication traps.
5. Teach a common language.
6. Have realistic expectations.

## Learn Their Language

Peter rescued Pearl just a few weeks ago. He noticed that Pearl spent most of her time hiding with her tail curled under, body crouched, and pupils dilated. Unlike previous kittens he had interacted with, Pearl could not be enticed closer by fuzzy mice or wand toys. When Peter approached Pearl, she hissed. She assumed a Halloween cat posture with an arched back and bottle-brush tail.

Peter thought that perhaps if Pearl knew he was in charge, she might be able to relax. Peter consulted the Internet, where he was instructed to "pretend to be the mother cat, scruffing the kitten firmly by the loose skin above her haunches while suspending her body in the air." When he attempted to implement this advice, Pearl yowled and sank her teeth into his skin.

In this case, Peter's misguided plan to act and "speak" like a cat backfired. Pearl, who was already fearful, became defensively aggressive and went into fight-or-flight mode. A mother cat may pick up her young kittens by the scruff, but this is mainly to carry them from one place to another, not as a form of discipline. When a human "scruffs" a kitten or adult cat, it can cause pain and stress.

We cannot replicate cat behaviors, and cats do not see us as members of their species. Our goal is not to mirror cat behavior in an attempt to "speak cat." Rather, we can use knowledge of our cats' language to better understand their emotional states and anticipate how they may react. Our ability to understand and predict our cats' behavior will help prevent miscommunication that may inadvertently diminish our bond or create more misunderstanding.

Realizing his mistake, Peter took a different approach. Instead of imposing himself on Pearl, he created a private suite just for her — a quiet sanctuary room with a litter box, food, water, some toys, and a perch next to a large bay window. For a few minutes several times a day, Peter sat at the threshold of the room with his body turned away from Pearl. He was silent or spoke quietly, almost in a whisper. He did not move and dared not reach for Pearl.

Slowly, day by day, Pearl came out from hiding and began to approach Peter. When Pearl bunted her cheek against Peter's knee, he knew that she was starting to relax. Once Pearl's anxiety diminished, she became increasingly social every day. After only a few more weeks, she began chasing the fuzzy mice Peter tossed down the hall. It was a slow process, but the result was well worth the wait.

Peter respectfully observed and interpreted Pearl's body language. He used this information to continually evaluate and adjust his interactions with her. He recognized that the direct and forthright approach humans use to greet each other could appear threatening to a cat.

By modifying Pearl's environment to help her feel safe and secure, Peter was able to diminish her stress and improve her comfort. Hideaways and vertical spaces in the form of boxes, shelves, and perches allow for easier escape in response to a perceived threat. Cats seem to enjoy an aerial perspective, which lets them easily spot both predators and prey. Had Peter restricted Pearl's ability to escape by approaching her or picking her up, Pearl's fearful behavior may have escalated to vocal and postural threats, and ultimately a physical attack.

This cat surveys her environment from above. Vertical spaces offer comfort and provide an opportunity for cats to escape from perceived threats. *Kathleen Spencer*

## Listen with All Your Senses

A cat's heavy reliance on nonverbal communication requires us to listen with all our senses so we do not miss important information. Observation is a skill that is developed and refined over time. Humans are not naturally adept at observing subtle body postures, facial expressions, and tactile cues, especially in another species. Recognizing and then deciphering what your cat is saying takes practice.

Strengthen your observation and communication skills by constantly observing how your cat's body language changes in response to your behavior and the environment. Your back-and-forth behavioral dialogue will make you a better tabby translator.

## Use Cues That Work for Cats

Cats respond to a variety of human cues, including gestures and vocalizations. Dr. Adam Miklosi and his team found that the cats in their study correctly interpreted their owner's pointing gesture, using it at a distance to find hidden food. In fact, cats performed just as well as dogs on this task.

In another study, by Dr. Atsuko Saito and Dr. Kazutaka Shinozuka, cats distinguished their owner's voice from those of several strangers, proving that cats can use vocal cues alone to differentiate humans. These cats oriented toward their owner's voice by turning their head or swiveling their ears, but made no attempt to respond by vocalizing or coming when called.

We consciously use gestures and verbal cues to communicate with our cats, but do cats pick up on our unexpressed emotions as well? In short, yes. Our emotional state may influence our cats' perception and behavior. Research conducted by Dr. Isabella Merola and her colleagues indicated that cats pay attention to their owners' facial and vocal emotional reactions to an unfamiliar object and may change their own behavior to match their owners' emotional response.

For example, in Dr. Merola's research, when an owner acted fearful of an electric fan that their cat had not seen before, the cat looked back and forth not only between the fan and her owner, but also between the fan and the exit route. If your cat looks to you for guidance in a novel situation, behaving calmly may provide a sense of security to your cat.

## Avoid Miscommunication Traps

To cats, humans may look and act like predators: we're giants with ominously fast movements and loud voices. In any interaction with a cat, we need to slow down and talk softly — take our shout down to a whisper — and allow the cat an easy retreat. When an interaction is not going well, it's okay to stop, reassess, and try again later.

Earlier we discussed how behaviors such as licking, tail wagging, and belly exposure are often misinterpreted as friendly or affection-seeking signals. How can you determine whether your cat truly wants to be petted or is going to deliver a bite that says *Please don't touch me*? How do you know whether licking is friendly allogrooming or a nervous displacement behavior?

Observe the rest of your cat's body language. Are her ears and tail telling you she's relaxed or worried?

Sometimes there is a lack of congruence in body postures that can be confusing. For example, the tail may say one thing and the ears another. This could indicate that your cat has conflicting motivations or is unsure of how to respond in a given situation. That conflict is frequently an indication of stress. To determine how your cat is feeling and avoid miscommunication traps, read your cat's entire body and behavior rather than focusing on just one body part or behavior.

## Teach a Common Language

Training is a common language that enables humans and cats to communicate more effectively. When our message is clear and the outcome is positive, cats understand and trust our intentions. Although people commonly believe that cats cannot be trained, you might be surprised to learn that cats can be trained in the same way that dogs are. But you must be patient! Just as we cannot expect humans to understand a foreign language without being taught, we cannot expect cats to automatically comprehend what we are saying.

You can teach your cat almost any cued behaviors — some with a practical purpose and others just for fun. These might include "go to your bed," "sit," "stay," and "high-five." The safest, most effective way to train a cat is using positive reinforcement. For example, you can teach your cat to go to her bed by tossing a treat onto the bed, saying "go to your bed," and then saying "yes!" and giving another treat when she is on the bed. That way, you are rewarding her for performing the desired response. The more often you reinforce the behavior, the more likely she is to do it in hopes of obtaining the reward.

Rewards might include a treat, a toy, praise, or petting. Which reward you use will depend on what motivates your particular cat. When deciding on a reward, keep in mind that what motivates a cat may be different from what motivates you or another animal. Treats may work for some cats, while others will do anything for petting or the opportunity to chase a toy mouse. (See chapter 6 for more on how cats learn and how you can use training in your home.)

## Have Realistic Expectations

Some humans sit around on the couch all day, while others are constantly on the go. One person lives by the mantra "The early bird catches the worm," while another may be a night owl. Cats, like people, have individual personalities and interests, which are influenced by genetics, learning, and environment. Although we can make some generalizations about cats of a particular breed, not every cat in that breed will respond in a similar way, and each cat is an individual. Unrealistic expectations will set your cat up for failure.

Dr. Benjamin Hart, DACVB, and Dr. Lynette Hart studied various pedigree cats and ranked their prevailing behavioral characteristics. Abyssinians and Bengals were the most active, while Persians ranked as the least active. Siamese were the most vocal. Familiarity with the general personalities and needs of different breeds can increase the chances of a good cat-owner match. For example, a household or environment best suited for a sedentary cat will not meet the physical needs of a Bengal. Likewise, undesirable behaviors can arise when the environment does not allow ample opportunity for a feline of any breed or type to express her normal behavioral repertoire of scratching, climbing, playing, and hunting.

The physical attributes of different cat breeds can affect how we interpret their body language. Brachycephalic, or flat-faced, breeds, such as Persians, Himalayans, and Exotic Shorthairs, may appear stoic and are difficult to read. The former Internet sensation Grumpy Cat, for example, always looked grumpy because of his physical attributes and fixed facial expression. Similarly, it's hard to tell if a Scottish Fold is pinning her ears back in fear or to evaluate tail carriage in a Manx or Japanese Bobtail, because these breeds lack most of their tail.

This Scottish Fold has small ears that are not as movable as a domestic shorthair's ears, making it more difficult to read his body language. *Carlo Siracusa*

Like people, cats have different tolerance levels for physical affection and handling. Some people enjoy hugs and massages, while others shy away from touch. Some cats seek out and enjoy petting and handling by strangers, while others become aggressive when even familiar people pet or pick them up. Because cats have unique personalities and preferences, it's important to read every cat's body language when you interact with her rather than assuming that she will behave similarly to cats you've known before. Just because a cat accepts brief physical contact does not mean she wants more. Likewise, a cat who does not like to be cuddled or cradled like a baby can still be a great companion.

Behavior is fluid and may change with the environment, with a cat's age, or due to pain or illness. Consider the case of Misty. Amy expected Misty to accept petting the same way she always had. But Misty's back pain changed her willingness to be touched. The bustling and highly active nature of children did not bother her before, but now she perceived their unpredictable movements as a threat. Misty felt safer in her own space, away from the hustle and bustle. Amy noticed this change in Misty's behavior but did not realize that her avoidance was a sign of pain. If she had understood Misty's physical limitations, she might have adjusted her expectations about physical interactions. Misty's reaction would not have surprised her. Instead, she may have been able to avoid triggers and provide a more comfortable environment for Misty.

By recognizing that changes in behavior and communication are often the first signs of illness, we can more actively care for our pets, intervene early, and ensure that all health issues are addressed.

### Avoiding Catastrophe:
### How to Recognize Signs of Pain and Illness in Your Cat

Generally speaking, any unexplained change in physical appearance or behavior can indicate that your cat is ill. Because cats evolved from animals who were solitary prey for larger animals, they can expertly hide signs of illness so as not to show how sick they really are. Early signs of illness are often hard to detect, and your cat's distress may become obvious only after a disease is quite advanced. By recognizing subtle signs, including those listed here, and consulting with your veterinarian, you can give your cat the best chance at an early diagnosis and successful treatment.

PHYSICAL SIGNS:
- Weight change (loss or gain)
- Unkempt coat or missing hair
- Weakness or loss of muscle tone
- Vomiting
- Change in the amount, frequency, or appearance of urine
- Soft or bloody stools, diarrhea, or constipation
- Reluctance to be touched in certain places
- Any change in appearance (cloudy eyes, drooling, new or changing lumps or bumps on or under the skin)
- Excessive skin twitching

BEHAVIORAL SIGNS:
- Change in mood (for example, a once friendly cat becomes aggressive)
- Change in activity or energy level:
  * Less outgoing and social
  * Hiding or sleeping more
  * Decreased activity level
  * Less interested in play or toys

- * Hyperactivity
- Increased or decreased vocalization
- Altered routines
- Changes in sleep-wake pattern
- Increased or decreased appetite:
    - * Dropping food out of her mouth
    - * Change in food preference (for example, no longer eats dry food)
- Increased or decreased water drinking
- Difficulty walking, or walking with a crouched gait
- Difficulty climbing stairs
- Difficulty jumping:
    - * Prefers to lie on the ground or on lower furniture
    - * Reduced height of jumping
    - * Jumping on low objects to reach higher locations
    - * Pausing to consider the height of a jump
    - * Loss of catlike grace, including clumsy or heavy landings or pulling herself up rather than jumping
- New or changing behavior problems:
    - * House soiling, aggressive behavior, excessive vocalization
    - * Problem worsening in frequency or intensity
    - * Previous behavior problem improves or resolves (for example, no longer jumps on counters, not aggressive because she spends most of the day hiding)

Unless they're very sick, unwell cats do not appear ill or uncomfortable all the time. Typically, behavioral signs of illness occur intermittently and are therefore easy to miss or overlook. An ailing cat may occasionally greet you at the door or run up the stairs, just not as frequently or easily as she once did.

Given the right motivation and mood, desire may outweigh discomfort. For example, an old, arthritic cat may still jump on the counter despite her pain if there is a good reason to do so (such as to eat off your dinner plate). Slight situational variations can also make a difference. A cat with a painful stomach may not vocalize when you pick her up if you happen to cradle her in a slightly more comfortable way. Rather than focusing on individual events, consider trends, such as increased frequency or intensity of a behavioral sign, when determining whether your cat is ill.

## Avoiding Pitfalls and Staying on Track

Instead of focusing on one body part or behavior, look at the cat's entire body when deciphering her feelings. Behaviors have different meanings depending on the context in which they occur. For example, a cat may purr either when she is content or when she is stressed.

Treat each cat as a unique individual, despite your past experience with other cats and knowledge of breed characteristics. Consider your cat's personality so as to optimize her environment and your interactions.

Remember that not every cat wants to be petted. And some like a little bit, while others prefer more. Where a cat likes to be stroked is also an individual preference.

Respect your cat's boundaries. Some cats may be more outgoing, social, and confident, while others prefer to have more space.

Pay attention to changes in your cat's environment and how they could affect her stress levels and the ways she communicates with you.

### Purring: Nature and Nurture

People around the world list cat purring as one of their favorite sounds. You may be surprised to learn, however, that purring is not unique to domestic cats and does not always mean the cat is happy.

As far back as the early 1800s, scientists such as the British anatomist Sir Richard Owen made a distinction between cats who purr and cats who roar. Most cat species purr, but lions, tigers, leopards, and jaguars do not. These large cats roar, but technically they do not purr. Similarly, other species as varied as bears, raccoons, hyenas, and rabbits make a purrlike sound, but they do not, in fact, purr.

So what is a purr? It's a continuous sound produced by the rapid vibration of a muscle between the cat's vocal folds during both inhalation and exhalation. Kittens begin purring around three weeks of age, often while they nurse. Adult cats typically purr in pleasurable situations, including friendly contact with humans and other cats, or when they are anticipating food. However, cats may also purr when they are sick or in pain.

Why do cats purr when they are ill? Depending on the situation, cats may purr not for pleasure, but to voice their desire to be cared for. It appears that cats' purrs may have different meanings depending on whether they are content or requesting attention and nurturing. Dr. Karen McComb and her colleagues at the University of Sussex in England analyzed recordings of purrs. She found that cats waiting to be fed, a soliciting event, purred differently than cats being petted, a nonsoliciting context. Soliciting purrs contained a high-pitched component that Dr. McComb equated to a hidden meow — an attention-seeking vocalization embedded within the purr. People listening to recorded purrs rated solicitation purrs as more urgent and less pleasant than nonsolicitation purrs.

Other researchers have a different explanation for purring. Dr. Elizabeth von Muggenthaler speculates that purring may be a form of self-healing. Similarly, several studies reviewed by Dr. Wing-hoi Cheung at the Chinese University of Hong Kong found that vibrations at frequencies similar to purring may stimulate bone healing. If this is the case, then purring may be an excellent way for cats to recuperate after a long day of hunting, and it may further explain why humans have a natural affinity for purring.

## What Did We Say?

- Cats rely on different forms of communication than humans. We are primarily verbal, while cats use tactile, olfactory, and visual signals in addition to vocalizations. Listen to your cat with all your senses to better understand and anticipate her reactions.
- We can't speak cat, but we can learn to read our cats' body language. Cats alter their body postures depending on how they feel. Their eyes, ears, tail, and body will all give you information, but you need to pay attention to the cat as a whole to really understand her mood.
- Avoid treating cats like small dogs. Some behaviors, like rolling over and wagging their tail, may look similar but have completely different meanings for cats.
- Use reward-based training to teach cats cues. This will allow you to communicate using a common language.
- Your cat's behavior will change with age, illness, and environmental

conditions. Being familiar with the normal behavioral and communication strategies of your cat will enable you to notice subtle changes and detect health or behavior problems at an early stage.

- Cats are sensitive to large gestures, fast movements, and loud voices. We need to slow down and reduce our shouts to a whisper.

# 2

# Welcoming Your New Best Friend

*Setting Up Your New Cat for a Lifetime
of Health and Happiness*

Kelly Moffat, DVM, DACVB

He strutted around the room with purpose. This one-year-old Bengal was friendly, engaged, inquisitive, and empowered. I knew right then that Nancy, a senior citizen, had a problem. "He is just so beautiful," Nancy gushed. "Isn't he the most gorgeous cat you have ever seen?" I nodded to show my attention and support. She added, "I just don't understand why he gets so angry."

I scanned her bruised hands and arms, marked with bite and scratch wounds in various stages of healing. Her thin skin and daily blood thinner medication made these wounds even worse. "I have already had several emergency room visits and was hospitalized for a few days after Zeus bit me particularly hard. I just don't know what to do, Doctor — I love him so much!"

As a general practitioner for twenty-five years and a veterinary behaviorist for fourteen years, I can identify a cat like Zeus in just a few minutes. The history I took from Nancy confirmed my suspicions. Zeus indeed was a gorgeous specimen of the Bengal lineage of cats. He was active, intelligent, and very outgoing. His personality, however, was a struggle for Nancy. She hadn't provided him with enough of the environmental and interactive enrichment he craved, so he used her as an outlet for his intense (and normal) predatory and play behaviors.

When Nancy became frustrated with the attacks, she began to use more verbal and physical punishments with Zeus, such as swatting at him and spraying water. This only made his rambunctious play worse. As he matured, his play became more demanding, and Nancy's rebukes were met with defensive and then more offensive aggression, as Zeus perceived these interactions to be more punitive than positive.

Nancy admitted that she would prefer a lap cat who would enjoy her more sedentary lifestyle. Yet despite my encouragement for her to find Zeus a more appropriate home, Nancy is still struggling to make the best possible environment for him and to change her interactions with him. And she continues to see occasional bouts of aggression from him.

Bringing a new cat or kitten into your home is a big decision. Many cats live fifteen years or more, so it's important to plan for this huge commitment. Often, owning a cat will dictate future living situations, partners, jobs, and activities. There are a lot of decisions to make, such as where to get your new furry addition; whether you should adopt an adult or a kitten, a male or a female; and whether you want a pedigree or mixed-breed cat. Choosing the right one is vital for both your and the cat's long-term well-being.

A fair amount of research is available showing how breed, sex, age, and other aspects of a cat's past can affect his lifelong personality and behavior. In this chapter, I'll clear up some questions and concerns in these areas and give you some facts that will help you choose the right feline friend for you. Then I'll focus on how you can provide the right environment for this new member of your family, what veterinary care and grooming he will need, and how to keep your cat and your house safe while also respecting the other members of your human and pet family.

## Facts, Not Fiction

Where should you get your new cat? Because of the pet overpopulation problem, getting your new friend as a stray or through a shelter or rescue group is a noble idea and one fully supported by the data on cats in shelters. Approximately 6.5 million companion animals enter US animal shelters nationwide every year — about 3.3 million dogs and 3.2 million cats. Each year, approximately 1.5 million shelter animals are euthanized (670,000 dogs and 860,000 cats).

According to a national survey of pet owners conducted by the American Pet Products Association for 2017–2018, 95 percent of cats were obtained someplace other than a pet store or breeder. The cat may have shown up on the doorstep or been adopted from a shelter, a rescue group, a coworker, or a friend who found a litter of kittens in their backyard or apartment complex.

Some people decide to actively look for a new cat and, being sympathetic to the feline overpopulation problem, visit a local animal shelter or another rescue organization. Most are not looking for a specific breed or even sex of cat. Many are open-minded about adopting either an adult cat or a kitten. They may choose their new pet by the way the cat approaches (or doesn't) the cage door, the beauty of his coat, or his laid-back or playful personality. Others are sympathetic to a one-eyed or three-legged cat, an older cat, or a timid cat — one they feel may have a poorer chance of being adopted.

## What Does That Mean?

**Open-admission shelter:** A shelter that accepts all animals surrendered to it and may work with the city's animal control agency. Not all animals surrendered to this kind of shelter get placed for adoption.

**Limited-admission shelter:** Generally, a privately funded shelter that may accept animals based on breed, behavior, adoptability, age, health, or other criteria. Many of these animals are transferred from open-admission shelters.

**Kitten mill:** A commercial or large-scale cat breeder, often criticized for having high numbers of kittens in tight spaces and lack of proper hygiene, medical care, and socialization.

**Microchip:** An implant that allows clinics and shelters to find a pet's owner if the pet gets lost. This information should be updated as your address and phone number change. This is *not* a tracking device; it's solely for identification.

**Pedigree, or purebred, cat:** A cat who comes from a known line of ancestors of a particular breed. These cats are bred for a specific look and often have behaviors that are characteristic of the breed.

**Mixed-breed cat:** A cat who is the result of random breeding, usually referred to as a domestic shorthair or domestic longhair.

**Hybrid:** The offspring of a wild species bred to a domestic cat. Ideally, this type of breeding leads to a cat who looks wild but has a safer, calmer, more domesticated temperament. Hybrids, including Bengals such as Zeus, typically require much more enrichment and a much larger environment.

**Temperament:** The aspects of an animal's behavior and personality that are genetically based.

**Heredity:** The act of passing traits from parents to their offspring. Many behavioral traits in cats, such as friendliness, can be inherited. Conditions that lead to diseases such as heart or kidney disease can also be inherited from a parent or other relative.

**Sensitive socialization period:** The time (two to seven weeks) when a kitten is most open to learning about his surroundings, including his mother, littermates, environment, other animals, and humans. During this period, kittens are more likely to approach, explore, and show little fear when encountering new animals, people, objects, and situations. Providing a wide variety of positive experiences during this period can help prevent a kitten from experiencing fear, anxiety, and aggression as an adult.

## Shelters

Many different types of shelters house stray, lost, abandoned, and surrendered animals. Some are run by the local government, but far more are independently operated as nonprofit animal welfare organizations. There is no national organization that oversees or regulates shelters, although many individual states and municipalities do regulate shelters within their jurisdiction.

If you adopt from a well-funded, responsible shelter, you will generally get a pet who has been examined by veterinary staff, vaccinated, evaluated for temperament, and often spayed or neutered. Many shelters lack funding, resources, and proper management, however, so it is important to make sure that any adult cat you are considering adopting has been tested and is negative for feline leukemia virus (FeLV) and feline immunodeficiency virus (FIV); any kitten has been tested for FeLV (FIV testing isn't accurate in kittens younger than six months old); and the cat has received his first core vaccines, including the one for feline viral rhinotracheitis, calicivirus, and panleukopenia (FVRCP). There is generally a modest adoption fee that helps the shelter cover the cost of care for the cat or kitten.

Many overcrowded shelters have discounted or even free adoption days. People flock to these events and often get caught up in the excitement of adopting a cat at little or no cost. Many of these potential owners, however, are unprepared to cover the costs of an initial veterinary visit, booster vaccinations, and medications for a cat who leaves the shelter with a respiratory infection, as many do. The financial commitment after adoption is the same whether the cat was free or not. Every potential cat owner should be prepared for the day-to-day expenses of providing and caring for their new family member.

## Rescue Groups

Numerous rescue organizations take in stray or unwanted cats, house them in group facilities or foster homes, and work to find them new homes. They may take in cats as transfers from overcrowded shelters or those placed on euthanasia lists because of various behavior or medical issues. They may also take cats from individuals who can no longer care for their pets. Some of these rescue groups are specific to a particular breed, but most are not. Many provide basic medical care, including FeLV and FIV testing, vaccinations, and spaying or neutering.

Not all rescue groups are created equal. Make sure you ask questions and see the medical records documenting testing, vaccinations, and spaying or neutering for the cat you are considering adopting. Some groups have fairly simple applications, while others have lengthy applications and require multiple home visits before approving a potential adopter. They generally charge an adoption fee to help cover the costs of caring for the cat. It's easy to find cat rescue organizations through an Internet search or by talking to local animal shelters or veterinarians.

## Cat Cafés

You may even get your little tiger at a cat café. The concept of the cat café started in Taiwan, based on the idea that customers can enjoy a hot beverage while also getting in some quality cat time. Since 2014, cat cafés have been spreading across North America. US cat cafés typically host animals from a local shelter and focus on adoptions. They may best be described as a cross between a coffee shop and an adoption center. Interacting with cats in this environment gives potential adopters a good idea of a cat's personality and can be a great socialization tool for kittens.

## Strays

There is typically no shortage of stray cats and kittens around housing complexes, mall parking lots, college campuses, and industrial parks. A wayward feline may also show up in your backyard or on your doorstep, looking for food or even companionship.

Before adopting one of these cats, make sure to have him scanned for a microchip and check "lost pet" postings online in places such as The Center for Lost Pets (www.thecenterforlostpets.com), the Missing Pet Network (www.missingpet.net), and Petfinder (www.petfinder.com). Occasionally, someone will find a cat who has wandered away from his owner, and that person has been desperately looking for him. If you can't find the owner and want to adopt the cat, assume that he hasn't had any medical care. He will need a veterinary checkup, including FeLV and FIV testing, a scan for external parasites such as fleas, a fecal exam, possibly a deworming medicine, vaccinations, and spaying or neutering. Check with local veterinarians about the costs for all these services; some offer discounts for rescued cats.

## "Free to Good Home"

These cats are found on social media sites such as Craigslist, community and work bulletin boards, or just about anywhere people post items to sell or give away. They generally have not been to a veterinarian, so you'll need to treat them the same as you would a stray: they'll need a general checkup, testing, vaccinations, and spaying or neutering. Be aware that some people may not disclose the real reason they are seeking a new home for their pet. Perhaps the cat has been urinating outside the litter box or destroying their furniture, and they don't want to deal with the problem behavior themselves. They may also misrepresent or misunderstand the degree to which the cat is social with people.

## Pet Stores

Pet stores turn a large profit selling popular purebred or mixed-breed cats who come from commercial breeders (known as kitten mills), middlemen, or brokers. The staff members often have little knowledge of the cats' true origin or the conditions in which they were born and raised. The cats often have illnesses, parasites, and congenital defects that end up being chronically difficult, as well as financially demanding, to treat.

Many pet store chains have stopped selling kittens and instead have created "pop-up" adoption centers hosting cats from local rescue groups or shelters. Be prepared to fill out an application and go through whatever screening process these groups require.

## The Internet

People use the Internet for everything, including looking for a new pet. This is a great way to start the search, because many animal shelters and local rescue groups have their own websites where you can view their adoptable pets and search the site to learn more about the group's background and mission. You can then call the organization and ask questions before you visit.

Breeders also sell kittens on the Internet, but be cautious if a kitten is coming from outside your area. You shouldn't buy any kitten sight unseen, and you should try not to have a kitten shipped to you by plane, as doing so will expose him to stressors that can affect him for the rest of his life.

## Choosing a Cat

Most cat owners choose a new cat of mixed ancestry rather than a recognized breed. According to the American Humane Association's *U.S. Pet (Dog and Cat) Population Fact Sheet* (2013), 95 percent of the cats in the United States are classified as domestic shorthair (DSH). As the name says, these cats have short fur. The rest are domestic longhair (DLH).

You may hear someone refer to their "calico cat," "tabby cat," or "tuxedo cat." These terms describe coat colors and patterns, not breeds. Mixed-breed cats come in a variety of beautiful colors, patterns, and unique combinations. So many need homes, and they can be a great choice for a new cat owner.

Maggie is a nine-year-old domestic longhair with a tuxedo coat pattern who was adopted from a local shelter. *Kelly Moffat*

T'Pring is a domestic shorthair kitten with a calico tabby coat pattern who was adopted from a cat café. *Craig Zeichner*

Some people really want a particular breed of cat. Perhaps they've seen this breed on television, in a magazine, or at a cat show. Unfortunately, some (such as Nancy) are seduced by looks alone and have not done enough research into the breed. They are not well-informed about the personality, activity level, medical concerns, and needs of that breed. Even if they learn about a particular breed, some people believe they will be able to provide for the special needs and behaviors of the breed, but later find themselves unprepared for or intolerant of the actual impact their new cat has on their lives, homes, and loved ones. This creates a heartbreaking situation for everyone — the cat and the people.

Pedigree cats have been bred specifically to exhibit a particular set of physical characteristics. Some of these characteristics may first have appeared as a genetic mutation, such as short legs, folded ears, or a lack of hair. Occasionally, a different species is bred with a domestic cat to form a hybrid, such as the Bengal.

If looks could kill, this Bengal, Sara, would be quite the assassin.
*Sheri Johnson*

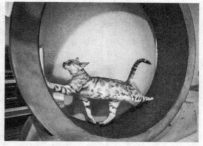

Bengals are a high-maintenance breed, requiring a lot of daily physical and mental exercise. Sara gets her exercise on the carpeted wheel her owners made for her. *Sheri Johnson*

---

### Top 10 Cat Fanciers' Association Breeds

1. Ragdoll
2. Exotic Shorthair
3. British Shorthair
4. Persian
5. Maine Coon
6. American Shorthair
7. Devon Rex
8. Sphynx
9. Scottish Fold
10. Abyssinian

Source: Cat Fanciers' Association 2018 breed registration numbers.

---

Pedigree cats are bred only to other cats of the same breed, to maintain the breed's particular characteristics. This means that the number of cats available for breeding is limited, and the gene pool is small. Problems can arise from a limited gene pool, and if there are heritable health problems or disorders, they are more likely to be passed on to the next generation. Certain conditions, such as heart and kidney disease, can be inherited and lead to a shortened life span.

---

### Diseases and Breed Genetic Predispositions

Problems that exist within a particular closed gene pool are considered inherited, or heritable, disorders. Some universities, such as the University of California, Davis, and the University of Pennsylvania, offer genetic testing to help breeders identify carriers of these conditions. Responsible breeders test all their breeding cats for the inherited disorders that crop up most often in their breed, then design breeding programs that avoid these health problems.

Following are some of the most common heritable diseases.

- **Hypertrophic cardiomyopathy (HCM)** has been documented in Ragdoll, Maine Coon, Himalayan, Burmese, Sphynx, Persian, and Devon Rex cats.
- **Polycystic kidney disease (PKD)** is a disorder caused by a single gene that has often been found in Persians, Himalayans, and Persian-derived breeds.
- **Progressive retinal atrophy (PRA)** has been seen in Bengal, Persian, Abyssinian, Somali, American Curl, American Wirehair, Balinese/Javanese, Colorpoint Shorthair, Cornish Rex, Munchkin, Oriental Shorthair, Peterbald, Siamese, Singapura, and Tonkinese cats, as well as some Ocicats.
- **Pyruvate kinase (PK) deficiency** can be seen in Abyssinian, Bengal, domestic shorthair and longhair, Egyptian Mau, LaPerm, Maine Coon, Norwegian Forest, Savannah, Siberian, Singapura, and Somali cats.

---

If you are considering buying a cat from a breeder, remember that not all breeders are created equal. Research them thoroughly by doing an online search. Investigate their reputation and find out if they've had any complaints lodged against them. Visit their cattery. Ask about testing, vaccinations, medical care, and socialization. A responsible breeder will put the time, energy, and money into producing quality kittens with the

Persians have a brachycephalic (flat) face and are predisposed to some health problems, such as polycystic kidney disease and hypertrophic cardiomyopathy. *Kelly Moffat*

best physical and mental health. They will be educated about congenital defects known in the breed and will have tested their breeding pairs to ensure that they will not pass on harmful genetic mutations.

Responsible breeders also consider the behavior and temperament of the cats they breed. A breeder should allow you to interact with the parents of a kitten you are interested in, or to talk to owners of cats from previous litters produced by the same breeding pair, so you can better predict a kitten's adult temperament.

A litter of Sphynx kittens awaits adoption at a veterinary clinic. *Meghan E. Herron*

Good breeders handle and socialize their kittens appropriately during the sensitive socialization period (between two and seven weeks of age) — something that doesn't always happen with rescued cats. This will have an impact on the kittens' future behavior. As mentioned earlier, there are breed-specific rescue organizations, both local and national, for all breeds of cats. While purebred kittens may be harder to find through a rescue group or shelter, they are out there if you keep a lookout for them.

British Shorthairs are big, round, mellow cats. Though more active than Persians, they are calm and friendly. *Carlo Siracusa*

Expect to pay hundreds or even thousands of dollars for a pedigree cat, depending on the breed. Even breed-specific rescue organizations might charge a hefty adoption fee. And, as with any cat, you'll also need to account for veterinary care and everyday expenses such as food, litter, and enrichment.

Exotic Shorthairs have the same body and head shape as Persians, without the problems associated with long hair. Typical of this breed, Mishka is a quiet, friendly cat. *Mariella Idonia*

Maine Coon cats are the gentle giants of cats. They are agile, active, and very affectionate. Their long, square muzzle and large ears with lynx tips give them a distinctive and very attractive look. *David Bernbaum*

### Learn More About Cat Breeds

Breed diversity in cats isn't quite what it is in dogs. Dog breeds were developed for a variety of purposes (hunting, herding, protection, and so on), whereas cat breeds were developed primarily for appearance. There are currently forty-four breeds recognized by the Cat Fanciers' Association (CFA) and seventy-one recognized by The International Cat Association (TICA) — the two largest American registries. These organizations have accumulated a fair amount of information about the temperament and characteristics of the various breeds.

Among pedigree cats, one must be mindful of breed disposition and special needs. (Again, think of Nancy and Zeus.) Before adopting a particular breed of cat, learn as much as you can about it — both good and bad — so you'll be prepared for the lifestyle the cat may require, his grooming needs, and any medical conditions to be alert for.

For more information on cat breeds, I recommend *Your Ideal Cat: Insights into Breed and Gender Differences in Cat Behavior,* by Dr. Benjamin Hart, DACVB, and Dr. Lynette Hart. Another resource is Purina's "Cat Breeds" web page (www.purina.com/cats/cat-breeds). You can also learn about cat breeds from the breed registry organizations, including CFA and TICA, online. Visiting a cat show and speaking with breeders is another option, but remember that they obviously love the breed they are raising and so will likely be biased.

## What Influences a Kitten's Behavior?

When you're adopting a kitten, his personality and behavior are far more important than his appearance. Personality and behavior traits are influenced by a complex interplay of genetics, prenatal conditions, early learning, and experience.

A kitten's individual genetics play an essential role in how social, playful, fearful, or confident he will be. Friendliness is likely a strong genetic trait and has been shown to be inherited from the father (called the tom). Unless you're adopting a pedigree cat, though, the father is often no longer in the picture when you meet a litter of kittens, so you usually don't know what he is like.

The mother (called the queen) contributes her part genetically, but normal development of a kitten relies strongly on a healthy mother who had proper nutrition during pregnancy and is attentive to him. Kittens who are raised together and learn from their mother (and one another) about both the world and feline social structures, social cues, and cat language are more well-adjusted than those who lack a healthy, attentive mother. Orphaned and hand-raised kittens have a tendency to be overly cautious, fearful, or aggressive as adults. Neglected kittens, or kittens from ill or malnourished mothers, may develop medical conditions or have behavior problems as they mature.

## Early Handling

In addition to the genetics of both parents and the health and early lessons provided by the mother, early handling, especially during the sensitive socialization period, also significantly contributes to a kitten's adult personality. Kittens who are handled just fifteen minutes a day from birth are more social, more willing to explore, and more able to handle stress as they develop. They are also likely to be more social with people when placed in a new home after weaning.

The most sensitive socialization period is thought to be between two and seven weeks of age, so the greater exposure a kitten has to humans of all ages as well as other pets, environments, and situations during that time, the better adjusted that kitten is likely to be.

That being said, there is evidence to suggest that gentle handling and exposure to people, other pets, and environmental stimuli even up to twelve weeks of age can be highly beneficial. So if your kitty is older than seven weeks, hope is not lost for helping him come out of his shell. And even if your kitten did get the opportunity to be socialized before seven weeks of age, you will still have work to do. Those early positive associations are best maintained through repetition and practice.

## Sex

There are some behavioral differences between male and female cats that can't be attributed to breed differences. According to research by Dr. Benjamin Hart, DACVB, and Dr. Lynette Hart, males show a much higher tendency for friendliness, playfulness, activity, and affection toward their human family than females, but they also rank higher in urine marking. Neutering greatly reduces this marking behavior, but it can still be seen in approximately 10 percent of neutered male cats, whether they are neutered as kittens or as adults.

Females show more aggressiveness toward both people and cats and are typically reported to be more fearful than males. They do rate higher on good litter box use, though.

Despite these tendencies, individual variations in personality and behavior are more important when choosing a cat. Picking a cat based solely on male vs. female can be less effectual than picking one based on individual characteristics.

## Is That Really True?

*Do temperament tests work?* Assessing very young kittens can be of limited value if they are still progressing through their sensitive socialization period. A kitten's receptivity to socialization begins to decline at about seven weeks of age; after that age, behavioral assessments may be increasingly more reliable in predicting a kitten's behavior as an adult. Assessing older kittens and adult cats can provide even more accurate information. Studies have shown that many aspects of cat personality remain stable over time once the animal is four to five months of age.

*How old should a kitten be before you adopt him?* Recent research recommends that if the kitten can stay in a stable environment with his mother and littermates, adoption is best after fourteen weeks of age. One study found that cats weaned at a later time had a lower likelihood of becoming aggressive toward strangers, as well as a lower probability of developing stereotypic behaviors (such as excessive grooming), than cats weaned earlier.

That being said, many kittens don't have the advantage of stable maternal care. Often kittens in shelters and rescue settings are adopted at eight weeks of age. If your kitten can't stay with his feline family until fourteen weeks of age, at least you can positively expose him to humans of all ages, other pets, and novel situations when you take him home.

*Is it better to adopt a kitten or a cat?* Kittens are undoubtedly cute and fun to watch and play with. However, kitten behaviors, though often YouTube-worthy, can be overwhelming. Kittens generally jump, scratch, and bite and are very active at night. If kitten antics aren't high on your wish list, consider adopting an adult or senior cat. Older cats are less likely to be noticed among the cages of frisky, playful kittens at a shelter and are adopted at lower rates. With fully mature cats, what you see is what you get. In other words, you already know their size and personality.

Adopting an adult cat may present its own difficulties, as he may not adapt as readily to your household and any other pets you may have. Adult cats generally have a longer and more challenging integration period with other adult cats than kittens do. If you adopt an adult cat from a shelter, he may have been surrendered for behavioral reasons that were not disclosed by the previous owner. Sometimes these behaviors are not evident in the first few days or even weeks of adoption. If there are behavioral concerns, many owners think that the cat just needs some time to adjust, which in many cases is true — but in many cases is not.

Despite these warnings, be open to adopting an adult cat. Many turn out to be terrific pets and live wonderful, enriched lives in their new homes. Just be careful, and if you have other cats in your home, introduce them slowly. (See chapter 5 for more about cat-to-cat introductions.) Also understand that on occasion, you may find a cat who, albeit adorable, may not be the best fit for your household, family, or other pets and is not suitable for your home.

*Should you adopt one cat or two?* If you're thinking about adopting a cat or kitten, consider taking home two. Cats need exercise, mental stimulation, and social interaction. Two cats can provide this for each other. Not all cats are going to be friendly with each other, so this works best with kittens and adult cats who came from the same home and ended up in the shelter together. Many shelters try to keep bonded cats together. Two littermates will have a closer relationship than two unrelated individuals, and a mother and kitten will generally have a close bond and do well together.

Dolce and Rudy are a pair of Burmese who were adopted together at a young age, allowing them to develop and maintain a strong bond throughout their lives. *Kathy Prinz*

Getting a new adult cat as a companion for an already established adult cat in your home is not always so successful, and introducing the two cats should be done carefully (see chapter 5). Adding a second cat can result in behavior problems, such as fighting or urine spraying. And make sure you are prepared financially, as having two cats means twice the food, twice the litter, and twice the medical care.

*Should a cat live indoors, outdoors, or both?* I find many cat owners are now allowing their cats outside for part of the day as an enrichment activity. Often they explain that the cat was taken in as a stray and continues to "ask" for outdoor time. The cat likes to climb trees, lie in the sun, chase birds, and hunt lizards. There is, indeed, no match for the great outdoors when it comes to feline enrichment.

That being said, the outdoor life comes with risks, and many owners choose to provide enhanced indoor enrichment rather than outdoor exposure. Fenced-in cat yards, cat patios (catios), and harness walks have fewer risks, but depending on the situation, they have their own dangers. Discuss all these risks with your veterinarian before allowing your cat outside.

Undoubtedly, an indoor cat is safer than an outdoor cat. Not only are outdoor cats susceptible to infectious diseases such as FIV, but there are other viruses, parasites, toxins, predators, and injuries to worry about as well. Whereas indoor cats live, on average, from twelve to fifteen years, cats who spend some time outdoors live two to three years less.

Risks for outdoor cats include:

- Infectious diseases, including FeLV, FIV, feline infectious peritonitis (FIP), feline distemper (panleukopenia), and upper respiratory infections spread by stray, feral, or un-cared-for cats
- Cat fight injuries
- Trauma (hit by a car or other trauma)
- Toxins (antifreeze, rodenticides, herbicides, fertilizers, and others)
- Predation (dogs, coyotes, cougars, large birds of prey, and others)
- Trapping by neighbors (who may then relocate the cat, take him to a shelter, or even kill him)
- Malicious actions by humans

There is no doubt that cats who have outdoor access have an assortment of enrichment opportunities to keep their minds and bodies active and engaged. As cat owners who want to keep our feline family member around as long as possible, and also be responsible pet owners and neighbors, we can provide similar enrichment for our cats indoors. Chapter 3 has some wonderful ideas for feline enrichment, and chapter 12 offers some suggestions for how to let your cat go outside in a safer and more controlled way.

## How Do We Begin?

Here are some tips for finding your perfect kitten.

- Look for a kitten who had a healthy mother and who was raised by her and with his littermates — ideally, until fourteen weeks of age.
- If both parents are present, look at their behavior. Friendliness toward humans is strongly influenced by the father. The mother contributes her genetics as well, and her mothering skills are important in shaping a healthy, social kitten.
- Try to find a kitten who has been handled frequently, preferably for at least fifteen minutes every day, during the sensitive period of two to seven weeks.
- A kitten who has been positively exposed to adults and children both inside and outside the home is more likely to develop into a socially stable cat. If your kitten is going to be around dogs, it is helpful if he was previously exposed in a positive manner to them as well.
- Does the kitten approach people, or does he run away or freeze? A kitten who freezes or runs away is fearful and will likely take more time to socialize or desensitize to people. If you are looking for a social, outgoing cat, a fearful kitten may not be your best pick.
- How does the kitten react to being properly picked up? To test this, gently pick him up with one hand under his chest and another cradling his back end, so he feels safe and stable. If he fights, freezes, or tries to flee, he is a timid, fearful cat and will require more of your time and effort to become more relaxed with you. He also may be unsuitable for small children, who may not be careful in handling him.

- Ask if the kitten is using a litter box. Kittens develop litter and litter box preferences before five weeks of age.

Here are some tips for finding your perfect adult cat.

- The sensitive socialization period is over, so what you see is what you get in an older cat. You'll have a fairly good idea of the cat's personality right away.
- Ask yourself what kind of personality you are looking for in a cat. Shelter staff, foster caregivers, and rescue volunteers can often help steer you to the right cat.
- Take into consideration where you are meeting this cat for the first time. Many environments, such as rescue organizations and shelters, can be stressful for a cat, so you may not get to see the best, most relaxed side of him. Try to meet him in a quiet area, and spend some time with him. Perhaps visit more than once.
- If possible, try to find out why the cat is available for adoption. Did he have behavior issues in his previous home, or was the family simply unable to keep him?
- If the cat has a medical issue, make sure you have the time and financial resources to take care of him.

## Avoiding Pitfalls and Staying on Track

When you bring your cat home, kitten or adult, a trip to the veterinarian to check out your new family member should be the first thing on your agenda. You want to make sure you are starting out with a healthy cat. And if you have other pets at home, you don't want to spread any infectious diseases or parasites to them.

If the cat or kitten had some veterinary or medical care before you adopted him, make sure to get a written record of what was done. That record should include medication and vaccination names, doses, and dates they were administered. Bring this to your veterinarian so that she can give you the best possible medical advice and recommendations. If possible, bring a fresh stool sample for a fecal parasite exam. The sample should be less than twenty-four hours old and can be placed in a small plastic bag or container.

A stray adult cat found on a doorstep gets her first full exam. *Sharon Witherspoon*

If you don't have any previous medical records for your new cat or kitten, the veterinarian will run FeLV and FIV tests, perform a fecal exam, and administer vaccinations. She also will do a thorough physical exam to check for common ailments such as upper respiratory infections, ear mites, dental disease, external parasites, and other skin diseases such as ringworm. She will talk to you about internal and external parasites, and depending on findings and the cat's circumstances, she may prescribe a deworming medication or flea and tick preventive.

If the cat is not already spayed or neutered, discuss the procedure, the cost, and the best time to schedule it.

Hopefully, your veterinarian will also ask about the cat's environment, whether you will be traveling with him in the future, and what his exposure will be to other cats and animals. This will help her develop the best medical plan for your cat.

Ask about microchipping as a means of identification. In this procedure, a small microchip, about the size of a grain of rice, is implanted under the cat's skin between the shoulder blades. That chip has a unique number on it that can be picked up and read by a scanner. Many indoor-cat owners do not think their cat needs one, but unfortunately many of these cats can and do escape. According to the research, the return-to-owner rate for cats is twenty times higher for microchipped pets than for all other stray cats in shelters.

## A Shopping List for Your New Cat

There are a few items you should have ready before you bring your new cat home.

- Food. Find out what your cat has been eating at his previous home and start with this. You can always transition to a different diet. If you decide you want to do that, do it gradually over about a week to avoid gastrointestinal upset or stress on the cat.
- Bowls for food and water.
- A cat carrier. If you are planning on airline travel, make sure the carrier is airline approved. A carrier with a removable cover works best for veterinary visits. Two kittens may fit in one carrier, but as they grow into adulthood, two separate carriers are better.
- Litter box(es). Choose a box that will be one and a half times the size of your cat when he has grown to adulthood. Most cats prefer an uncovered box. A kitten may need a box with lower sides to begin with.
- Litter. Most cats prefer sandy, clumping litter. You may want to ask what the cat has been using and start with that. As with food, transition slowly if you want to make a change.
- Toys. Avoid toys with long strings or small parts that could be ingested.
- A scratching post. It should be heavy and sturdy enough that it won't get knocked over, and tall enough to allow the cat (as an adult) to reach up and fully stretch to use it. Many cats also like a horizontal scratching surface.
- Cat trees and perches. These are excellent enrichment items. Place them in areas where your family spends time and in front of sunny windows. They might include tents, boxes, or other hiding spots for those times when your cat wants to be out of sight.

## What Did We Say?

- Find a cat whose personality will fit your present and future lifestyle. That may be an adult cat or a kitten, a particular breed or a mixed-breed. Don't forget to consider the other pets in your household and how they may be affected by and respond to a new addition.

- Realize that cats often live more than fifteen years. Take into account their longevity and the care your cat will need over all that time.
- Do you know the history of the kitten you plan to adopt? A kitten raised by his mother, with his littermates and with human contact and a variety of environmental exposures, is likely to be friendlier and less fearful in his adult life than one who didn't have these advantages.
- Look into your options for finding a new cat or kitten. The pet overpopulation crisis may point you to the more socially conscious decision to adopt from a shelter or rescue group, or to take in a homeless stray. Several medical and financial decisions come into play here, as shelter cats have generally already been evaluated medically, vaccinated, and spayed or neutered.
- If you choose a cat from a rescue group, make sure the group is reputable and you obtain the cat's medical records.
- With a stray, you are starting with little or no history and should have the cat immediately checked out by a veterinarian for infectious diseases, parasites, and any other health issues.
- If you want to adopt a pedigree cat, make sure you research the breed extensively and are aware of breed behavior traits, grooming needs, and disease susceptibilities. Choose a reputable breeder.
- Select a veterinarian ahead of time and schedule a visit within the first few days of getting your cat.
- Purchase food, bowls, litter boxes, litter, a carrier, and toys for your new arrival *before* you bring him home.
- Enjoy your new best friend!

# 3

# The Feline Dream Home
*Creating an Enriched Environment
for Your Cat's Mind and Body*

Kelly Ballantyne, DVM, DACVB,
and Amy L. Pike, DVM, DACVB

Jessica loved her new cat, Fiona. She was the most playful cat Jessica had ever had. Fiona greeted her at the door when she came home from work, and Fiona's antics were usually very entertaining. However, Jessica wasn't sleeping well because Fiona pounced on her and meowed repeatedly in the early morning hours.

Jessica had tried closing Fiona out of her bedroom, but the few nights she did so, Fiona meowed and scratched at the door most of the night. The only thing that seemed to stop the meowing was to feed Fiona, but it seemed like Fiona was waking her up earlier and earlier. Jessica was exhausted and not really sure what to do. While she loved Fiona, she was also really frustrated by some of her behaviors.

Unlike dogs, which humans actively domesticated, cats just came along for the ride. We encouraged cats to remain nearby as long as they controlled the rodents that threatened our food supply and homes. In return, we asked for very little change in their daily habits.

Fast-forward thousands of years, and instead of wandering outdoors, working hard to survive, our cats are now our indoor pride and joy. But with this new closeness comes a responsibility to remember what cats really are: active climbers, hunters, stalkers, and hiders. The inability to spend their days doing "cat stuff" and instead living in dull — or, worse, stressful or frightening — environments can take its toll.

Poor environmental conditions (too many pets; no safe places; lack of easy access to needs such as food, water, and litter boxes; nothing to do;

lack of predictability) have been linked to stress, anxiety, obesity, and poor health. In this chapter, we will explore and explain the link between environment and medical health, and how certain medical conditions, such as feline interstitial cystitis (FIC), can be treated or prevented with environmental enrichment and stress-lowering techniques.

Enriched environments for cats should include safe and acceptable climbing, perching, and hiding areas; hunting excursions to find and procure their daily food; and soft bedding in safe places where they can sleep and dream. All these things strengthen a cat's mind and body. This chapter will help you create a home where your cat will be fulfilled and enriched, and the envy of all her feline friends.

## Facts, Not Fiction

There is a long-held misconception that cats are low-maintenance pets. In other words, if you have a busy lifestyle, work long hours, or travel a lot, but want the companionship and joy of a pet, you should get a cat. Many people think all a cat needs is a home, a litter box, and bowls of food and water to be happy and thrive.

However, there is strong scientific evidence to the contrary. It shows that cats living without the benefits of an enriched environment are more prone to stress and anxiety, which can cause chronic diseases that may shorten their life span. These diseases also can lead to behavior problems that are frustrating to deal with — that may cause you to want to scream at your cat, confine her, or, worse, immediately take her to the shelter. Urine marking, using household areas as a bathroom, scratching your furniture, and aggression toward human and animal members of the household are common symptoms of stress.

### What Does That Mean?

**Enrichment:** Provisioning your cat's environment so that it improves the quality and value of her life. Enrichment goes way beyond providing for a cat's basic needs of shelter, food, water, and a litter box. It enhances the environment by giving your cat opportunities to express species-typical behaviors such as hunting, climbing, and playing in desirable, appropriate ways, and has a direct correlation with her well-being.

**Stress:** A state in which stimuli (stressors) have disrupted the optimum mental well-being of the animal. In this chapter, we will be talking about emotional stress. Stressors can be obvious (such as strangers in the home or a new cat housemate) or subtle (the owner leaves for work thirty minutes earlier, or the couch was moved to the other wall). Stress is closely related to anxiety.

**Anxiety:** A state of anticipation that is not necessarily about an actual stressor being present, but the worry about what might happen. The stressor can be real or imagined.

**Sympathetic nervous system:** The part of every mammal's nervous system that is activated when the animal needs to react quickly. Known as the fight-or-flight system, the sympathetic nervous system is responsible for all the changes in the body when a cat is stressed. This stress response will not only suppress normal behaviors (such as playing, grooming, eating, sleeping, and social interaction), but it also can suppress the cat's immune system, making her more prone to infections. Perpetual activation of the sympathetic nervous system can lead to chronic vomiting and allergic skin disease, as well as a cascade of changes associated with the bladder, known as feline interstitial cystitis.

**Feline time budget:** How a cat spends a typical twenty-four-hour period. Cats sleep on average about 40 percent of the day and spend another 22 percent resting — likely not a surprise to any cat owner. The hunting process (traveling, stalking, killing) takes up anywhere from 15 to 46 percent of their day, while eating their kill takes only 2 percent. Grooming takes up another 15 percent of the day.

**Crepuscular:** More active at dawn and dusk. Domestic cats are considered to be a crepuscular species.

**Marking:** An important form of communication in cats. Cats may mark their environment by bunting (rubbing their face on an object or animal), scratching, or urinating. Cats who urine mark typically spray urine on vertical surfaces while standing with their tail erect. Some cats will urine mark by depositing urine on horizontal surfaces. While urine marking is a normal form of communication in cats, those who urine mark frequently are often experiencing distress — such as having frequent conflicts with other cats in the home.

**Pheromones:** Species-specific chemicals released by several animals, including cats. These chemicals convey information to other animals of the same species. Cats deposit pheromones on objects in their environment when scent marking.

**Sickness behaviors:** A group of nonspecific medical and behavioral symptoms that can include a combination of any of the following: vomiting, diarrhea, decreased appetite or water intake, fever, enhanced painlike behaviors, decreased activity, decreased grooming, and a reduction in social interactions. Urinating and defecating outside the litter box can be considered sickness behaviors in cats. Sickness behaviors are believed to be a coping strategy to promote recovery. They are seen in response to both physical stressors (such as infections or other diseases) and psychological stressors (such as changes in the environment).

**Feline interstitial cystitis (FIC):** An inflammation of the bladder, with no known or identifiable cause (such as an infection), which can cause blood in the urine.

## Is That Really True?

*Cats can take care of themselves.* We like to think of cats as independent animals, but, in fact, cats need our help to live safe and happy lives. Cats who spend 100 percent of their time indoors are entirely dependent on their human family members to provide them with an environment that meets their physical and mental needs. Cats who have outdoor access need our help to keep them safe and avoid outdoor perils such as vehicles, exposure to diseases, and harm inflicted by other animals or humans.

*Cats are lazy.* The image of a popular large orange cartoon cat may come to mind — an obese and lazy animal who sleeps and eats all day. This stereotypic image of cats misrepresents what cats actually are — active and agile predators. Remember, cats who fend for themselves can spend up to 46 percent of a twenty-four-hour period searching for food and hunting. Cats are opportunistic hunters and evolved to catch small rodents, such as mice. The size of their prey means cats need several small meals every day, and these meals may be few and far between. Cats need to be prepared to catch their prey whenever it appears, even after they have just eaten.

Your cat's eyes and ears are attuned to the movement and noises of rodents. Once she detects potential prey, she will stalk it. Her body will be low to the ground, and she will wait nearly motionless in this crouched position, then suddenly pounce on the unsuspecting prey. This hunting style is very successful, with studies reporting only two to five pounces needed to capture prey, depending on the animal being hunted.

Cats learn hunting early in life, with lessons from mom beginning as early as four weeks of age. Young cats are particularly active hunters and may spend a large percentage of their time exploring and hunting.

Our mistaken view of cats as being lazy has probably developed from how we keep our cats. Indoors, cats have few options for entertainment. Inactivity is a result of their limited options, and they can quickly become uninterested and overweight. Once overweight, they may become even more inactive. A recent study comparing lean and overweight cats of similar ages found that the lean cats were significantly more active than their overweight counterparts and also interacted more with their caretakers.

*Cats don't care about human companionship.* One recent study by Dr. Matilda Eriksson and her colleagues showed that cats interact for a longer time with their owners after extended periods of separation. This rebound effect of contact-seeking behavior after a prolonged absence demonstrates the importance of human companionship in a cat's environment. Another study, by Dr. Kristyn Vitale Shreve and her colleagues, found that when given a choice, most cats will choose social interaction with humans over food. This is an interesting finding, considering that food is necessary for survival, and it highlights how important human companionship can be for cats. They benefit from positive and regular interactions with their owners, and a cat's caregivers are actually the most important determinant of her mental and physical well-being.

Cats who live exclusively indoors require more time to interact with their owners compared with cats who have some outdoor access. We are their primary source of entertainment! Although cats benefit from social interaction, they also need time to be alone to rest and avoid conflicts. So while it's important for you to interact with your cat regularly, it's equally important to provide her with a space that she can retreat to when she needs time to herself.

## How Do We Begin?

Jessica realized that she needed help with Fiona and scheduled a behavioral consultation. During the consultation, we determined that while Jessica provided Fiona with food, water, and a litter box, the cat lacked the enrichment she needed to entertain herself and be a cat while Jessica was at work. Jessica was Fiona's only real source of entertainment, and Fiona was bored!

Enriching your feline's environment can seem overwhelming — for you and for her. Abrupt change is hard for everyone, but it can be especially problematic for our sensitive cats. We recommend making incremental changes over the course of several weeks to months. Implementing one new thing every few days or weeks will cut down on the stress that the novelty itself can cause.

There are four areas of enrichment to address: cognitive, physical, sensory, and social. Cognitive enrichment focuses on mental stimulation and encourages your cat to think about and puzzle through a problem or task. Physical enrichment focuses on the structure and layout of her environment. Sensory enrichment focuses on the five senses: taste, sight, smell, hearing, and touch. Social enrichment focuses on your cat's interactions with you, other cats in the household, and any other pets you may have. Each kind of enrichment we discuss here can address one or several of these areas.

### Food and Food-Dispensing Toys

As we know from the feline time budget (see "What Does That Mean?" earlier in this chapter), about one-third to one-half of your cat's day is spent acquiring and eating food. If you feed your house cat one or two meals out of a bowl, it likely takes her no more than ten minutes to eat, which is less than 1 percent of her day. So how should she fill the rest of her time? Perhaps by munching on your houseplants or finding a hair tie in the bathroom to chew on, leading to a visit to your veterinarian's office. Or maybe just by sleeping more, which can further contribute to inactivity and obesity.

Her wild feline counterpart eats ten to twenty small prey each day, and up to half of her hunting trips are unsuccessful. One easy way to extend the time your cat takes to find and eat her meals is to place her food in food-dispensing toys. These toys deliver food only when your cat plays and interacts with them. So instead of imitating the vacuum cleaner at mealtimes, she can show off her inner hunter.

Introduce each food-dispensing toy by placing your cat's favorite treats inside. Place the toy in the spot where you normally feed her right before her normal mealtime, so she is especially hungry. Put a couple of treats next to the toy to pique her interest in it. Some cats like to imitate their owners, so you might want to play with the toy to show her how it dispenses the food.

Your cat's interest in her regular diet and how savvy she is with the new toys will determine how quickly you can switch her completely from eating out of a bowl. Once she is comfortable eating solely out of the toys, the next step is to start moving the toys to various locations throughout your home. When she has mastered several toys, you can vary which ones you put out each day, so that she can hunt and eat in different ways throughout the day and night.

Since she is crepuscular, it would be ideal to have food-dispensing toys available at dawn and dusk, when she is likely to be more active. To avoid any thieving canine housemates, place feeder toys on elevated surfaces or only in rooms that are inaccessible to your dogs (because of baby gates or microchip-activated cat doors).

We determined that not only did Fiona need more entertainment, but she also needed a change in feeding routine, as she had learned that the best way to get food was to pounce on or meow at Jessica. To address both issues, one of the first things we introduced into Fiona's home was food-dispensing toys. Once Jessica was sure Fiona was eating out of the toys, she began a new routine of hiding a few of these toys around the house before she left for work, as well as hiding a few around the house before bedtime. When she started this new routine, Jessica was also careful never to feed Fiona when she was meowing.

Some of our favorite commercially made food-dispensing toys include the Trixie 5-in-1 Activity Center, the Indoor Hunting Feeder from Doc & Phoebe's Cat Co., PetSafe's SlimCat and Egg-Cercizer, the Pipolino, and Kong's Cat Wobbler. You can also make your own toys using materials found around the house, like empty cardboard paper towel or toilet paper rolls, tissue boxes, plastic yogurt or cottage cheese containers, egg cartons, or ice cube trays. (See "The Three-Minute Food-Dispensing Toy" in chapter 11.)

A young cat excitedly plays with the Indoor Hunting Feeder. She hunts for a portion of her daily food in a way that allows her to express her natural inclination to work for food. *Sarah Millet*

A homemade tower of toys and treats can provide hours of investigative fun for your cat. Tino's tower is made from cardboard tubing. *Deborah Crosier*

Another way to make feeding time more enriching is to vary the type of food you give your cat. Cats develop food preferences as young kittens, so to increase the chances that your cat will accept different types of food later in life (for example, if your veterinarian prescribes a diet change), it is important to introduce a variety of food types, brands, and flavors early on. This includes dry and canned, different meats, pâtés and chunky stews, and various kibble shapes.

It is also important to remember that you do not want to frustrate your cat by introducing enrichment that is too difficult for her skill level.

This is especially true with food-dispensing toys. It can be very danger-ous for cats to go several days without eating, so when you try a new food toy, make sure your cat is getting enough food out of the toy or is getting supplemental meals as needed.

## Safe Places

Your cat's safe place is a private area that allows her to retreat and feel protected; it gives her a sense of security and control. Put one safe place up high — your cat will want to climb up to observe her home, especially when there's been a change (such as a visitor arriving) or when she's frightened. Provide her with a few different options, including an open resting spot such as a shelf or windowsill and an enclosed resting spot such as a box or bed with high sides. You can encourage your cat to use these spaces by lining them with washable fleece bedding to make them extra comfy.

---

### Can the Carrier Be a Safe Place?

While the carrier can be a good option for a safe hiding place, your cat may have learned to fear her carrier if you have only brought it out before frightening experiences, such as going to the veterinarian or riding in the car. To improve the way your cat feels about her car-rier, make it a normal feature of her environment.

Set it in an area that she uses frequently and leave it there. You may find that she will use it more often if you put it on an elevated and stable surface, such as a shelf. Encourage her to explore the car-rier by hiding food or catnip inside, and line the bottom with com-fortable bedding so that she can curl up for a catnap.

Turning your cat's carrier into a safe space will not only give her a great option for resting when indoors, but it can also offer her com-fort and a sense of familiarity when traveling or taking trips to the veterinarian. This is especially important for cats with chronic ill-nesses, who may need to make several trips to the veterinary clinic every year. (See appendix A for more tips about carrier training.)

---

Safe spaces are especially important in multicat homes. While many cats can tolerate living in homes with other cats, they're most successful when they have enough space to keep their distance from one another and get out of sight when needed. A study by Dr. Sharon Crowell-Davis, DACVB, that evaluated the habits of indoor cats found that most cats prefer to maintain a distance of at least three to nine feet when they are within sight of one another, and they may spend as much as 50 percent of their time out of one another's sight.

You can help your cats avoid social stress caused by too much contact with their housemates by providing as many safe places in the home as you have cats. Even if you live in a small house or apartment, you can increase the amount of vertical space for your cats by adding perches, shelves, and cat trees. You can also divide rooms into several sections using vertical room dividers. These dividers make rooms more complex and give your cats more choices about where they want to be — and whom they want to see.

The "cat library" is a concept started by a few creative architects with an interest in feline furniture. Hobbes and his housemates enjoy the increased vertical space and hiding spots this homemade version provides. *Anne Gallutia*

## Separate Core Areas

Although cats are a social species, they can be quite possessive of their space and resources, especially with other cats they were not raised with or are not directly related to. We cat owners choose which cats will live in our household — the choice is not theirs. This is like your college picking your dormitory roommate; you may not necessarily like the person they pick!

In a household with multiple cats, it is important to create a separate core area for each cat. This is a specific area within the cat's territory (the space the cat actively uses and defends) where you should put all the resources she needs. Observe where each cat tends to hang out when left to her own devices, and choose the location of the core area accordingly. That area should include the cat's food, water, litter boxes, toys, resting places, perching and hiding spots, and enrichment opportunities. Two cats who spend all their time together may share their core areas.

Having an environment of plenty that offers each cat a separate space for her wants and needs will help alleviate tension among your cats and also help prevent, and sometimes eliminate, fighting, urination and defecation outside the litter box, and episodes of feline interstitial cystitis.

Junebug enjoys her own core area, where she has access to food, water, scratching options, and toys in an upstairs bathroom. Her housemate has a separate and similar area downstairs. *Meghan E. Herron*

## Structure, Predictability, and Consistent Interactions

Cats benefit from regular, positive, and consistent interactions with their human family members. In fact, a cat's human family is likely the most important determinant of her mental and physical well-being.

During our discussion with Jessica, she mentioned that she had never been able to create a consistent routine with Fiona. She loved talking to, petting, and playing with Fiona, but her work schedule was demanding. She found that more and more she rarely had the energy to interact with Fiona during the week. She felt very guilty about this and ended up trying to give Fiona lots of attention on the weekend.

Jessica is not alone. Many pet owners balancing the demands of jobs, family responsibilities, social lives, and caring for their pets feel stretched thin. It's tempting to just meet your cat's basic needs of providing food, water, and litter box care during the workweek, then focus on play and interaction on your days off, when you have more time. However, a study by Dr. Judi Stella and her colleagues showed that a simple change in routine (like skipping daily playtime or varying mealtimes) can result in sickness behaviors such as decreased appetite and vomiting, as well as house soiling. These findings highlight the importance of keeping a consistent routine for feeding, playtime, and interaction with your cat. Since she has little control over her environment, a regular schedule will provide predictability and reduce stress.

Rather than trying to interact with your cat a lot on just a couple of days a week, set up a regular schedule for playtime and interaction every day. It helps to time this around other daily activities, such as mealtimes, so it becomes a habit for both of you. A little can go a long way — just two to three minutes of daily playtime can be a positive addition to your cat's daily routine. And if you want to add more mental enrichment, try positive reinforcement training (see chapter 6).

Keeping a consistent routine for interactions is an important aspect of cat care. However, change is part of life, so when you need to make a change in your schedule, do it gradually so your cat has time to get used to the new routine.

*How* you interact with your cat is as important as how regularly you interact. Cats experience less stress when they're allowed to choose whether to interact or not rather than having interactions forced on them.

While Jessica was tempted to cuddle with Fiona frequently on weekends, she admitted that this often happened when the cat was napping, and Fiona occasionally hissed and swatted at her when she was trying to show Fiona affection. A simple switch to *inviting* Fiona to interact with her and not disturbing her during her naps resolved the swatting and hissing. Jessica was also careful to respect Fiona's limits, so when the cat moved away during a cuddle session, Jessica didn't force the issue by following her or picking her up.

## Toys

Each cat is an individual when it comes to the types of toys she enjoys playing with. Yours may prefer chasing the laser pointer, swatting a ball around a track, attacking a feather attached to a fishing pole, or chasing a remote-controlled mouse through the living room. There are also motion-activated toys that turn on when she walks in front of the sensor, and ones that can be set to move around at certain time intervals, which can be very useful if your cat is home alone for long periods of time.

Sophie grabs, bites, and kicks at her Kong Kickeroo, mimicking a normal predatory behavior. *Amy L. Flom*

Toys and playtime should mimic hunting opportunities for your cat and include stalking, chasing, and capturing. Be aware that some cats may get frustrated by laser pointers because, since the cat can't capture the light, she is unable to complete the full hunting sequence. It is best to end laser pointer play by landing on a treat or toy that she can actually attack and so feel fully satisfied.

## The Importance of Scent

Cats depend much more on their nose than we do. Your cat's sense of smell provides her with important information — helping her to detect potential threats as well as giving her a sense of familiarity and security. She deposits pheromones around your home by scent marking — both rubbing on and scratching objects. These pheromones are used to communicate with other cats and to establish her core living area.

Whenever possible, it's important not to interfere with your cat's sense of smell. Don't use strong cleaners and detergents around your home, and always use unscented litter in her litter box. You also need to provide your cat with scratching posts, pads, and boxes where she can deposit her scent. Ideal locations for scratching surfaces are near entryways and your cat's resting areas, as these are places where she will naturally want to deposit her scent by scratching and rubbing. Providing her with appropriate scratching options may help prevent her from scratching on furniture.

## Catnip and Cat Grass

One of the best types of scent enrichment is catnip, which comes from the perennial herb *Nepeta cataria,* a member of the mint family. Only 50 to 60 percent of cats actually respond to catnip, and there is a genetic basis for this trait. Although most responder cats become lovable and relaxed when exposed to catnip, some become reactive and aroused. The first time you offer catnip to your cat, make sure she is in a room by herself, away from other pets and small children in the household, so you can see what her response is.

Many cats enjoy playing with toys that contain catnip, or simply just rolling around in some freshly crushed catnip strewn on the floor. As with cooking herbs and spices, catnip loses its aroma over time, so you should periodically refill or replace any catnip toys to increase their desirability.

Chewing on edible plants such as mint, parsley, or cat grass is another kind of enrichment that satisfies a cat's senses of taste and touch. Cat grass is grown from a variety of nontoxic grass seeds, including barley, oat, wheat, and rye, and can be a great alternative for cats who enjoy munching on your houseplants, many of which are toxic to cats. To make sure the plants in your house are not toxic, visit the ASPCA's plant database at www.aspca.org/pet-care/animal-poison-control/toxic-and-non-toxic-plants.

## Auditory Enrichment

Cat-specific music can be a good form of auditory enrichment. Music for cats is specifically composed and played at frequencies, tones, pitches, octaves, and tempos that your cat will enjoy. The types of music that cats like are even supported by research! There are tunes created to help them relax and those that can stimulate them, which are good at playtime and feeding time. Two sources for such music are Music for Cats (www.musicforcats.com) and Through a Cat's Ear, a CD/MP3 series available from various outlets.

## Visual Stimulation

Many cats enjoy watching birds from their window perches, so placing a bird feeder in the yard or near the window can increase your cat's enjoyment. Watch her after installing the feeder to make sure she isn't bothered by the sight of prey without having the opportunity to chase it. If she appears nervous or frustrated while watching birds from the window, remove the feeder. And, of course, if your cat goes outside, then luring birds to your house is not a good idea.

Your cat may also enjoy watching fish in a fish tank or turtles in a terrarium, but make sure the top of the tank is closed so she doesn't inadvertently fall in or make one of them a meal.

There are several high-tech ways to visually stimulate your cat, including games and apps for your phone or computer that mimic bugs and prey for her to swat at. These can be both fun

Smokey Joe and his best friend, Peanut, are captivated by a movie made for cats, with birds and other prey animals moving around the screen. *Brittany Vance* for her and entertaining for you! Just as with laser pointers, if your cat becomes frustrated by not being able to capture the "prey," avoid these visual activities, which will likely be more detrimental than enriching.

## Access to the Outdoors

While keeping your cat exclusively indoors can protect her from many dangers, such as vehicles, diseases, fights with other cats, malicious humans, and predation by larger animals — as well as protect sensitive wildlife populations such as migrating songbirds — it also limits variety in her environment and can result in boredom and behavior problems.

If you want to allow your cat outdoors, make sure she is microchipped for identification, properly vaccinated against contagious diseases, and protected from both internal and external parasites, such as fleas, ticks, and mosquitoes. If your cat doesn't have access to the outdoors, she should at least have access to natural lighting and a window where she can look outside. If you have more than one cat, make sure there are perches by several windows to limit competition for this valuable resource.

You can make going outdoors safer for your cat and for the local wildlife by creating a secure screened-in enclosure in your yard or on your deck — a catio! Another option is to enclose your yard with cat-proof fencing, which can give your cat access to your entire yard while preventing her from getting out (and other animals from getting in). Even with adequate fencing or an enclosure, cats should not be allowed outdoors without your supervision, because of the risks of potential escape and other animals entering the space.

Spotty enjoys the safe outdoor view from her catio. *Kelly Ballantyne*

Although you may view giving your cat access to the outdoors as a special treat, if she has had limited experience outside, she may become overwhelmed and frightened. Watch her body language carefully for signs of fear, and provide her with elevated perches and enclosed areas to hide in, just as you do indoors.

Depending on your cat's temperament and experience with the outdoors, you can train her to wear a harness and leash so you can take her on a walk around the neighborhood. Due to the risk of entanglement, cats should *always* be supervised when on leash.

Dobby enjoys a little outdoor time with his big sister, safely restrained by his kitty harness and leash. *Amy L. Pike*

Jessica lived in a third-floor apartment that did not have a balcony. While she had plenty of windows, Fiona could not access any of them. The windowsills were narrow, and there were no nearby perches or shelves where Fiona could rest and observe the outdoors. Despite these initial challenges, we came up with several options to provide Fiona with this important source of enrichment, including setting a low side table below one window and installing window perches near a few others. Within a few weeks, Jessica reported that Fiona was spending much of her time on these window perches, and they appeared to be her new favorite resting spots.

## Grooming and Petting

Some cats enjoy being groomed and petted, which can be another form of tactile enrichment. If you watch cats grooming each other, they focus on the head and neck areas, so it is a good idea to concentrate your petting and grooming on those areas — especially if your cat is not that fond of being petted in the first place. A recent study by Dr. Sarah Ellis and Dr. Helen Zulch found that petting the back half of a cat produces more negative reactions than petting the front half.

## Social Enrichment

Food and human interaction are typically the forms of enrichment cats prefer most. However, providing your cat with one-on-one social enrichment can be difficult, depending on your schedule. Make sure you carve out time to spend with her that is purposeful and meaningful for both of you.

Many of the activities discussed in this chapter are intended for you and your cat to do together and will provide enrichment to both your lives. If your cat likes the company of other people, having friends come by to interact with her, especially when you are away for long periods, can give her some much-needed social interaction and perhaps satisfy a need for those friends who want some cat snuggles.

## Avoiding Pitfalls and Staying on Track

*My cat won't play with food-dispensing toys.* Introducing food-dispensing toys to a cat who has never had to do anything other than scarf down her food can be challenging for both you and her. It's important to take your feline's current skill level into account when introducing food-dispensing toys and never offer anything that may be frustrating for her. To encourage a toy's use, take it apart and place treats around and inside it to lure your cat over. Some cats will even play with the toy if they see you doing so.

If your cat likes to bat toys around, consider food-dispensing toys that require her to use her paws to get the food. If she's more of a couch potato, stationary food toys may be more up her alley. Increase her motivation to interact with the toy by introducing it when you know she will be hungry, and initially use high-value treats instead of her regular kibble to entice her to use it.

Gradually reduce the amount of food in your cat's bowl each time she readily eats out of a food toy. Start with about a quarter of her daily ration in one or more toys, and every few days increase that proportion. Once she is fully comfortable playing with the toys to retrieve her food, eliminate the bowl entirely. You should still keep track of her daily intake, though, because a change in food consumption is an indication of an illness.

*I set up a perch for my cat, but she won't use it.* While most cats prefer a safe spot that is several feet off the floor, some cats may not be able to reach elevated resting areas because of their age or reduced physical capabilities. If you have a kitten or an elderly cat, if your cat has arthritis, or if your cat is overweight, she may need assistance getting up to her preferred perch. Provide ramps, pet steps, or a series of perches spaced at strategic intervals to help give her access to her safe space without much jumping.

Elsa loves watching the birds perched on the tree outside her window. This strategically placed cat cubby gives her the boost she needs to reach her favorite spot. *Carlo Siracusa*

*I gave my cat scratching posts, but she is still scratching my furniture.* Your cat's failure to use the scratching surface you've provided could be related to a variety of factors, including the type of surface, the location of the surface, and whether it is vertical or horizontal. Most cats prefer surfaces covered with wood bark, cardboard, or sisal rope for scratching, but some may prefer carpeting or fabric. Offer a few different options, both vertical and horizontal, and make sure you place them in key areas around the house that your cat visits often.

If you have a vertical scratching post, make sure it is tall enough for your cat to stand up on her back legs to scratch. Whether vertical or horizontal, the scratching surface must be stable and not slip or wobble, as that may scare your cat. And if your cat appears to have a particular penchant for scratching your favorite couch, try covering a scratching post with a similar fabric.

This scratching post offers two vertical scratching options close to resting places. *Carlo Siracusa*

Both of these horizontal scratchers have rubber bottoms to prevent slipping during scratching. *Carlo Siracusa*

To encourage your cat to investigate her designated scratching area, rub catnip on it and reward her with a small treat whenever you see her using it.

A newly available treatment for unwanted scratching involves applying a synthetic feline interdigital pheromone (Feliscratch by Feliway) to your cat's scratching post. This product leaves a visual mark (blue dye) in addition to the pheromone, mimicking the visual and scent marks created when cats scratch, thus encouraging your cat to scratch in desirable locations. A recent study testing this product over twenty-eight days showed it was effective in decreasing unwanted scratching in house cats.

## Keeping Life Interesting

Cats will lose interest in toys and other enrichment items that are simply left out all the time. There are so many new enrichment items that hit the market daily that you could likely buy a new one every single day of your cat's life. That could get rather expensive. So unless you want to spend as much on these items as on a college education, try rotating her toys as a way of introducing novelty. Put a few away when she appears to have lost interest in them and bring out a few to replace them. And voilà, what once was old is new again!

Homemade toys can also be very effective in stimulating play. Dr. Sagi Denenberg, DACVB, studied cats' preferences for several different types of toys and found that most of the cats preferred to play with one simple homemade toy — a hair band tied to a string — more than all the others, including store-bought items such as plastic balls or feathers on a stick. You may find that your cat likes playing with similar toys or other common household objects, such as plastic bottle rings or wadded-up paper balls. Just make sure you put away toys with strings or other easily ingested objects between play sessions.

## Adding a Playmate

If you already know your cat gets along well with other cats, and you have the time, money, and space to open up your home to another feline friend, she may enjoy having a buddy. Sometimes a full-time roommate can be the best enrichment of all.

When adopting another feline friend, make sure you set up a separate core area for her. Use this area initially to separate the newcomer from your current cat, then turn it into her own special space to retreat to once they are integrated. (See chapter 5 for how to do proper introductions.) You should be able to completely close off the new area from the other cat with a door or multiple baby gates stacked on top of each other to prevent escape. It is important to make this core area an environment of plenty, with food, water, litter boxes, hiding spots, her favorite toys, and the other enrichment resources discussed in this chapter.

Now that your cat has a buddy, don't forget to continue playing with and paying individual attention to both her and her new friend. Remember, cats do not like to share resources, including attention from their owners!

Jessica gradually made many of the changes discussed throughout this chapter to enrich the home she shared with Fiona. After a few months of living in this feline dream home, Fiona was playing with her food-dispensing toys, enjoying her daily play sessions with Jessica, and no longer pouncing on or meowing at Jessica in the middle of the night. Jessica was sleeping better and felt that her bond with Fiona was stronger than ever.

As Jessica found out, enriching your feline friend's world is one of the most important strategies to prevent stress and promote good health. Making simple changes in the way you feed her, providing her with safe places to retreat to and rest, increasing the consistency and number of times you play with and groom her, and stimulating all five of her senses can give her the kind of environment that will make her the envy of all the other felines in your neighborhood. She will truly be the cat's meow.

## What Did We Say?

- An enriched environment is key to your cat's well-being, health, and happiness.
- Enrichment means providing an environment of plenty, with outlets for all her species-typical behaviors of playing, hunting, and climbing.
- Options for enrichment include safe outdoor access, toys, food-dispensing toys, nontoxic edible plants and catnip, cat-specific music and movies, the companionship of a buddy, and much more.
- Human companionship is an essential source of feline enrichment. To decrease stress and increase predictability, make time for daily play and interactions.

# 4

# Social Butterflies
*Cats Are Not Really Solitary Animals*

Sharon Crowell-Davis, DVM, PhD, DACVB

Topaz was rescued from a filled-to-capacity animal control facility after living there with her eight-week-old daughter Opal for more than a month. The two were huddled in a small cage in a roomful of dogs barking so loudly you had to step outside to have a conversation. Shelly, their soon-to-be rescuer, opened the cage door and slowly reached for them. Crouched in the back corner, Opal snuggled up against her mother. Neither hissed or growled. Their hair did not stand up. They did not try to bite. They just quietly crouched in the back of the cage, frozen with fear, as Shelly petted them and decided to take them home.

Once released from the carrier into her new home, Topaz quickly ran from Shelly, Opal in tow, taking what seemed to be permanent refuge under a low shelf of a bookcase, avoiding any human who came near. Both refused to come out of hiding. For the first few days, Shelly kept the door to the room Opal and Topaz were in closed so the eight other cats in the house could not bother them while they were getting accustomed to their new home.

As the days passed, Topaz and Opal gradually ventured out of their hiding place, only to find new hiding places. Even when the door was open, they avoided the other cats, who looked at them curiously but did not attempt to interact with them. It was pretty clear that Topaz and Opal didn't want to be sociable. The humans in the household gave them their space, sometimes tossing delicious treats in their direction and talking to them in soft voices.

As the weeks passed, Topaz and Opal still didn't seem inclined to trust humans. But cats learn from one another, and they saw that the other cats liked to be petted and cuddled. Opal started watching when this happened, and the humans noticed. She had a look of curiosity on her face. She could see the other cats holding their tails up, a sign of contentment, as the humans petted them. She could hear the other cats purr and meow as they interacted with the humans.

Over time, Opal seemed to ponder this strange phenomenon of cats trusting humans. She watched and listened and eventually approached within Shelly's reach. At first Opal quickly moved away if Shelly extended a hand to her. Soon, though, she started staying still and eventually allowed Shelly to touch her. Within a few weeks, Opal arched her back and enjoyed a gentle massage along her head, neck, and back. That was the beginning of Opal trusting humans and becoming a pet.

Although Topaz remained in hiding, she observed her daughter's brave interactions with her human and feline housemates. Opal was beginning to really enjoy being petted. She would walk up to Shelly with her tail in the air and stay close for a long, delightful petting session. She clearly liked this interaction and obviously was not afraid of Shelly. Topaz watched this relationship develop — always from the safety of her hiding places.

The first time Topaz was petted, it was an accident. She had been following Opal, and as Opal approached Shelly for petting, Shelly reached down to pet Opal and moved along to pet the next cat without realizing it was Topaz. Topaz fled, but as this scenario was repeated, Topaz stayed closer and closer. Eventually, Shelly was able to pet her without triggering fear, and Topaz started to allow Shelly to pet her more often and for longer periods. Shelly's heart melted when, many months later, in the early morning hours, Topaz jumped on the bed and walked up to Shelly, purring loudly. This was the start of their morning cuddle routine.

During this time, Topaz and Opal remained fast friends. They groomed each other and snuggled next to each other to sleep. This wasn't surprising. Related cats and those who become close friends often maintain that closeness throughout their lives, sleeping together, rubbing and grooming each other. They also started to show more and more curiosity about the other cats. For a long time, interactions with them were simple — just a drive-by nose touch or a quick moment of contact as they passed in the hall. In time, they developed bonds with the other cats, showing physical affection that included grooming and head rubbing.

These girls had come a long, long way from crouching in fear at the back of a cage. It took time and patience, but Topaz and Opal were able to learn that they were safe and that life could be good.

Opal and Topaz snuggling. *Sharon Crowell-Davis*

There are a number of unfortunate myths about cats and their behavior, and when people believe them, they are unable to see cats for who and what they really are. Each cat is a unique individual, shaped by genetics as well as early experiences and specific events throughout the cat's life. Some cats are bold, outgoing, and fearless. Others are timid and fearful. Many fall somewhere in between. Some are social butterflies with their own kind but timid with people. Others love and trust their human companions but fear other cats.

The domestic cat is a social species, but how social each individual cat is will be based largely on his early experiences. And how each cat expresses this sociability to people and to other cats differs from one cat to another. The fact that Topaz and Opal developed friendships with both Shelly and the other cats suggests that, perhaps prior to their traumatic experience at animal control, they'd had pleasant experiences with humans and members of their own species.

## Facts, Not Fiction

It is often said that cats are asocial, solitary creatures who don't like other cats. This is simply not true. Domestic cats often form social bonds with other cats, as well as with members of other species. This is confirmed by the fact that feral and semi-feral cats form large colonies with highly complex social dynamics. Cats who prefer not to be around other cats likely were not well socialized to other cats when they were kittens.

It is also said that cats don't really bond with us — they just view humans as staff. This, too, is false. Like any pets, cats want the humans they live with to provide basic resources such as safety, food, and water. But as a social species, cats also want to have friendly relations with their human companions. Some cats even develop separation anxiety when their people are gone, and they may go through a prolonged period of grief after the loss of a human companion. Again, their early experiences influence how social they will become.

## What Does That Mean?

**Feral cat:** A cat who lives entirely outside, with minimal or no interaction with humans. Feral cats are afraid of humans and avoid them. Unless they are being monitored by an animal control agency or a caretaker group, these cats are not spayed or neutered and regularly breed and produce offspring.

**Semi-feral cat:** A cat who lives entirely outside but has regular interaction with humans, usually volunteers who feed a colony. Over time, these cats become less and less afraid of humans, and many will eventually allow petting. Many semi-feral cats are spayed or neutered as part of trap-neuter-return (TNR) programs and do not produce offspring.

**Colony:** A group of feral or semi-feral cats that includes multiple adult males, multiple adult females, and a number of kittens and juveniles. These groups are matrilineal. That means the mothers (called queens), with their daughters, granddaughters, and great-granddaughters, make up the core of the group.

**House cat:** A cat who has been raised by and socialized to people from a young age and is living in a home with one or more humans. Some house cats are kept inside all the time, while others have varying amounts of outdoor time.

**Socialization:** The process by which a kitten learns about the world and all the objects and people in it. Kittenhood, particularly the period from two to seven weeks of age, is an especially important time for psychological development. The kitten's rapidly growing brain is learning what is safe and what isn't; what is fun and what isn't; who is nice and who isn't. It is important for proper socialization that appropriate input occurs during the first two to seven weeks, and even up to twelve weeks and beyond.

**Queen:** An unspayed, sexually mature female cat.

**Tom:** An unneutered, sexually mature male cat.

## Is That Really True?

Often veterinary behaviorists are asked what the best way is to make sure cats become social animals. To raise cats to be socially healthy, several things have to happen during that especially sensitive time from two to seven weeks.

- The kitten should be kept with his mother, unless the mother is feral and afraid of humans — in which case the kitten could learn from her to be afraid of humans. If the mother is calm and friendly with humans, the kitten will take his cues from her.
- As with Opal and Topaz, if a kitten and his mother are together after weaning, they often form close, lifelong social bonds. This might be a good point to consider when adopting. Instead of adopting just one kitten, adopt a kitten and his mother, so the kitten will have the reassuring presence of his mother for many years.
- If the mother is very fearful of humans, it may be necessary to remove the kitten from her at a younger age than is ideal. In these cases, the health and nourishment of the kitten from mother's milk must be weighed against the adverse effect of the kitten learning that humans are scary. In such situations, it is ideal, if possible, to place the kittens of a feral mother with a friendly queen who is already nursing her own kittens. Fostering kittens this way is usually easy, since queens take care of one another's kittens in feral situations. If a foster mother is not available, then in addition to bottle-feeding

the kitten and ensuring that he has many positive experiences with his human caregivers, it is best to place him with some older, friendly kittens or some well-socialized, friendly adult cats, so that he can learn how to be a cat.

- The kitten should be exposed as much as possible to other kittens, juveniles, and adult cats who are behaviorally and physically healthy. This is important for the kitten to learn how to behave socially with members of his own species.
- The kitten should also be exposed to a lot of people, frequently. Periods of exposure should always include kind and gentle handling and opportunities to play. The kitten should always have the option to join or leave the interaction as he pleases, and should never be forced to interact with someone he finds frightening.
- If you want the kitten to be comfortable and unafraid with other species, such as dogs, expose him to pets who are well mannered and gentle before he is nine weeks old — even better, before he is seven weeks old, if you have the opportunity. Friendships can still form when the kitten is older, but it is easier at this time.
- The kitten should experience various sights, sounds, and odors that are safe. A kitten who grows up in a diverse, somewhat complex environment will learn that the world in general is a safe place, and he is less likely to be timid and fearful of novelty.

*Is it true that only related cats can live together?* At the very least, kittens in a litter who have grown up knowing one another and their mother will generally get along very well. That little nuclear family is not, however, the limit of their sociability. Kittens, and adult cats who were properly socialized as kittens, can meet new cats, both unrelated and related (such as an aunt or a cousin), go through a period of getting to know them, and then get along very well. Both Opal and Topaz, as they became acquainted with the cats already in Shelly's household, became friendly, or at least socially neutral, with the other cats.

While some individual cats will be true social butterflies, particularly with their best friends — hanging out together, walking around together, grooming each other, playing together, and rubbing on each other a lot — others may not seek out each other's company, but also will not have significant conflicts. Some pairs of cats can be together in the same room and not fight, but they don't particularly act like friends either.

Also, just like people, sometimes certain cats simply don't get along. If this is a mild problem, limited to hissing when the cats accidentally encounter each other, the situation is probably best left alone. However, if this is a significant problem, you should ask your veterinarian for professional help.

*How do you know if cats are getting along or not?* Cats who get along well have a variety of friendly social interactions. Whether you are watching a group of feral cats, semi-feral cats, or house cats, you will see many examples of how cats demonstrate friendship. They tend to just hang out together. Outside, they will walk down a road or forest path side by side; inside, they are likely to hang out within a few feet of one another. Whether inside or outside, they will often curl up close to one another to sleep.

In contrast, if two particular cats are never seen close to each other or engaging in the various social behaviors of nose touch, head bump, rubbing on each other, or playing together, and instead they hiss at each other whenever they meet, they're not getting along too well. Sometimes, this situation will improve on its own with time. Sometimes, professional help is needed. Occasionally, two cats are just seriously incompatible, and it may be best for all involved to remove one of them from your home.

Three semi-feral cats walking down a road together with tails held high—a friendly signal. *Ali T. Ozer*

These three house cats resting together are clearly friends. *Sherry Lynn Sanderson*

A very common social behavior for two cats is rubbing their bodies against each other. This is roughly the equivalent of a human hug, but since cats' forelimbs don't work well for hugs, they rub instead.

Rubbing is also important for maintaining a common scent. Cats have a much better sense of smell than humans do, and social odors are important to them. In cat colonies, we tend to see a surge of rubbing when cats are rejoining one another after being separated for a time, usually to go hunting. We see less rubbing among cats who live together indoors 100 percent of the time than we do among outdoor cats, presumably because indoor cats do not need to reestablish the communal scent that may be lost when a cat has spent several hours stalking through tall grass, hunting for dinner.

Semi-feral cats doing a full-body rub. Socially, this is roughly equivalent to a human hug. *Rhonda Van*

When a house cat is hospitalized for a few days or is otherwise away from home, the group scent may be lost, compromising the ability of the other cats to recognize him when he returns. Talk with your veterinarian about how to minimize this problem. For example, it may help if you bring a fresh blanket or towel that the other cats have been resting on at home to the hospital every day. In addition to helping the hospitalized cat maintain the group scent, smelling his friends on the blanket may provide him comfort.

If he is hospitalized for a long time, it may be necessary to reintroduce him to the other cats as if he were new to the home. In addition to smelling like a foreigner, he will probably not be feeling all that well and may display unfamiliar or unpredictable behaviors compared with how he used to act.

Cats commonly transfer this feline rubbing behavior to humans they trust, especially if there is an established social bond. So, when you get home and your cat runs up to you and begins rubbing back and forth against your lower legs, he is essentially saying *Welcome home!* He is also probably trying to make you smell right, at least from his point of view.

This semi-feral cat is rubbing his body against a person's leg in a friendly greeting. *Rhonda Van*

*How do cats show friendship?* Cats use many parts of their body to show friendship. They use their heads in three ways.

- **The nose touch.** They simply walk up to each other and briefly touch noses in greeting.
- **The head bump.** They push their foreheads against each other quite firmly. This gesture is more forceful and lasts a little longer than the nose touch.
- **The head rub.** They rub the sides of their heads back and forth against each other. More than two cats may do this at the same time, and several cats may exchange head rubs in sequence as part of a greeting ritual.

Two pet cats greet each other with a brief nose touch. *Sharon Crowell-Davis*

Two semi-feral cats greet each other with a head bump. *Cimeron Morrisey*

Cats also use their tongues to show affection, often grooming each other, primarily on the head and neck. If an overzealous groomer ventures away from those areas, the cat being groomed may take offense and swat at him or even bite him. The equivalent for us humans might be someone dropping their hands a bit too low during a hug.

This is an important thing to remember when considering how to handle cats. While many cats learn to be comfortable with whole-body strokes from humans, especially if they are petted this way as kittens, some take offense when humans engage in petting behavior that can feel inappropriate to them.

An adult cat cleans the head and ears of an older juvenile. *N. Prince/PrinceRoyal Bengals*

Hindquarters and tails are also used to communicate. One cat approaching another in a friendly way will hold up his tail. Sometimes the tail will be pointed straight up, like a flagpole. "Tail up" means the cat is approaching with friendly intentions and a desire to move closer.

This cat is approaching with his tail up, a sign of friendly intentions. *Rhonda Van*

Cats will sometimes pause when passing each other, crossing and often intertwining their tails kind of like a corkscrew. They also use their tails to stroke each other along the back.

Two semi-feral cats do a partial "tail wrap" with their tails upright. This is a sign of friendship and greeting. *Cimeron Morrisey*

Cats often use their hindquarters when they are socializing, pushing against each other in a behavior that says *We're buddies.* Sniffing each other under the tail is also a normal part of cat interactions. They obtain scent information about each other in this way, and not objecting to being sniffed is a sign that they get along well.

If the only cats you've known have been shy and solitary, preferring their own company to that of both other cats and humans, you have known only cats who were raised to behave that way. Our historical habit

Three semi-feral cats socialize by pressing their hindquarters together. *Cimeron Morrisey*

of removing kittens from their mother at the age of four to six weeks, then raising them in an environment where they interact only with a limited number of humans and no other cats, has produced asocial individuals — even though cats, as a species, are social.

If you want a kitten to grow up to be sociable, ideally he should be raised with his mother and littermates, then with other cats who have good social skills, in an environment where he has plenty of exposure to and friendly handling by people. He may not need to nurse past eight or nine weeks of age to physically survive, but keeping the litter together for fourteen weeks is best to allow him to develop mentally and socially. A kitten needs his mother's presence to feel secure and safe and to learn important skills from her, and he needs the presence of other cats to learn further social skills. Occasionally, an individual cat will not become very sociable even in this environment, possibly due to genetics. But the care of his mother and the exposure to friendly cats, both related and not, lays an important foundation for good cat citizenship.

Keeping a kitten with his mother and littermates may not be ideal, though, if the mother is feral or the environment does not offer much social contact with people. As mentioned earlier, in that case temporarily housing the cat with friendly kittens and adult cats will enable him to learn the important feline skills he will need as an adult.

Kittens who grow into full-fledged members of a cat colony — where they are raised by their mothers (who ultimately teach them how to hunt) and educated by other cats in the group in appropriate feline etiquette — are quite social. The same is true for kittens who grow up in a home where socially competent adult cats and, most important, their mother teach them how to be cats. As we learned from Topaz and Opal, cats look to other cats they know for information about what and who in the environment is safe or dangerous.

Of course, as with any extended family, not every cat will get along with all of his roommates or relatives. In some ways, cat colonies are reminiscent of high school. There are cliques who hang out together, grooming, rubbing, nose touching, tail wrapping, and head butting one another regularly. Cats outside of a particular clique might get the cold shoulder from its members. Still, most have their own clique where they can socialize and feel accepted.

---

### Where Do the Males Go in a Matrilineal Society?

Intact (unneutered) male feral and semi-feral cats often wander off to seek new colonies when they are young adults, at about two years of age. This is good for the colony because it prevents the cats from becoming inbred and facilitates genetic diversity. Joining a new colony can be a challenging experience for a young male, however, because the cats in the colony will not automatically trust him. He must earn their trust and friendship while living on the periphery of the group. It can take many weeks before a new male is accepted into a colony.

In the environment humans have created for cats, new adults of either sex may be brought home to an established group. As in feral cat colonies, newcomers are generally not automatically accepted into the group, even if they've been spayed or neutered. They may even be perceived as invading strangers and aggressively attacked.

Because of this, when you bring a new cat home, it is best to keep him separate from your other cats and to introduce them all gradually (see chapter 5). The speed at which the other cats accept the newcomer, and the speed at which the newcomer becomes comfortable with them, will vary depending on the cats' individual temperaments and degrees of socialization. In the household that Topaz and Opal moved into, the other cats were well socialized and readily accepted the newcomers.

## How Do We Begin?

Logistically, there can be some difficulties in accomplishing both cat-to-cat socialization and cat-to-human socialization. Ideally, when you're adopting a cat, his mother and littermates are physically healthy, and there are several kittens in the litter. Kittens from the same litter also can have play parties with kittens from other litters who are known to be physically healthy and not carrying contagious diseases.

For more structured education and socialization, kitten kindergarten (a program first designed and implemented by Dr. Kersti Seksel, DACVB) is gradually becoming more and more popular. The term "kitten kindergarten" is used because it is a learning environment for kittens. Ask your veterinary office if they offer kitten socialization classes or if good classes are available elsewhere in your area.

To ensure that such classes do not lead to the spread of diseases, several health standards should be followed for participation.

- Every kitten must have been examined by a veterinarian and found to be healthy.
- He must have had his first set of vaccines and be free of intestinal parasites.
- He must not exhibit any signs of illness, such as diarrhea, runny nose, or runny eyes, during the time between the veterinary exam and the first class, or during the time between classes.
- He must not have been exposed to other cats who could potentially have been carrying infectious diseases.

Once a kitten has started a class, it is important to monitor him closely for any signs of illness. If he becomes sick, he should not attend class.

In a rescue facility, queens commonly arrive from a variety of sources and in various states of health. If possible, once a litter of kittens is two to three weeks old, the family should be housed together in an enclosure that allows the kittens to run and play, socializing with one another and with their mother. If there are two or more healthy families with older kittens (seven weeks and up), it can be beneficial to allow all the families to be housed together, if possible. If the queens do not get along well, the kittens can be put in the same area together for twenty to thirty minutes a day and spend the rest of their time with their mom and littermates.

To set kittens up for social success and companionship with their own species in your home, consider adopting two kittens at the same time. Even if they are not related, juvenile cats tend to get along well with other juveniles, and they often have a happy relationship for life. When cats are well socialized to other cats, their lives are richer if they have others of their own species with whom they can play. Since most cats don't get to go on walks and meet other cats regularly, having friends within their household is even more important. Don't worry — they'll still love and need you!

In a multicat household, owners can facilitate friendly interactions by appropriately petting and otherwise rewarding cats when they are being sociable and friendly with one another.

These four house cats line up side by side first thing in the morning, waiting for their owner to come downstairs and start petting them all. Note the relaxed facial muscles, the whiskers turned forward, and the raised tails. This body language indicates that the cats are happy and friendly with their companions.
*Sherry Lynn Sanderson*

## Increasing Social Behaviors in an Adult Cat

What if you already have an adult cat and didn't know the importance of exposing him to various people and other cats as he was growing up in your home? Perhaps this cat is comfortable with you and your immediate family but hides when guests arrive. Adult cats who were not socialized as youngsters can still become social. They'll just require more time and effort.

If kittens of a feral mother who avoids humans are not captured until they are twelve weeks of age or older, all is not lost either. That being said, they'll need more time and effort to help them learn how to feel safe in someone's home, surrounded by people and other animals.

As we learned from Topaz and Opal, cats watch what happens in the world around them and learn from what they see and hear. Even cats who have been through very frightening experiences can learn to feel safe with at least some humans. And humans who provide yummy food treats may not be so bad after all!

For both the feral kitten and the unsocialized adult cat, one place to start is teaching the cat a verbal cue or trick. You can teach your cat lots of cues, but one will be enough to help him feel less timid. Contrary to popular belief, cats like to learn and are motivated by food — like most animals. Sometimes we just have to be a bit more creative in finding a tasty treat the cat is willing to work for. And remember that cautious cats typically sniff and investigate a new treat before they eat it, rather than gulping it down. Experiment with various things until you find the one your cat is crazy for. Once you have found that treat, you can train simple cued behaviors using positive reinforcement.

Always train the behavior first, then add the cue word. To teach your cat to sit on cue, begin by waiting for your cat to sit, then immediately give him a treat. You may be able to facilitate this process by holding the treat over his head, pinched between your fingers so he can't grab it. Many cats will sit and look up if the treat is over their head. Again, as soon as your cat sits, give him the treat.

What if your cat does something else, such as standing or sitting up on his hind legs, as he tries to figure out how to get the treat? This is fine, too. Your goal is not to teach your cat a specific behavior. Your goal is to teach your cat to engage in some kind of behavior in response to a cue and to earn a reward. So if your cat likes to sit up on his hind legs, then train him to do that.

Once he is doing the behavior consistently, add a word cue, such as "up" or "sit." Now your cat will associate that word with the particular behavior and the pleasant reward of a treat.

Practice the trained behavior regularly until your cat is really good at it. For the transition to having people he doesn't know interact with him, it can be helpful to always practice the cue in a particular place or on a particular item that can be moved, such as a small mat — although that's not essential.

Once the cat has a lot of experience with his trained cue, invite a friend to come over around training time. Have her sit quietly in a place where your cat can see her while you train him and give him treats. Even if your cat is not ready to approach your friend, she can toss treats toward him, making sure they land near him but don't hit him.

With time, have more and more visitors come over. These people need to be comfortable with the cat but also understand that if he's acting shy, it is important not to push him. You and your friends need to accept your cat's natural personality and let him be who he is. Allow him to get closer and closer to the visitors at a pace that works for him. When he seems comfortable, have them start cuing his trained behavior and rewarding him with treats.

Once the cat is comfortable approaching and being near a particular visitor who is giving him familiar cues to engage in a specific behavior and then receive a treat, she can attempt to pet him in ways that you know he likes. This petting should be very brief and limited to the head and neck areas.

If your cat is not able to make progress in becoming comfortable with other people through treats and then petting, your veterinarian may recommend a medication that could help him be more confident and less afraid while he is learning that people are safe. As Topaz and Opal showed us, when cats have been through major psychological trauma, it takes time to recover.

## The Best Petting

What is the best way for you and others to show affection to your cat? As with many things, there is wide individual variation in the types of petting by, the attention from, and the interactions with humans that cats enjoy. Let's review different types of petting, and then you can think about whether your cat likes them or not.

**Gently scratching and rubbing around the head and neck.** People who are experienced with cats know that this is one of the ways most cats prefer to be petted. It closely mimics how a cat would be groomed by another cat, who would use his tongue to rub and scratch at the head and neck. Odds are your cat will like this.

**Stroking the entire body.** Some cats like this, and some find it offensive. We need to remember that we are giants in a cat's world. Imagine if a giant ten times your size reached down with their giant hand and fondled you over your entire body. That could feel very threatening. On the other hand, if your cat really trusts you, this type of petting mimics cats rubbing against each other to some degree, so your cat may interpret your gesture as friendly rather than dangerous. For sure, reserve full-body petting for cats who know you really well.

**Rubbing his belly when the cat is on his back.** The great majority of cats do not like this type of petting. As with stroking the entire body when the cat is upright, the cat may perceive this as threatening. Remember, this is a very vulnerable position.

The small number of cats who appear to enjoy having their belly rubbed include queens who have previously nursed a litter. If a queen becomes socially bonded to a human and trusts them, the queen may roll onto her side and partially onto her back, in the same position she was in while nursing. Nursing her kittens was probably a happy experience. The kittens rubbing on her belly caused the release of oxytocin, a hormone that triggers the release of milk. Oxytocin also affects mood and makes the mother very happy. If you have a queen or former queen (one who's been spayed) who rolls over into this nursing position, she may experience you gently rubbing her belly as reminiscent of when she was nursing her kittens. Some males are comfortable with this type of petting as well. It all depends on their early experience.

If your cat acts stressed, afraid, or aggressive if you try to pet his belly, don't do it. There are plenty of other ways to interact socially with him. If you have previously had a cat who was okay with, or even liked, having his belly rubbed, don't assume a new cat is going to be the same. As we said, this is rare.

**Scratching at the base of the tail.** As with rubbing the belly, there is wide individual variation in whether cats find this pleasant, frightening, or even painful. If your cat enjoys this type of petting and pushes into your hand, it can be a good way of interacting. If he quickly turns around, swats, hisses, growls, or starts avoiding you, don't pet him there. If he has a strong reaction to you trying to scratch him at the base of the tail, take him to the veterinarian to determine if there is pain in that location.

## Scaredy-Cats Love Boxes

An important part of understanding and helping timid, fearful cats is to respect their fear. Although they are predators of small animals, cats are also preyed upon by larger animals such as coyotes, foxes, bobcats, eagles, and even dogs. Because of this, some of their behaviors are driven by the need to stay safe.

Cats love boxes. One reason for this preference is that many cats may feel safer in an enclosed space, such as a box or tented cat bed, than out in the open. A study done by Dr. Kathy Carlstead and her colleagues found that cats in stressful situations have lower stress hormone levels if they have a place to hide. A more recent study by Dr. Judi Stella and her colleagues found that cats housed in environments that offer hiding and perching options exhibit fewer sickness behaviors, meaning they eat better, use their litter boxes, and show fewer signs of gastrointestinal upset.

For your timid cat to learn to be confident, he must know that he has a place to retreat to that feels safe. Make sure everyone in your household and all your visitors know that when he is in his safe space, it's important to leave him alone.

## Is There Such a Thing as Too Social?

Yes and no. Healthy cats who have friendly, trusting relationships with others — be they other cats, humans, dogs, or other creatures — may want to engage in a lot of social play. This involves chasing, jumping, and grabbing. In some circumstances, this can be a problem. For example, if there is an old cat in the house who doesn't feel like moving very much anymore and you bring home a kitten or young adult who wants to play, play, play, this can be very stressful for the old cat. Sooner or later, he will respond with aggression, driving the young cat off. Now the old cat is stressed and afraid, and the juvenile is afraid of him.

This situation can be prevented or fixed by addressing the individual needs of each cat. It is normal and healthy for a young cat to engage in a lot of vigorous play. The solution may be to get a third cat who is approximately the same age so that they can play "chase and tumble" together. Alternatively, the humans in the house can spend enough time with the young cat to satisfy his need for social play.

Sometimes a young cat's vigorous social play is directed at a human rather than another cat. This behavior can include jumping on the person's legs or feet or grabbing at them as they walk by. If the vigorous social play is causing injury, we call it misdirected play behavior. It can seem vicious, but the cat is really just trying to play with his family. (See chapters 7 and 11 to learn more about this problem.)

## Avoiding Pitfalls and Staying on Track

One potential concern in a multicat household is inter-cat aggression. One of the most important and basic ways to avoid this problem is to make sure there are enough resources for all your cats. These resources should be distributed in various places throughout the house.

Some cats have a preferred core area, or place where they typically rest and hang out. Make sure all the necessary resources are present in each cat's preferred area. Think of everything that is important to your cats, then make sure there are multiple options available. This includes food, litter boxes, warm and soft places to sleep, toys, scratching posts, and high resting perches.

Cats who must compete for limited resources will exhibit aggressive behavior, and some cats will be able to monopolize resources and prevent others from having access to them. Cats who live in a household where they know everyone has what they need and want and they do not have to fight to get it are much less likely to develop aggression issues.

Cats use the same friendly behaviors with other species that they use with one another. *Sharon Crowell-Davis*

## What Did We Say?

- Cats in general are neither asocial nor solitary. A cat can become asocial if he is raised in isolation from his own species and from friendly human contact.
- Cats are social creatures, with the queen, who is the matriarch, forming the core of an extended family.
- Every cat is an individual with his own temperament. This temperament is derived from a combination of genetics, early experiences, and specific events.
- Appropriate social behavior must be learned as the cat is growing up. His brain has the template to learn and retain social behavior, but he must learn from actual experiences.
- To grow up to be behaviorally and socially healthy, a kitten and a juvenile cat need exposure to multiple friendly cats and people. If it's available in your area, enroll your kitten in a socialization class, often called kitten kindergarten.
- Cats develop strong social relationships with the humans they live with, as long as the people are kind to them and respect their preferences.

- Cats behave toward humans they are friendly with the same way they behave toward cats they are friendly with. That does not mean cats actually think humans are cats. It means they have a specific set of behaviors they use for friendly interactions, and they use those behaviors regardless of the species they're being friendly with.
- Because they are prey animals, cats may be slow to accept new people and locations. Novelty can represent danger. Provide your cats with enclosed areas where they can feel safe. Make introductions pleasant and slow, allowing them to determine the pace of getting to know new people.
- Ask visitors to your home to offer treats and toys to your kitten or juvenile cat, so that he learns that even non-household humans are sources of pleasant experiences.
- As Topaz and Opal showed us, the bond between feline family members can remain very strong for many years.

# 5

# Living with Multiple Cats
## *Creating Harmony in the Multicat Household*

Leticia Mattos De Souza Dantas,
DVM, MS, PhD, DACVB

Lili was a nine-year-old cat who loved her life with her owner, Maria. One day Maria was browsing a list of adoptable cats on a rescue website and saw a beautiful younger cat who looked as if he could have been Lili's offspring. Tiger was a two-year-old stray who had been picked up by the rescue group. Maria hoped he would become Lili's best friend.

When Maria brought Tiger home, Lili seemed to be okay with him initially. She got along with other cats she'd lived with before, so Maria didn't worry too much about introducing the two cats slowly. Tiger acted shy and hesitant but did not show any obvious signs of fear or aggression. But one day, during an attempt to get them to like each other by feeding them together, Tiger approached Lili's food bowl, and she attacked him. She was out of control, hissing and growling. When Maria approached, Lili bit her on the leg, causing a deep wound. Maria separated the two cats.

As time went on, Tiger and Lili learned to coexist separated by a gate. But they were never friends, and Lili continued to hiss and growl at Tiger through the gate. Then Tiger developed a bone marrow disease. When he was under stress, his symptoms became worse. Maria thought Lili's aggression was taking a toll on Tiger's health and eventually separated the two cats completely. This saved them both from living with chronic stress.

Then Lili passed away. Understanding that Tiger would have a difficult time living with another cat and that his illness was worse when he was stressed, Maria decided not to replace Lili. Since then, Tiger has been the happiest cat ever. His disease has been in remission for years, and he does not seem to miss having a companion. Although Maria would love to get one of the kittens she sees all the time on adoption websites, she understands it is best for Tiger to be her only feline companion.

If you have cats in your home, chances are you have more than one. Most cat owners do. But how do cats feel about that? As humans, we know that living with someone can be difficult. Sharing space, sharing your things, not having silence and solitude when you want it — it doesn't always work out with roommates. It's not very different for cats. Some cats willingly live with other cats, but many cats seriously resent the company or take quite a long time to adapt, and then only if behavior modification is part of the introduction process.

In chapter 4, you read about the social behavior of domestic cats. In this chapter, I will explain how feline social behavior regulates interactions in a multicat household, and how you can make it work if you decide to add a new kitty to your family. I will discuss realistic expectations, basic guidelines to increase the chances of peaceful feline coexistence in a multicat household, how to fulfill every cat's needs, and how to introduce a new cat so the situation is less stressful for everyone (humans included!).

## Facts, Not Fiction

Do cats enjoy the company of other cats? Mixed messages abound: *Cats are not social. Cats are not as social as dogs. Cats are highly social.* What is really true?

If cats are social, why can it be so hard to introduce a new cat to a household? Why do so many cats never get used to having a companion of the same species? The answers are in the evolution and biology of their behavior.

The ancestor of all domestic cats, *Felis silvestris lybica,* or the African wildcat, was a solitary animal. But through centuries of domestication, this wildcat developed into *Felis catus,* the domestic cat, with the amazing ability to be social. This makes our cats (along with lions and cheetahs) part of a very select group of feline species that exhibit social behaviors and form groups. They are capable of complex and fascinating cooperative behaviors, such as taking care of and nursing one another's young.

Free-roaming cats often form matriarchal groups of related female cats. They rely on chemical communication in their environment to establish a group identity, often using scent before sight to verify individuals. Strangers are most definitely not welcome in these groups. Males tend to leave the group around one year of age, and the resident cats will aggressively chase away strangers if they come too close.

When we decide to share our lives with more than one cat, we force unrelated cats into an artificial social group. For many cats, this can be difficult and even unacceptable. While cats can show affiliative (friendly) behaviors to other cats, their evolutionary history (eons of solitude) means they lack the conflict-defusing behaviors that other animals, such as dogs, have mastered. So if they have an uncomfortable encounter, they typically default to avoidance and dispersal — that is, they run away. When cats live indoors in a house ruled by humans, however, they cannot just leave and find another place to live. That is why introducing your cats to one another the right way (stay tuned) is so important. First impressions are everything; you want to avoid that initial squabble at all costs.

Feline social preferences are also influenced by personality, genetics, prenatal and postnatal brain development, early life events, and adult life experiences. Every cat is unique, and when integrating cats into a harmonious home, you must consider this individuality.

On the bright side, cats have developed several amazing ways to coexist without conflict — *if* the environment they're living in affords each cat her own space, resources, and coping mechanisms. We now understand what enables some cats to live together with minimal stress and in many cases to truly bond and become friends.

In a multicat home, some cats will form their own groups, while some might behave as solitary cats. This is totally acceptable. The key, as I will explain later in this chapter, is to provide separate and multiple resources to support each group and each cat.

## What Does That Mean?

**Ancestor:** An early type of animal from which others have evolved.

**Affiliative behaviors:** Social behaviors meant to communicate affection, reduce tension, and maintain a bond.

**Antagonistic behaviors:** Social behaviors related to aggression, fighting, or an altercation. These can include stress or fear signaling, threatening behaviors, retreat or avoidance behaviors, and attacking.

**Anxiety disorders:** A group of mental disorders or behavior pathologies characterized by significant feelings of anxiety and fear that interfere with the ability of an individual to live a normal life.

**Anxiety:** A state of worry or unease about something that may happen or an outcome that is uncertain.

**Appeasement and reconciliation behaviors:** Behaviors meant to make peace, de-escalate a situation, or avoid a fight. Although cats show some of these behaviors, they have a less extensive repertoire than dogs due to their evolutionary history of using physical avoidance and scent to avoid conflict.

**Behavior therapy or behavior modification:** The systematic use of learning procedures to treat psychological problems and modify dysfunctional behaviors.

**Fear:** The emotion of being scared or afraid of some situation, animal, person, or event.

**Pheromones:** Naturally occurring species-specific scents that cats use to delineate territory or calm nursing kittens. Synthetic analogues (copies) are available commercially.

**Stress:** The biological response triggered when a stimulus, called a stressor, challenges the peaceful balance of an individual's body or mind. Stressors can be external (coming from the physical environment or from social interactions) or internal (illness, pain, discomfort). Stress can initiate the fight-or-flight response, a complex reaction of the nervous and endocrine systems that affects the whole body.

## What Does It Look Like?

Let's review the signs of stress and of friendly interactions discussed in earlier chapters. What are those signs? How do you know when your cat is happy to meet another cat and when she's not? Here's a quick body language dictionary, looking specifically at the signals that are most important in a multicat household.

**Affiliative or friendly behaviors.** For cats, greeting with the tail relaxed and up straight is a common signal of a friendly approach. The gaze is soft, and some cats slowly blink. Rubbing and grooming one another, playing, resting in close proximity, and snuggling together are other examples of these behaviors.

**Threatening behaviors.** Freezing and staring, sometimes with hissing and growling, are common feline threats.

**Retreat or avoidance behaviors.** These include breaking eye contact, backing up, walking or running away, and hiding.

**Attacking.** This can be swatting, biting, or clawing.

**Stress.** Cats can present stress signs using facial expressions, body movements, and behaviors. Common facial signs are tension in the facial muscles, typically accompanied by ear movements such as flicking them, fixing them forward while staring at something, or rotating them toward the back of the head. (Ears rotated backward and flattened is a sign of extreme fear.) Other signs of stress that can be easily noticed on a cat's face are rapid blinking or squinting (which is usually accompanied by a head turn as the cat breaks eye contact), dilated pupils, and lip licking and gulping. Movements of the tail are also meaningful. Some cats will tuck their tail close to their body, and some will flick it as a sign of increasing agitation.

Some stressed cats might exhibit behaviors that seem out of context, such as quickly grooming. Cats also show tension in the muscles of the body, often followed by behaviors such as flinching, lowering the body close to the floor (crouching), or arching their back. Their fur might be raised or fluffed up, and their head might be low.

Many stressed cats are hypervigilant, constantly scanning the environment and reacting to movement and noises they detect, while others act sedate and simply freeze and look catatonic. These behavior changes can be accompanied by active attempts to avoid whomever the cat is interacting with (or any scary stimulus), such as moving backward, walking away, running away, hiding, jumping, or climbing up to a high spot. Some cats might not move until they are touched or the scary individual gets too close.

Nervous cats will often vocalize, which can vary depending on a cat's socialization history and arousal levels. Some cats produce a high-pitched meow, some hiss and growl, and some might even scream or spit.

When stressed cats feel cornered or pushed into a situation, they may show aggressive behavior. Or they may alternate their stress signaling with freezing and staring, then attacking (biting and clawing). Some cats might actively chase and attack as well.

## Is That Really True?

How worried should you be if your cats are showing signs of stress due to living together? Does stress actually cause disease? The answer is yes, it really does. When a cat perceives a potential threat or challenge, her body responds, activating the stress mechanisms that may also lead to anxiety and fear. Cats experiencing acute stress show a specific body language that may help you detect when your cat needs help (see the previous section, "What Does It Look Like?").

Even though the brief stress response is an important defense mechanism for all species, living under chronic stress is detrimental to a cat's mental, emotional, and physical well-being. Chronic stress can cause medical and behavior problems, such as anxiety disorders, aggressive behavior, and house soiling.

For example, stressed cats can develop an inflammatory condition in which urination becomes painful, their urine may contain blood, and they may start urinating outside the litter box. Eliminating outside the box is not a complaint or a protest against anything, but rather an attempt to eliminate somewhere that feels safe and comfortable. (See chapter 8 to learn more about this topic, other reasons cats might eliminate outside the litter box, and what to do about it.)

## How Do We Begin?

Imagine you just got home from a long day at work. You cannot wait to pour yourself a glass of wine and relax, maybe even binge-watch your favorite TV show. Suddenly, someone knocks on your front door. You open the door and a stranger walks in, picks up your glass of wine, sits on your couch, and changes the channel. What would you do? Probably call 911.

Cats can't do that. But we bring strange cats into our home and let them make themselves comfortable. How terrifying this must be for the resident cats!

Planning ahead for a multicat household is an investment in your cats' health and relationships. Using science-based methods when introducing a new cat, rather than just letting the cats "work it out," will make things go a lot smoother and prevent serious problems down the road.

The first impressions cats have when they meet has a long-lasting effect, and cats who fight at their first meeting are less likely to get along. A 2005 study conducted by Dr. Emily Levine, DACVB, and her colleagues at Cornell University Hospital for Animals found that the factor most frequently associated with fighting in the weeks immediately following the introduction of a new cat into a household is unfriendly or aggressive behavior at the first meeting. In other words, first meetings described as unfriendly or aggressive by the owners in the study were significantly more likely to be associated with fighting in the following weeks than first meetings described as friendly or nonaggressive.

That's why a successful introduction of a new cat requires careful planning and proceeds slowly, never pushing either the new cat or the resident cats beyond their threshold and into fight-or-flight mode. It's a gradual process, and what that means is different for every cat. For some cats it may take only a few weeks, while for others it may take months.

### Go to Your Room

Before you bring home a new cat, prepare a room for her. The room should have a door that shuts it off from the rest of the house and contains everything the cat needs: food, water, litter box, toys, scratching post, hiding spot, and elevated resting area.

Bring your newly adopted cat directly into her prepared room, keeping her apart from your resident cats. Do not stop to let them interact with her — not even a sniff. Being placed in a new environment with new sights, sounds, and smells is scary! A separate space will allow the new cat to get comfortable and relaxed in her new home and give the resident cats time to take in what is going on. Do not allow your resident cats and the new cat to see or touch each other at this stage.

The cats will likely react to each other through the closed door, so make sure they are truly separated. You can, for example, use a draft stopper or box to prevent the cats from seeing each other under the door. When all signs of stress, fear, and anxiety have ceased in all the cats (see "What Does It Look Like?" earlier in this chapter), you can progress to the next stage.

## Introducing Scents

At this point, your new cat and resident cats are probably ready to be introduced to each other's scents. Cats are guided by smell and chemical communication, so scent is more important than sight. Before we get started, though, a word of caution: Artificial scents on their body are not well tolerated by cats, not even if all the cats carry the same artificial scent. Do not put perfume or any other scent on your cats! That's really stressful for them. They will naturally and gradually create a group scent based on their own odors, not ones added by you.

You can start by exposing each cat to minor items used by another cat — for example, by swapping blankets or small toys. To maintain their sense of security, make sure you do not place these items in the cats' safe places, such as beds or cat trees.

Give the cats time to familiarize themselves with the new scents. Always present these items paired with a high-value treat. You'll want to use a treat or food that is very enticing to the cats in order to promote the most positive association possible, so take time to identify which treats are most rewarding for each cat. Remember, different cats have different tastes.

## Time-Sharing

When you observe that none of the cats are showing signs of stress when presented with the other cats' scent items, you can start a time-sharing experiment in the common areas of the home — the rooms that are not any cat's respective safe haven — to further expose them to each other's scents. Do not introduce more than one cat's scent at a time to the new cat, as this can be really overwhelming for her.

Begin by allowing each cat into the common areas for a few minutes every day, then progress to longer periods. Remember to always give small, high-value treats to the cats as you practice this step. Progress to the next step when there are no signs of stress, fear, or anxiety.

## Sneaking a Peek

If possible, allow your cats to see each other without the opportunity for physical contact. Glass or screen doors or baby gates with transparent acrylic panels affixed to them can make this step as safe as possible. A hook-and-eye latch that allows the door to be open just a crack may be a suitable alternative to a glass or screen door. Pair these introductions with high-value treats or play to keep the cats focused on you, while striving to create a positive association between them. Only if all the cats are calm and friendly should they be allowed to shift their attention to each other.

Do not overwhelm or push your cats. A couple of five- to ten-minute sessions twice a day is more than enough to begin with. Do not let them focus their attention on each other unless they are both calm, and make sure they have some distance from each other to begin with, even with the barriers separating them. If they start staring at each other or showing any other signs of stress, call one of the cats to you (it is very useful to teach cats a verbal recall cue to help manage them without having to touch them) or, if it can be done safely, pick one up or cover her with a thick blanket or towel to block her vision.

When none of the cats show any signs of stress, fear, or aggression when they see each through a barrier and happily approach the barrier in spite of another cat being on the other side, you can move to the next step.

## Eating Treats Near Each Other

Start feeding the cats at the same time, without a physical barrier between them but at a distance — as far apart as it takes for them to remain calm. You can use high-value small treats or high-value food that can be eaten quickly instead of their regular meals.

It's better and safer if you have one or more people to help you, so that each person is paying attention to the body language of one cat. Reinforce calm and friendly behaviors by rewarding the cats with high-value treats and praise, and redirect any stress signs or antagonistic behaviors (such as staring) by happily calling the cat's name and focusing her attention back to the food or to you.

If you notice that one of the cats is becoming fearful, anxious, or aroused, remove her from the situation or cover her with a large blanket, then try again the next day.

## Playing Near Each Other

When the cats are consistently meeting with success in the previous step (all of them are calm and not aroused or stressed in each other's presence, and they are able to hang out without focusing on each other), try playing with them while they are all together in the same room. Food-dispensing toys are great at this stage, because they can help the cats show social and play behavior without focusing too much on each other

Eliciting play is an effective way to promote positive interactions between cats.
*Leticia Mattos De Souza Dantas*

— all the while making the positive association you want between food and the other cats. Games where cats search for food can serve the same purpose.

Another type of activity that can promote a great experience while not allowing the cats to focus on each other is teaching them a new task or trick that they can do when asked. For example, you can ask the cats, one at a time, to touch an object or your hand with their nose, then reward them with a treat. (This is a form of operant conditioning. See chapter 6 to learn more about how amazing cats are at learning and how fantastic it is for their mental health.)

If this phase goes well, start allowing the cats to be in each other's presence without so much guidance and control from you, but still with supervision. Allow short interactions, ending while everyone is still calm, and gradually increase the time together if all the cats remain relaxed and stress-free.

If you are afraid that an altercation may suddenly arise and escalate, consider keeping each cat on a harness attached to a long, loose leash. Do not put any tension on the leash at any time during the positive interactions; use it only to separate the cats should a fight occur.

## Unsupervised Interactions

Unsupervised interactions (and eventually, being allowed to live together freely) should come only after several weeks or months of no stress signs and no antagonistic behavior from any cat. Whenever your cats show any friendly behaviors toward each other (approaching with tail up, gazing with soft eyes as opposed to staring, purring, nose touching, head or

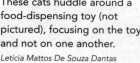

These cats huddle around a food-dispensing toy (not pictured), focusing on the toy and not on one another.
*Leticia Mattos De Souza Dantas*

body rubbing, grooming each other, attempting to play), give them lots of praise and a high-value treat immediately — this is gold!

You might experience a setback at some point, but do not despair. Behavior is dynamic and ever-changing. This means everyone — your cats included — can have bad days from time to time. Just take a deep breath, go back to the previous step, and pick up from the stage at which no cats showed any signs of stress.

---

### What Not to Do

Now that you know what to do, let's examine the things you need to avoid.

- Never bring a new cat in and let her loose to explore the house while the resident cats are free to roam as well.
- Don't plop down the new cat in her carrier and let the resident cats surround her. This "shark tank" method will cause the poor newcomer to be trapped in a box while being menaced by strangers. Meanwhile, the other cats will be freaking out over the intruder in their house. This is a lose-lose situation and no way to do an introduction.
- Don't reprimand or correct any negative responses from any of the cats, because this is likely to add tension to the situation. Hissing, growling, and swatting are behaviors that come from stress and fear, and your cats have the right to express those feelings. For the same reason, forget spray bottles, making loud noises, yelling, throwing things, and so on. All these punishments will only hurt the bond the cats have with you and will certainly not teach them to love each other. You must do this the right way and the respectful way, to ensure that things turn out for the best.

---

## Avoiding Pitfalls and Staying on Track

The most common pitfall when introducing cats is rushing the process. Trust the method you have learned in this book and take your time with it! Remember, your cats' behavior is your guide for when to move on to the next step. They need time to adapt, and how they feel is all that matters.

Cats commonly do not express stress, fear, and anxiety with signs that are obvious to us humans. Instead, they have evolved to show avoidance behaviors (hiding) and scent marking (urine spraying or increased scratching) when they are stressed or frightened, to signal to other cats how they feel. Some cats are more active about how they show their emotions, and others are more passive. Signs of heightened fear and aggression (such as hissing, growling, charging, swatting, pawing, and biting) definitely mean that a cat is severely stressed. However, some cats who are stressed do not show these signs. Often cats simply freeze in fear and do not move, or they move very slowly. In other words, the absence of obvious aggressive behavior does not mean that your cats are okay.

If you notice any of what veterinarians call sickness behaviors (decreased grooming, decreased appetite, a change in sleep patterns, increased vocalizations, missing the litter box), these may be signs that a cat is nervous or stressed about what is happening. Do not proceed with the introduction, and keep the cats separated until they are all calm.

Other signs that a cat is stressed include a decrease in playfulness, avoiding social interactions (with both humans and cats), frequent hiding, or a tendency to remain on the periphery of the room. Paying attention to these changes is very important, especially for cats who have a more stoic or passive temperament. A change in attention-seeking behaviors (usually seeking more attention or acting needy for active cats, and fewer social interactions for more passive kitties) is another important clue that a cat is stressed. (See chapter 1 to learn more about cat communication, body language, and signs of illness.)

## Enough Resources for Everyone

In 2013, the American Association of Feline Practitioners and the International Society of Feline Medicine published a terrific booklet, *AAFP and ISFM Feline Environmental Needs Guidelines* (https://journals.sage pub.com/doi/pdf/10.1177/1098612X13477537). Several distinguished veterinarians, including veterinary behaviorists, got together and organized years of research into a comprehensive and objective document that outlines what cats need to have an excellent quality of life. Check out the AAFP website (www.catvets.com) for other important guidelines and handouts for cat owners.

Long before these environmental needs guidelines were published, decades of studies had shown how enriching an animal's environment can significantly benefit her health in several ways. Some of these studies (including ones I was involved in) were conducted in shelters or laboratories where cats were kept, with the goal of improving their quality of life and decreasing their stress levels. Other studies and review papers focused on house cats and how to optimize their well-being, including a 2012 study by Dr. Meghan Herron, DACVB, and Dr. C. A. Tony Buffington. And still others explored using enrichment to treat feline interstitial cystitis (FIC), a common feline pathology for which stress is a major risk factor and trigger. (See chapter 8 to learn more about this problem.)

When it comes to multicat households, some of the enrichment strategies described in the environmental needs guidelines can give cats coping mechanisms to deal with the stress of group living. Here's what you need to know about how to set up your home environment for multicat success.

## Key Resources

Cats should have multiple and separate resources. When your cats have the option *not* to share their most important resources, they have more control over the things that are important to them, and this decreases the likelihood of conflict.

Key resources are food and water stations, litter boxes, scratching surfaces, toys, play areas, elevated resting areas, and safe spots. It is very important that these resources are provided in multiple locations throughout your home, as opposed to crammed into one area or even one room. This is a common problem with litter boxes. If they are all in one area of the house, for cats this counts as just one elimination location. If a cat is afraid others will block her access to the box or ambush her when she's in it, she may avoid the area and eliminate in what she considers a safer place.

Avoid feeding the cats in a situation where they must be close together. When a cat is trying to get her meal, it can be stressful to eat side by side with other cats or have to fight for access to one large bowl. Eating should be a safe and peaceful process, or anxiety levels may go up.

Carriers can be great safe places for your cat, but you need to have one for each cat. Leaving each cat's carrier accessible all the time has the added bonus that it can make the trip to the veterinarian less stressful for your cat, because she sees the carrier as a safe haven. *Leticia Mattos De Souza Dantas*

(Small treats that can be quickly consumed are used in training and introductions. At those times the space between cats is carefully controlled. We're talking here about their regular meals.)

## Play Alone or Together?

Even adult and senior cats need to play! Play is important for their mental and physical well-being, and it is an indicator that all is well with a cat. Cats may play by themselves, with each other, or with their human family members. Some cats are enthusiastic and will play with anything and anyone. Others are more particular, preferring certain types of toys and styles of play. Some prefer one-on-one playtime with their owners and are not really into social play or sharing toys with other cats. If you have a cat who behaves this way, play with her in a separate area apart from your other cats.

Have fun experimenting with your cats, so you get to know their preferences. Toys can be as simple as a wadded-up paper ball or as sophisticated as a battery-operated toy that triggers hunting behavior. Our household cats may be domesticated, but they still retain some wild tendencies. Many cats have a strong preference for toys that spark parts of the predatory sequence: stalking, chasing, pouncing, grabbing, clawing, and biting. If cats are not given the opportunity to display these predatory behaviors through play, they may develop inappropriate behaviors (chasing, pouncing, biting) directed at their housemates, which would not be conducive to peaceful coexistence!

Games where cats are encouraged to search for food or toys keep them busy while helping them have a good time together.
*Leticia Mattos De Souza Dantas*

## Predictable Routines

Having a predictable routine gives cats an additional sense of control and reduces their stress levels. Make changes slowly and gradually. Knowing what to expect and how their lives will unfold every day (from feeding to playtime) can significantly decrease cats' stress and anxiety, and help our feline companions understand how to distribute their time and space to coexist peacefully. For example, if there are conflicts between two cats living together, they may decide to be more active at different times of the day and in different areas of the house.

## Positive, Consistent, Predictable Human-Cat Social Interactions

Often our cats are more attached to us than to their feline companions. This is more important than most people realize. One study published in 2017 by Dr. Monique Udell, Dr. Lindsay Mehrkam, and Dr. Kristyn Vitale Shreve showed that most of the cats they studied actually preferred human interactions to food, toys, and the scent of food.

Offer your cats predictable times when they can get one-on-one attention and affection. Make this time special for both of you by exploring your cat's favorite activities. This is especially important if your cats are separated during an introduction period and need to be moved from room to room in the house — which means each one will get less time with you.

## Outdoor Space

It is generally accepted that cats are safer and will live longer if they're kept indoors. However, it is obvious that even the most amazingly designed indoor living space cannot mimic the excitement and stimulation of being outdoors. An acceptable compromise (when space and budget allow) is to net or completely fence in an outside area for your cats. The additional space and stimulation can greatly increase cats' welfare and help with their cohabitation by offering more exciting enrichment, more opportunities for normal behavior, and more spacing — all of which will help prevent and defuse conflict. (See chapter 3 for more information on environmental enrichment and fulfilling feline needs.)

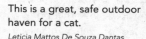
This is a great, safe outdoor haven for a cat.
*Leticia Mattos De Souza Dantas*

## I Don't Remember You!

What about when one cat leaves the house and then returns? Her buddies may act as if they don't know her, even if they have been living together for years. What's happening here?

Scientists believe that through all their marking and rubbing behaviors, cats create a group scent. They may lose this scent after extended boarding or hospital stays and return home smelling like a stranger to the other resident cats. In fact, some resident cats can get nervous and even become aggressive toward a cat who has been gone for less than a day at a veterinary appointment.

The cat coming home is also likely to be returning stressed and upset. Take an active approach and put her in a room by herself for a short time, so that she can calm down and groom off the foreign scent.

If the other cats still act as if they don't know her, the introduction protocol outlined earlier in this chapter will come in handy. Take the returning cat to a separate area of the house and give her separate resources and time to calm down. Give the cats who stayed behind time to reacclimate to her smell and sounds. Go through all the steps in the introduction protocol, but often a reintroduction is much quicker than an initial introduction.

You might have cats who have gotten along well for months or even years, then suddenly show signs of conflict. This situation can sometimes be triggered by a frightening external event that made one of the cats nervous and reactive, such as a shelf falling off the wall or a stray cat or wild animal coming up to the window. Some cats also develop fear and anxiety as they age and have scary life experiences.

Once the primary cause of the stress that triggered the conflict has been removed, you can address the problem exactly as you do when you introduce a new cat to the home. Separate your cats, give them time to calm down, and then gradually start the protocol of exchanging scents and reintroducing them to each other, using lots of high-value treats and praise.

## What Else Can Be Helpful?

When stress spikes or becomes chronic, some kitties might benefit from medication that can decrease their arousal levels and support better functioning of the brain areas that regulate fear and anxiety. This is not a decision to be taken lightly. Talk to your cat's primary care veterinarian and perhaps discuss a referral to a behavior specialist. Knowledge is empowering, and the veterinarian will be able to give you all the information you need to decide how best to help your cat.

You have probably noticed that there are several commercially available products that promise to decrease your cat's stress levels and even help with specific problems, such as getting cats to coexist without conflict. These include synthetic pheromones, herbal supplements, homeopathic remedies, essential oils, nutritional supplements, and many more.

Beware of guarantees or promises of quick fixes. The truth is that these products are not FDA approved, most of them have had little or no research to test their efficacy, and often the active ingredients and chemical structures are unknown or not revealed. While some pheromone analogue products and nutritional supplements have been shown to help decrease stress, no homeopathic remedy or essential oil has.

Feliway Classic is a synthetic version of the feline facial pheromone that cats deposit in the environment when they rub with their faces on objects, and Feliway MultiCat is a synthetic version of the maternal appeasing pheromone that queens produce when nursing their kittens. They come in both a spray and a plug-in diffuser. These products claim to produce a sense of safety to help cats remain calm. In a 2014 clinical trial of forty-five families who reported social conflict among housemate cats, Dr. Theresa DePorter, DACVB, found that using a Feliway Multi-Cat plug-in diffuser reduced the level of conflict compared with using a placebo. Although there are a number of other products available that may list pheromones in their ingredients, the Feliway products are the only ones with scientific research behind them and are, at the moment, the only ones available in a spray or a diffuser.

There is some evidence that the amino acid L-theanine (Anxitane) and the milk protein alpha-casozepine (Zylkene) can be used to treat anxiety in dogs and cats, including research by Dr. Gary Landsberg, DACVB, but large, controlled studies on cats are lacking.

Ask your veterinarian before medicating your cat with anything, no matter how "natural" it is. And remember, even the products with some science behind them are not meant to be used as a substitute for appropriate management and behavior therapy strategies that can make your cat truly feel safe.

## What About Catnip?

Catnip can be one of those special treats you use to create a positive association when cats are being introduced. Typically, cats become relaxed and exhibit play behavior when exposed to it, and that's just what you want.

You can grow catnip and give your cats fresh leaves, or buy dried leaves or toys that are stuffed with them. Not every cat responds to catnip, though — only 50 to 60 percent of cats respond behaviorally. Their response has a genetic basis. In other words, do not feel offended if you spend money on a catnip toy and one of your cats totally ignores it.

Some cats who have a behavioral response to catnip get aroused and cross to the dark side. Their eyes get big (they look this way because their pupils are dilated), and they might act tense, vocalize (in a way that sounds more alarming than fun), and twitch their backs. Some will swat at or bite whoever comes close.

If that is your cat's reaction, do not bring catnip into your home. When cats get aroused, they can redirect their aggression to the nearest target. You don't want to put anyone — human or feline — at risk. The relationship between your cats also can be seriously damaged if there is an aggressive incident. At the end of the day, cats who have this type of extreme response should not be exposed to catnip.

## Can All Cats Live with a Feline Companion?

As with some humans, some cats just can't get along, despite our best intentions and even if we do all the right things. Remember Tiger and Lili? Their socialization to other cats might have been deficient, or they might simply have not been able to handle the stress of being around an unfamiliar cat. Even cats who peacefully shared part of their life with another cat in the past may find it very difficult living with a new cat.

In theory, cats who cannot get along can live in separate areas of your home, as long as you provide each with all their key environmental needs. Some cats will adapt to living this way with low stress levels. Sadly, others will remain severely stressed, resulting in a poor quality of life and decreased longevity.

If your cats are not adapting, even after you have diligently tried the introduction process described in this chapter and given it plenty of time, consult with a veterinary behaviorist or a certified behavior consultant. A specialist can help you figure out if the cat who cannot adapt could benefit from a medication that treats fear and anxiety, or if one of your kitties would be much happier in a different home.

Having cats who need to be separated for the rest of their lives (especially if they show aggressive behavior) can also take a toll on the humans in your home. You need to consider what is best for your family's well-being. But before you give up on your cats, we strongly encourage you to give them another chance by consulting with a veterinary behaviorist.

## If You Really Want More Than One Cat

As you have already learned, being related increases the likelihood of cats getting along. Research also has shown that early socialization to each other greatly increases the chances of feline bonding. So, when you think of adopting again, consider taking home a mother cat with one or more of her litter, siblings, or pairs or trios of unrelated kittens.

But the most important consideration is, does your resident cat, or an older cat you're thinking of adopting, want a companion? Certain cats with certain personalities prefer to be alone, and you need to give careful thought to how your decision will affect them.

When your resident cat cannot adapt to living with a feline companion, her well-being should be your priority. It may be best not to adopt another cat. Likewise, if you had a long and difficult introduction between two cats but things are finally going well, you don't want to upset the harmony you have finally created by adding a third. This might be disappointing, but living under chronic stress and anxiety can be devastating for your cat (and your family). In the end, every cat deserves a peaceful, stress-free life.

## What Did We Say?

- Cats form matrilineal social groups in a free-roaming situation, but they typically do not allow unfamiliar adult cats into their group.
- Cats lack the conflict-defusing abilities that dogs possess, and they quickly default to avoiding each other and dispersing after an alter-

cation. It is important not only to introduce newly adopted cats slowly and carefully but also to prevent conflict between cats who get along.

- Stress is a serious health concern for cats. Kitties *really* need places to hide, feel safe, and calm down.

- Cats might coexist without conflict if the environment supports giving everyone her own space, resources, and coping mechanisms. Instead of being forced to share, cats should have multiple, and separate, environmental resources spread throughout the space they occupy.

- When introducing cats, take your time and use the step-by-step plan in this chapter. Don't rush introductions. Your cats' behavioral responses are your best barometer for knowing how and when to proceed.

- Don't use punishment-based techniques or devices, which will only raise the stress level and promote conflict.

- If, despite your best efforts, one of your cats is not adapting, discuss it with your cat's primary care veterinarian or seek the help of a veterinary behaviorist or certified behavior consultant. Medical treatment for fear and anxiety might be warranted.

- Some cats just prefer to be solitary, either by themselves in a separate area of the house or simply living with no other cats in the house at all.

- When adopting cats, consider taking home a mother with one or more of her litter, siblings, or two or three unrelated kittens. Being related or being introduced at a young age will greatly increase the chances of cats bonding and living together in peace.

# 6

# Unlocking the Feline Mind

*What Learning Really Is and How Cats Learn*

Lisa Radosta, DVM, DACVB

Sugar, a snow-white, doll-faced Persian cat, has lived with Leslie since she was three months old. Before Leslie moved to her current home, she and Sugar lived with Leslie's mother and sister. The most memorable encounters Sugar had with men before moving there were with Leslie's loud, boisterous uncle and a visiting handyman, all ending with Sugar hiding under the bed for the entire day. When Leslie started dating Joe, now her fiancé, Sugar disappeared under the bed every time he visited the house and came out only after he left.

Over the course of the year that Leslie and Joe have been dating, there has been some improvement in Sugar's behavior, but she still won't get within five feet of Joe. Leslie is torn between her kitty and her fiancé. Joe, a cat lover, is hurt by Sugar's behavior. How could she *not* love him? From his perspective, it seems like Sugar is acting out of spite or jealousy so that she can have Leslie all to herself.

Sugar is afraid of Joe because she learned through her earlier experiences that men are loud and scary. Sugar could have inherited from her parents the likelihood that she would become a scaredy-cat, since the tendency to be fearful is known to be passed on from parents to their offspring. However, exposure and training early in life can either reduce that tendency or reinforce it. In Sugar's case, the learning that occurred when she was a kitten confirmed her suspicions that men were scary. When Joe came along, Sugar couldn't accept him because her fear was too overwhelming.

Like many cat owners, Leslie considered Sugar's behavior around men to be "normal cat behavior," and it never occurred to her that she should intervene. Don't all cats hide under the bed? The answer is, sometimes, but not for long periods, and some never hide when company comes.

As you will see in this chapter, the learning associated with fear overshadows virtually all other types of learning. But even if a cat has a genetic predilection toward fear, early and proper conditioning and training, before the fear becomes too intense, may help prevent problems like the one Sugar has with Joe. Hope for Sugar is not lost, however; training can still help forge a loving relationship between her and Joe.

Surely you have heard, or possibly said yourself, that cats can't be trained. The truth is that cats are highly intelligent and can be trained with relative ease, if you know how they learn and how to motivate them. With effort and time, your cat can become more relaxed and better able to cope with stress, and the two of you will be closer than ever.

In this chapter, I'll discuss:

- How your cat learns
- Why you must train him
- How to motivate him to work with you
- How to train him effectively
- How to determine his specific training needs

The difficult truth is that while cats are treasured members of our families, the environments we have created for them can be stressful or unfulfilling. Life changes as owners get married, have children, add pets, move to a new home, or switch jobs. And let's not forget about the scariest experience of all: veterinary visits.

To add insult to injury, cats have little or no control over what happens to them. Imagine if you got out of the house only when you went to the doctor's office — and someone else made all of your decisions for you, including adding feline roommates who will share your food, water, loved ones, and even your toilet. You would be stressed, too!

Without training, cats are ill-equipped to deal with these situations, and they may lead to aggression, depression, fear, or compulsive behaviors. Training is a constant that will enable your cat to cope with life and its challenges with more resilience. Who wouldn't want to give these gifts to their kitty?

Training will also help your cat understand simple but useful tasks, like coming when you call his name or make a specific sound. With the tools in this chapter and a little time and effort, you'll be surprised how readily your cat learn to lead a less stressful life.

Even if your cat seems pretty happy, training can help him be happier.

**Problem:** Your cat hides under the bed when you have visitors.
**Solution:** Teach him to lie on top of his cat tree, out of reach of visitors, helping him to cope with his fear. (Teach your visitors not to touch him when he's there, and he may even start to relax.)

**Problem:** Your cat sometimes bites you when you go to pet him.
**Solution:** Teach him a signal, such as touching your hand with his nose, so that he can tell you when he wants to be petted.

**Problem:** Your cat chases your other cats.
**Solution:** Teach him to come on cue so that you can interrupt the chase.

**Problem:** Your cat hates the veterinarian. (What cat doesn't?)
**Solution:** Teach him to go into his carrier, ride in the car happily, and allow an examination without fuss.

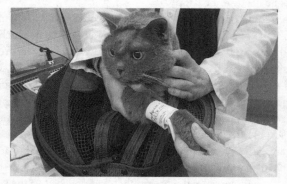

Marcos, who suffers from high blood pressure that affects his vision, has his blood pressure checked by the veterinarian while still in his carrier, which he loves because he uses it as a comfy bed at home. *Carlo Siracusa*

## Facts, Not Fiction

Many people believe that their cats can't be trained, so they don't try. Whether your cat is scared, mischievous, or predatory, understanding what influences his learning will give you a head start on changing his behavior. Every problem has a solution. Once you understand the foundational concepts of how cats learn, the possibilities are endless!

## What Is Learning?

From the outside, learning looks simple. But inside the brain, learning causes developmental changes, changes in electrical impulses, and the release of neurochemicals. Behavior scientists define learning as the process by which experiences change the neurons and neurochemicals in the brain and body, in turn causing an outward change in behavior. Powerful!

Just like his wild brothers and sisters, your cat has learned many things by paying attention to events in his environment. As long as he is awake, he is learning by associating events with consequences ("I do this, and that thing happens"). These associations enable him to predict what will happen in his environment, adjust his behavior to stay safe, and get the things he needs to be happy.

What is going on in your cat's brain neurochemically will affect his ability to learn at any given moment. In particular, the neurochemistry associated with fear, anxiety, and stress (what we call the stress response) will block your cat's ability to reason properly — such as when he scratches you as you try to get him into the carrier to take him to the veterinarian's office. To make things worse, this stress response promotes vivid sensory memories of the environment, people, animals, and inanimate objects involved in certain situations. Memories created when a cat is scared are easily retrieved when he is in that situation again, facilitating very powerful learning.

Now you can understand why it only takes one visit to the veterinarian for your cat to never forget the horror of that place, but ten tries to get him to stay off the kitchen table! If your kitty is fearful, anxious, or stressed, he will have a difficult time learning what you are trying to teach him.

## Cats Are Unique

The scientific principles of learning apply in the same ways to every animal, from honeybees to humans. But each species also has its own predispositions and inclinations. Let's look at some of the things that make cats unique.

Compared with your brain, your cat's brain has more real estate devoted to sensory processing and less to deep thinking. Sensory processing describes the way your cat's nervous system receives input from his senses and turns that input into behavioral responses.

To go along with a brain that is highly skilled at sensory processing, his body is well developed to collect information about what he hears, sees, and smells, then quickly feed it to the brain. For example, your cat can move his ears independently in several directions, enabling him to home in on sounds that we can't even hope to hear. The ridges inside his ears alter a sound so that he can locate the distance and height at which the sound originates to an amazing level of precision. His enhanced hearing enables him to hear subtle cues given in training sessions and notice sounds in the environment that predict scary events. That's why he may be more distracted during training sessions if the room is noisy.

Cats have excellent vision that is adapted to predation. Your cat is somewhat farsighted and has better night vision than you, so be sure to give your training signals at least six inches away from his nose so that he can see them clearly.

As with most predators, cats have a highly developed sense of smell — about a thousand times more sensitive than yours. Because of this, smells that you are completely unaware of are apparent to your cat. He can associate these smells with past situations that trigger specific behaviors, or he can create a new association that he will then store in his brain. For example, did you ever notice that one of your cats is suddenly repelled by another when he returns from the veterinarian's office? That is partly due to the change in the cat's scent.

## What Does That Mean?

**Stimulus:** Anything in the environment (object, person, animal, event) and any sensory factors (sight, smell, taste) associated with that object or event that cause a sensory (such as pupil dilation) or a behavioral (such as hiding) response.

**Habituation:** A type of learning where a cat learns to ignore repeated stimuli in his environment that are not frightening or stressful.

**Sensitization:** A type of learning where a cat becomes more likely to react to something in the environment.

**Conditioning:** Another word for learning; used to indicate the change in behavior that results from the association of two stimuli or events.

**Desensitization:** The process of exposing a cat to a stimulus that he is afraid of, in a manner that is the least threatening possible and incites no or a minimal fear response (such as playing recordings of fireworks or storms at very low volume). This process works well when paired with classical counterconditioning.

**Classical conditioning:** A kind of learning that occurs when a word, a sound, a smell, or the sight of something that was previously without meaning comes to predict a particular outcome. This association causes an involuntary emotional response and reflex behavior in a particular cat; the cat does not control the response. Also called Pavlovian conditioning. Emotional responses might include fear or happiness, and reflex behaviors might be physiological changes such as increased heart rate or respiratory rate.

**Classical counterconditioning:** The process of changing a cat's fearful emotional state by pairing a stimulus that triggers fear with something that naturally triggers a positive emotional response, such as food or play with toys.

**Operant conditioning:** A kind of learning that takes place when a cat makes a conscious choice to perform a behavior, resulting in a consequence for him. The cat can control the result of his actions by changing his behavior.

**Punishment:** Something that is applied (positive) or removed (negative) from a situation to decrease the frequency of a behavior. Also called a punisher.

**Reinforcement:** Something that is applied (positive) or removed (negative) from a situation to increase the frequency of a behavior. Also called a reward.

**Continuous reinforcement:** Reinforcement for every correct attempt at a behavior.

**Intermittent reinforcement:** Reinforcement for some but not all correct attempts at a behavior.

**Conditioned reinforcer:** A neutral stimulus (something that has no meaning for the cat) that is paired with a reward until the conditioned reinforcer comes to predict the reward. Conditioned reinforcers such as clickers are especially helpful for training cats. The cat hears a click and knows that a reward is coming.

## Different Types of Learning

Certain types of learning do not require much obvious effort from you or your cat. Habituation and sensitization are two such types. When a cat habituates to something, he adjusts to it and learns to ignore it. The result is a decreased response to that stimulus, because he has not learned a positive or negative association with it.

For example, your cat may have habituated to the family dog because the dog has been very calm and quiet around him. You did not make a particular effort to help them get along. Nonetheless, they have adjusted to each other. If the cat is very afraid of the dog, he may not habituate (fear overrides all other types of learning), but instead he may become sensitized.

Sensitization is the opposite of habituation. When it occurs, a cat's reaction to something becomes more pronounced. In the example with the dog, if your cat is afraid of the dog and does not show some improvement in about a week, he might be sensitized. A different behavior of the dog — for example, barking instead of being very quiet — may have caused a different outcome. Over time, if nothing is done to change this association, the cat will become more fearful and stressed. If you think your cat is becoming sensitized to a stimulus in your home, act immediately to prevent long-term harm.

Whether individual cats habituate or sensitize to a stimulus depends not only on their experience with that object or event but also on their personality. More fearful animals are more likely to become sensitized to a specific stimulus.

## Classical Conditioning

Isabella was very timely in her daily feeding routine for Chewie, a super-size shorthaired black cat with big amber eyes. Each time she was ready to put down his food-dispensing toy, she also called his name. Over time, Chewie learned that whenever Isabella called his name, she would give him food. So now he comes running, with a cute meow of excitement, 100 percent of the time when Isabella calls him, no matter where he is in the house.

Is this a testament to Isabella's incredible training skills? Not really. It's a result of Chewie's ability to associate events with outcomes and to learn even when Isabella wasn't consciously training him.

Two types of learning occurred here, resulting in a reliable behavior. The first type is called classical conditioning ("conditioning" is another word for "learning"). The second is operant conditioning, discussed in the next section.

When he was adopted, Chewie had no idea what the word "Chewie" meant. It was just a sound his new owner made. But every time Isabella made that sound, she put food inside his dispensing toy. In Chewie's brain, the following association was made:

"Chewie" = food

You can probably think of a time when you have been classically conditioned to feel a certain way. Maybe there is a particular scent or song that triggers a happy feeling for you. Classical conditioning caused Chewie to feel happy when he heard his name — as happy as he was when he actually received a yummy treat. Now his name alone, without any food, evokes a happy feeling.

"Chewie" = food
food = happiness
"Chewie" = happiness

Classical conditioning can be positive or negative, and therefore can either enhance or diminish your cat's well-being. You can condition your cat to be stressed, fearful, and upset just as easily, if not more easily, than you can condition him to be happy. In Chewie's case, he has also been classically conditioned to be afraid of the cat carrier, because it means he will be going to the veterinarian's office. When he sees the carrier, he panics and runs away. Classical conditioning is extremely powerful and is difficult to change once it has occurred.

## Classical Counterconditioning

What if your cat has been classically conditioned to be fearful of his carrier or the veterinary clinic? Fortunately, classical conditioning works both ways, and you can change, or "counter," a negative emotional response through classical counterconditioning. For example, if you associate the stimulus (the carrier or clinic) with a food your cat particularly likes, with repetition you can change his negative response to a positive one, and he will begin to feel good about getting in the carrier or going to see the veterinarian.

## Desensitization

What if your cat won't enter his carrier to eat the special food you're offering him? In that case, you may need to incorporate desensitization into the counterconditioning process. This means that you must start at a level that will not trigger any fearful response. Remove the top of the carrier and place the food on the bottom. Once your cat is comfortable eating there, place the top over just a portion of the bottom. As he gets more comfortable with this arrangement, gradually move the top of the carrier over more of the bottom until eventually the top is in place without the door. When your cat is willing to enter the carrier and eat in a calm, relaxed state, add the door and then gradually close it. The process is complete.

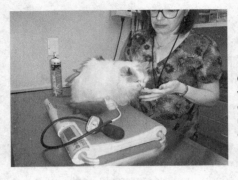

Offering cheese during a veterinary visit helps classically condition a positive emotional response to the veterinarian's exam. *Lisa White/Courtesy of Karen Pryor Academy's Better Veterinary Visits Course*

## Operant Conditioning

Operant conditioning takes place when the cat makes a conscious choice to do something that results in a consequence for him. In this case, Chewie (now feeling quite happy due to classical conditioning) chooses to run to Isabella when he hears his name. The consequence of this choice is that he gets food. In fact, he can control whether he gets food by choosing to either run to her or to stay in his comfy bed. This is the association that has formed in Chewie's brain due to operant conditioning.

"Chewie" + running = food

With operant conditioning, there are four possible consequences of an action, and each consequence causes either a decrease or an increase in the behavior to which it is applied. The four possibilities are:

1. Positive reinforcement
2. Negative reinforcement
3. Positive punishment
4. Negative punishment

Understanding these concepts, and which one makes a behavior more likely or less likely to be repeated, will enable you to effectively teach your cat almost anything.

Let's start with reinforcement. If you want your cat to continue performing a behavior, no matter what the behavior is, it has to be rewarded. Behavioral scientists call the act of rewarding something "reinforcement"; rewards are called "reinforcers." Reinforcement increases the strength of a particular behavior, much like the beams on a building reinforce its strength. It makes the behavior more likely to occur in the future.

Punishment, on the other hand, decreases the likelihood of a behavior occurring. See the chart "Four Consequences in Operant Conditioning" below for details on what reinforcement and punishment do.

### Four Consequences in Operant Conditioning

|  | The Cat's Point of View | What Happens to the Behavior | Example | What the Cat Does Next Time in That Situation |
|---|---|---|---|---|
| **Positive Reinforcement** | Something good happens | Increases | Your cat meows, and you pet him | Meows more |
| **Negative Reinforcement** | Something bad is taken away | Increases | Your cat meows, and you take him out of his cat carrier | Meows more |
| **Positive Punishment** | Something bad happens | Decreases | Your cat meows, and you squirt him with water | Meows less |
| **Negative Punishment** | Something good is taken away | Decreases | Your cat meows, and you stop petting him | Meows less |

## Reinforcement Schedules

For Chewie, what is reinforcing the behavior of coming when called? Food! If Isabella stopped giving Chewie food when she called him, eventually he would stop coming to her. To keep this behavior strong, Isabella will have to continue to reinforce the act of him coming to her when she calls.

How often you reinforce a behavior is called a reinforcement schedule. There are several schedules you can use to reinforce your kitty for his fantastic behavior. Chewie is on a continuous reinforcement schedule — every time he responds to his name by running to Isabella, he gets food.

When a cat is first learning a new skill, a continuous reinforcement schedule is the most effective. But once Chewie is well trained, meaning he responds nine times out of ten the first time Isabella calls him to come (90 percent accuracy), she can start reinforcing him on an intermittent reinforcement schedule. That means Chewie's behavior will be rewarded some of the time, but not all of the time.

Once a skill is learned, an intermittent reinforcement schedule is actually more powerful than a continuous reinforcement schedule, creating strong behavioral responses that are difficult to change. This is the same reinforcement schedule that causes otherwise cautious people to sit at a slot machine for hours, hoping for a payout. The gambler can't predict which coin will produce a big payout, so he or she spends the entire day feeding money into the machine.

If you want to create a strong, reliable response to a training cue, teach first with a continuous reinforcement schedule, then switch to an intermittent reinforcement schedule when your cat is about 90 percent accurate.

That being said, negative emotions like fear and anxiety can make learning more difficult and decrease the accuracy of the cat's response. That's why fearful and anxious cats may need to stay on a continuous reinforcement schedule for longer to obtain good training results.

Keep in mind that behaviors that are not reinforced will eventually be extinguished (they will disappear). If Chewie never gets rewarded or is not rewarded frequently enough, he will stop coming to Isabella when she calls his name.

On the other hand, sometimes we want our cats to *stop* performing a certain behavior. In this case, removing all reinforcement is an excellent, permanent option. One word of caution, though: behaviors that were previously rewarded, even with only your attention, and then are ignored will increase before they decrease. In other words, expect your cat to be very, very persistent for three to five days before the behavior starts to disappear.

## What About Punishment?

So far, we have talked about reinforcing your cat for desirable behavior. You may be wondering what you should do when your cat does something you don't like. It's about time we talked about punishment. If we punish a behavior, it will stop, right? Problem solved! Not so fast, because it rarely works that way.

Punishment, simply defined, means a consequence that, when applied correctly, causes a behavior to decrease or stop. Punishment can take many forms, from removing attention or a toy to a stern "No!" to squirting with water or hitting. Most important, the animal receiving it must think of it as a punishment. Remember, to be successful, it must be motivating enough to cause a behavior to decrease.

Milo, a long, lanky orange tabby cat, loves being on the kitchen counter. He likes to lie with his long tail and back feet precariously hanging off the edge as he sleeps. He also enjoys walking across the counter to the stove to visit Judy, his owner, when she is cooking dinner. Judy, however, does not want him on the counter where she prepares food, considering that his feet have been in the litter box. There is family conflict: Milo wants to be on the counter, and Judy doesn't want him there.

Judy's first reaction was to sternly tell him "No!" and place him on the floor. Milo, confused about Judy's behavior, jumped back onto the counter and sidled over to her again to see what was on the stove. This process repeated itself every day before dinner until one of them gave up. When Judy was too frustrated and tired to put him on the floor again, Milo took up his usual spot on the counter. Sometimes she would have the perseverance to continue putting him down, and Milo would give up. In other words, sometimes Milo would be rewarded (allowed to be on the counter) for his behavior (jumping up there), and sometimes he would not.

Take a moment to test yourself. What type of reinforcement schedule was Milo on? What do you think happened with the jumping behavior?

Judy noticed that Milo became even more persistent over the next few months. It took more and more tries to get him to stay off the counter. She was losing the battle.

What was happening? Judy was using positive punishment. Behavioral scientists use the word "positive" here to mean adding something to the situation. Positive punishment means you're adding something your cat doesn't like with the goal of decreasing his behavior. Judy added a stern "No!" to decrease the likelihood of Milo jumping on the counter. When you add things like yelling, hitting, or squirting with water, you are using positive punishment.

However, Judy soon discovered that things were not going as planned. She had not considered Milo's point of view. Maybe Milo's motivation to be on the counter was stronger than her loud "No!" Plus, she was inconsistent in applying the training: When Judy's back was turned, Milo would jump right back on the counter, and sometimes Judy would just give up and let him stay. She was trying to teach:

Jump on counter + yelling "No!" = less jumping on counter

But Milo actually learned that sometimes he could not only get on the counter but also stay there. If punishment isn't delivered within about one second of the behavior, *every time* the cat performs the behavior, the cat is being intermittently reinforced. In other words, sometimes the behavior works, and sometimes it doesn't. As we just learned, intermittent reinforcement makes a behavior stronger. So Milo actually learned:

Jump on counter + sometimes reinforced, sometimes not = more jumping on counter

Let's see what happened next. Judy did what a lot of people who use positive punishment do: she escalated. Judy decided that Milo had to receive a more uncomfortable punishment. The next night at dinner, she had her squirt bottle ready. When Milo jumped up on the counter, she said in her sternest voice, "Milo!" and squirted him with water. Milo jumped off the counter immediately.

But because Judy had always been inconsistent in delivering punishment, causing Milo to be intermittently reinforced for jumping on the counter, he jumped on the counter again — although it was a good ten minutes before he made the attempt. As his feet touched the counter, the interaction was repeated: "Milo!" then squirt. This continued for several nights, until all Judy had to do was leave the squirt bottle out when she was in the kitchen, and Milo wouldn't jump on the counter.

Problem solved? Nope. And, unfortunately, now there was a bigger problem. Judy noticed a change in Milo's behavior. He no longer responded to his name when she called him. He used to happily run to her whenever she called his name, greeting her at the door when she came home. But that behavior had stopped. Milo had learned that Judy calling his name was followed by a squirt of water. Why would he come for that?

To make matters worse, when Judy was at work and checked in on Milo by watching her webcam, she could see him resting comfortably on the counter with the squirt bottle nearby. The problem wasn't solved.

## The Problem with Positive Punishment

Mistakes like the one Judy made, or simply poor timing, end up punishing the wrong behavior. Judy ended up teaching Milo to associate his name with punishment. Unfortunately, positive punishment can quickly — after only one or two instances — cause powerful classical conditioning of fear of the owner. In some cats, this fear can lead to swatting and biting. Sometimes the biting is directed at the owner, but sometimes it is directed at someone nearby, like a cat, dog, or child.

Remember that classical conditioning is a powerful kind of learning. Milo didn't want to be around Judy because he had been classically conditioned to feel differently about her. He was no longer running to her with happiness. How sad for her and Milo!

Now, in Milo's mind, the following associations had been made:

"Milo!" = squirt of water
squirt of water = fear
"Milo!" = fear

Positive punishment also causes a decrease in a cat's willingness to interact and offer spontaneous behaviors, making it more difficult to train him. In Milo's case, Judy is no longer able to use his name to get him to come, because now he is fearful when he hears his name. What previously was a useful tool to start training sessions is lost. In addition, the fear of being punished makes Milo reluctant to try new things during training sessions. Better to stick with what he knows or walk away than to be squirted with water.

Positive punishment also causes confusion, because it doesn't teach the cat what he should do, but only what he shouldn't do. In Milo's case, if Judy had just set up a cat tree near the kitchen counter and taught Milo to go there, he would have been able to be high up and near her (which is what he wanted) and also get rewarded for it.

When there's confusion, the behavior we don't want may decrease. But because the motivation for the behavior is still there, cats often exhibit a different behavior that we want even less. In Milo's case, he still wanted to be close to Judy, but he didn't know how to get her attention. He may have started rubbing in between her legs and meowing as she tried to move in the kitchen, creating an annoying and dangerous situation.

Let's review the pitfalls of positive punishment.

- It's difficult to use consistently and becomes reinforcement when delivered inconsistently.
- It must be delivered within about one second of the behavior.
- Classical conditioning results in fear of or aggression toward the owner.
- It reduces the cat's willingness to offer spontaneous behaviors.
- It teaches the cat what he shouldn't do, not what he should do.

In short, try to avoid positive punishment, in particular when it is associated with you. Sometimes you can use positive punishment in a way that it won't be associated with the people or other animals in your household. If you want to consider this option — only with cats who are not fearful or aggressive — we strongly encourage you to discuss it with a certified animal behavior consultant or veterinary behaviorist.

Positive punishment often results in learning: think of touching a hot stove and learning not to do that again. But teaching a new behavior that is incompatible with the undesirable behavior — for example, teaching Milo to go to a cat tree — is the best way to go.

## How to Use Negative Punishment

At this point, you are probably wondering how you can tell your cat that he has done something wrong. Isn't it important for him to know when he is *not* right? Yes, it is. But when cats are not right, they need clear, consistent feedback. This type of feedback can be helpful in the learning process. This is the place for negative punishment.

Remember, with negative punishment, something the cat likes is removed in order to decrease a behavior. Take the example of Ted, a cat who meows to get his owner, Scott, to pet him. Even when Scott is petting Ted, he keeps meowing, as if to say *Don't stop.*

Scott loves Ted dearly, but he is tired after work and would rather have some peace and quiet while he's petting Ted. So, when Scott is petting Ted and Ted meows, Scott withdraws his hand. He removes the petting that Ted likes in order to decrease the meowing. This type of negative punishment is highly effective.

However, if you remove something a cat enjoys without redirecting him to another activity, frustration can build, causing negative behaviors such as biting and swatting. If your kitty is easily frustrated, make sure to immediately follow a negative punishment with a new activity that is enjoyable or relaxing for your cat.

---

**Do** use positive reinforcement and, when appropriate, negative punishment.

**Don't** use positive punishment or negative reinforcement.

---

## Is That Really True?

*Are cats jealous and spiteful?* Let's go back for a minute to the example of Leslie, Sugar, and Joe. Joe believed Sugar was acting out of spite or jealousy. Do cats really do that?

The cerebral cortex, the part of the brain involved in conscious thought, occupies a larger portion of your brain than it does your cat's. Because of this, behavioral scientists believe that cats spend little time pondering the mysteries of existence and instead spend most of their time watching their environment and forming associations based on sensory input.

In other words, cats can't plot to take revenge on you for dating the wrong person or changing your work schedule. They can't understand the concept of money or that your comforter cost $300. If your cat urinated on your bed, most likely he was responding to a dirty litter box, intimidation by another pet in the family, or a major stressor in his life. No, your cat is not filled with vengeful thoughts about you. He simply had to urinate, and that was the most convenient, safe, and comforting spot at the time. He is very intelligent, but he isn't conniving or spiteful.

Another thing we know about cats is that they live in the moment. That means they also learn in the moment. That's not to say cats can't remember what happens to them from day to day. Of course they can! If your cat didn't form long-term memories, he wouldn't remember that sleeping on your head is comfy or that going to the veterinarian is scary.

The cat's predisposition to live and learn in the here and now means we have to be careful to deliver rewards and consequences within seconds after desired or undesired behaviors. In the example of the cat urinating on your bed, he will remember how pleasurable it was to relieve his bladder on such a soft, clean surface. That will cause him to return to that spot in the future if nothing else in the environment changes.

If you enter the room later in the day and yell at him, he will remember that as well. Unfortunately, he will not associate urinating on the bed with your reaction, because too much time has passed. Instead, he will associate you and the bedroom with your anger. This could cause several unintended learned responses, such as avoiding you when you are in the bedroom.

We are not suggesting that because cats' brains are different from ours, they lack emotions. Most cat owners have seen fear, pleasure, grief, and joy in their cats. Cats display body language that shows us how they feel in most situations. They have emotions just as we do. They may not spend hours deep in thought about those emotions, but they are real, and they shape how cats learn.

## How Do We Begin?

Are you ready to start training your cat? Before you begin, you need to have a very clear idea of what you want to accomplish. Think about the following:

- What is the new behavior you want to train or the exact behavior you want to change?
- What will the new behavior look like?
- If you want to change an existing behavior, what is your cat's motivation for that behavior? What in the environment, the social situation (with people or other cats), or unmet needs is creating his motivation to engage in the behavior? Remember, behaviors are maintained by their consequences. Therefore, you need to figure out what is happening with the cat that encourages him to continue the behavior.

Take a moment to think about what motivates your cat. Does he like food, being brushed, playing, or petting? Write down in detail all the things he enjoys, then rank them from the most desirable to the least desirable. These will be your positive reinforcers.

Commit to using only positive reinforcement and, if necessary, negative punishment. Get in the right frame of mind by thinking positively. If you are in a cranky mood, skip training until your mood improves.

Consider your cat's overall health before you start training. Can he have treats? If so, what kind? Is he overweight? If he's an older cat, are there pain issues that might limit his ability to perform certain tasks? These are all important considerations.

Consider your cat's personality. Is he a wild child or a couch potato? His personality will influence how you train him. Try to train around mealtimes so your cat is hungry — but beware of a hungry kitty! Some cats become frustrated when they are hungry. This will interfere with learning and may cause them to be more physical about getting their food exactly when they want it, perhaps swatting your hand as you hold the treat. For cats like that, train an hour or two after a meal.

Most cats will need a conditioned reinforcer for the most effective training. A conditioned reinforcer is a sound or word signaling to the cat that the behavior he just performed was correct. It's a very efficient way to train a cat, because it's a clear signal and is delivered immediately — faster than you could give him a treat or another reward. A clicker with a soft "click" sound would certainly do the trick, but you can also use a specific phrase, like "Good job!" Just remember to just be consistent about using the exact same sound or words every time you train, or they will not become conditioned reinforcers.

A clicker can be an effective conditioned reinforcer that tells your cat his action was correct and a treat is coming. This clicker comes with a loop so you can slip it on your wrist. Some cats may be startled by loud clicks, so make sure to choose a clicker with a soft tone. *Carlo Siracusa*

### Your Training Tool Kit

Pull together a tool kit with all the things you'll need for a training session. Put the kit away when you aren't using it so your cat understands when the training session has ended.

THINGS TO PUT IN YOUR TRAINING TOOL KIT:

- Conditioned reinforcer (a clicker, but you can also use a word or short phrase)
- Training diary, to track your cat's progress
- List of training goals
- Treats
- Toys
- Mat for teaching the cat to go to his spot and settle
- Bowl for holding food rewards or so you can deliver a food reward at a distance
- List of behaviors to be taught
- List of your cat's body language when he is upset or disengaging

Save your cat's favorite treats and toys for your training sessions. Cats are attracted to novelty, so keep at least three different types of treats handy each time you train. Make sure the treats you use are about the size of a pea (break them up if you have to). In addition to your training tool kit, keep some treats and another conditioned reinforcer around the house so you can reward your cat throughout the day for desirable behaviors, such as lying on the cat tree instead of the countertop.

Keep sessions short, about five to ten minutes at the most, and always end on a high note when your cat is having a good time and is successful. When he loses interest, the training session is over. Consider even a one-minute training session a success. If your cat works with you for only a minute, make it your goal to work with him twice a day when he is most hungry for attention.

Before training a specific behavior, take a couple of days to practice your own training skills. You will need your conditioned reinforcer and small treats. Whenever you see your cat doing something you like, click the clicker or say your conditioned reinforcer word and hand him a treat. This exercise will put you in a positive frame of mind and hone your observation skills. You will notice that your cat will take more notice of you as well. He may start to pay attention as you walk through the room, as if to ask *Do you like what I am doing now?* Practicing your skills before you start training will help your cat learn more quickly.

Observe your cat throughout the day and make a list of the body language he exhibits when he disengages from you or is upset. Maybe he thumps his tail or puts his ears back. He may turn his head away or start grooming to avoid you. If he exhibits body language of this sort while you are training him, go back to the point where he was easily successful and increase the reinforcement by rewarding him more frequently or with a higher-value reward.

## Luring and Shaping Behaviors

There are two primary ways you can teach your cat new behaviors: luring and shaping.

*Luring* means holding a reward and using a physical gesture to get your cat into position so that you can reinforce him. For example, if you want your cat to sit, you might hold the treat up in the air just above his nose and then move it back slightly, so that as he follows it with his nose, he has to sit. If your kitty swats at the treat or doesn't move to sit, you may need to just wait until he sits. When he does, click and reward with the treat.

## Teaching "Go to Your Spot"

This example shows how to use operant conditioning to teach your cat a behavior on cue. It uses luring to get him into position.

1. Choose a comfy spot for your cat that is also convenient for you. A cat tree usually works well.

2. Stand one foot from the spot.

3. Get your cat's attention by calling his name or shaking the treat bag.

4. When he comes to you, click the clicker and hand him a small (pea-size) food reward.

5. Immediately toss a food reward onto the cat tree. When he steps onto the tree, click and place another food reward on the tree.

6. Call your cat off the tree and repeat step five twice more — or until he gets the idea.

7. When your cat is reliably going to the tree before you toss the food onto it, add the cue "go to your spot." Always click and reinforce when he gets to the tree.

8. When nine times out of ten he goes to his tree on cue the very first time you give it, increase the distance between you and the tree.

9. As he gets better and better at responding to the cue, gradually increase the distance. Eventually, you will be able to send him there from anywhere in the house.

*Shaping* entails rewarding successive approximations of the final behavior. If you were teaching your cat to get on a cat tree using shaping, you would reward him for getting near the cat tree, then getting on the lowest platform, then getting on a higher resting place. This is where a conditioned reinforcer such as a clicker can help with your timing, because you have to reinforce your cat at the exact moment he does what you want.

Another cool way to use a conditioned reinforcer is to capture behaviors. This works very well with cats. Think of capturing a behavior as similar to taking a photo. You associate a verbal cue with a behavior that your cat offers spontaneously, and then you ask your cat to do the behavior using the cue. To capture a behavior, when you see your cat doing what you like, click the clicker and give him a reward. If you are teaching him to sit, whenever you see him sitting, just click and reward. Soon he will be offering to sit whenever he sees you.

---

### Teach "Touch"

Cats naturally use a gentle nose touch as a greeting behavior. If you want to promote this positive behavior as an appropriate way to seek attention, as opposed to biting your hand or climbing on your leg, you can capture the nose touch and put it on cue.

1. When your cat is approaching you with a relaxed and friendly body posture (tail up, ears straight forward, relaxed gait, meowing), gently extend your hand toward him. If he seems intimidated by you extending your hand, try using a single finger.

2. The cat will likely smell and touch your hand. Use your conditioner reinforcer, then give him a good treat.

3. If the cat repeats this behavior, use your conditioned reinforcer and reward him again. However, if you anticipate that he may start to become overexcited and bite your hand, toss a few treats away from you before he gets too excited.

4. Repeat this association — touch, then treat — every time your cat approaches you to interact.

5. When he gets the idea and starts to approach you and touch your hand to get a treat, you can say the word "touch" a few seconds before he touches your hand.

6. Quickly, he will associate the word with the interaction, and you will be able to say "touch" to trigger the behavior.

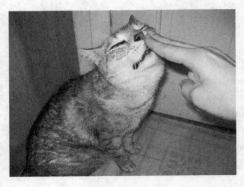

Primo offers a nose touch on cue. *Meghan E. Herron*

## Revisiting Judy and Milo

Remember Judy and Milo? Let's see what Judy decided to do next to keep Milo off the counter.

Judy knew her plan so far hadn't worked. Milo was on the counter when she wasn't home, and he was distancing himself from her at other times. She loved Milo, but she just didn't want him on the counter! A friend suggested that she put one of those shock mats on the counter, but Judy didn't want to hurt Milo, and she knew that more positive punishment wasn't the answer. She had already seen the difference in him when she used the squirt bottle. It was time to go in a new direction.

Instead of focusing on what Milo was doing wrong, she focused on what was motivating him to get on the counter in the first place and how she could satisfy that need. She took some time to observe him and noticed that he hung out in lots of high spots, like the back of the sofa and her dresser. She figured Milo wanted to be on the counter to be close to her and also to be up high.

Judy invested in a cat tree and put it in the dining area near the counter. Each day before dinner, she put catnip and a couple of treats on the cat tree. Sure enough, he ran to the top of the tree, ate the treats, rolled in the catnip, and fell asleep. Judy continued to do this each night before she started making dinner.

Then, on the weekends when she had time to work with Milo, she used a clicker and treats to teach him to run to the top of the cat tree on her verbal cue ("go to your spot"). Within a couple of weeks, she was able to send him to the cat tree before she started cooking dinner and rewarded him intermittently while she was cooking. She had taught Milo to stay off the counter and also taught an alternative behavior that worked for both him and her. He was getting the interaction with her that he craved, and she was enjoying Milo and a clean counter!

Providing cats with lots of elevated comfortable spots where they can be near us helps prevent conflict and gives them alternatives they can be rewarded for.

*Craig Zeichner*

Here's your chance to test what you've learned as you've read this chapter. What associations were made in Milo's brain?

Judy = treats and catnip
Judy = happiness
Cat tree = treats and catnip
Cat tree = happiness
"Go to your spot" + going to the top of the cat tree = treats from Judy

What types of conditioning did Judy use to help Milo learn these associations?

Classical and operant conditioning

## Avoiding Pitfalls and Staying on Track

While we love our cats for their individuality, sometimes it can make training that much more difficult. Let's look at some examples of how you can overcome training challenges with your cat.

## Older Cats

If your cat is over age ten, he is considered a senior cat. Cats are notoriously good at hiding their pain and discomfort. In one study done at North Carolina State University, Dr. Elizabeth Hardie and her colleagues looked at one hundred cats over twelve years old whose owners reported the cats had no pain; they found 90 percent had arthritis. If your cat is older, it's likely he has some discomfort, so take things slow when training him. You may want to start with a stationary exercise, such as "watch me," where your kitty learns to make eye contact with you on cue.

## Overweight Cats

If your cat has a little extra meat on his bones and you are concerned about weight gain, reduce the amount of food you give him in his bowl by about a tablespoon, and consider feeding him using a food-dispensing toy. Make sure to ask your veterinarian, of course, before you make any changes to his diet. When training him, keep the food rewards to about the size of a pea. You can use his kibble for training, but take it out of his daily ration.

## Different Personality Types

Cats who are full of energy and prone to frustration may swat at you when they don't get rewarded quickly enough during training. If your kitty is a wild child, he may respond better to reinforcement that is remotely delivered from a treat-dispensing device or placed in a bowl off to the side of where you are working. Alternatively, you can use a clean, squeezable travel shampoo bottle filled with thinned canned food and let him take a taste from the nozzle. That way, you can deliver the food without having it come from your hand.

If you are going to place the treat in a bowl or use a remote dispenser, be sure to use a conditioned reinforcer, whether that be a word or a clicker. That way, you will instantly reward the correct behavior — even if the food is a little slow in coming. If your kitty is a couch potato, make sure to use very high-value food such as canned cat food or tuna or chicken, and train before mealtimes.

### Cats Who Aren't Foodies, Eat Slowly, or Are on Prescription Diets

Keep in mind that cats eat more slowly than dogs. Your cat's naturally suspicious mind may cause him to investigate new foods at first. Don't take this as a lack of interest. Be patient and let your cat explore. It may take a couple of attempts to get him to feel comfortable eating a treat. Try out new treats before you start training so you know what he likes.

Try training with toys, grooming, petting, or a chance to rub against a knobby brush as rewards. Not every cat is motivated by food. If your cat is on a prescription diet, you will have to use that diet or veterinarian-approved treats to train him. If the diet comes in a canned version, stick with that for training purposes (dole out a little on a spoon or from a squeeze bottle). You can also try training before meals, when he will be motivated to eat.

### Cats Who Walk Away Before You Are Done Training

If your cat is showing you disengagement signals and walking away from training, he may be tired, frustrated, or just done training. Keep your training sessions very short, maybe as short as a minute, always end on a good note leaving your cat wanting more, and use the very highest-value treats. Keep the best treats, grooming tools, and toys for training so that they maintain their special value.

## What Did We Say?

- Cats are highly intelligent and trainable. They are also unique in the ways they perceive the world, process information, and make the associations that are so important for learning.
- Cats have a strong self-protection mechanism, which can quickly result in classically conditioned fear responses. Fear will override

your hard work when training your cat, so do your best to avoid fearful situations or try to lessen how scary they are for him.

- Cats feel emotions just as we do, but they aren't spiteful or vengeful.
- To change unwanted behaviors, find what motivates your cat and try to satisfy that need in a way that is acceptable to you both.
- Use only positive reinforcement and, if necessary, negative punishment when training your cat.
- Practice using conditioned reinforcers for more effective training.
- What are you waiting for? Get out there and train your cat!

# 7

# Do Cats Mean to Be Mean?

*Understanding Why Cats Aggress Toward Humans
and What to Do About It*

Terry Marie Curtis, DVM, MS, DACVB

Molly, a two-year-old orange tabby, was hand-reared as a kitten. When she was small and cute, her owner used to play with her using his hands and feet as toys for Molly to wrestle and bite. As Molly grew, so did the sharpness of her teeth and claws. Now playing with Molly often results in scratches and bites. Is Molly really aggressive? Should her owner stop playing with her?

Sid, a ten-month-old black and white kitten, was separated from his brother when he was eight weeks old. Sid is still very playful and is the only cat in his home. He often stalks and attacks his owner "out of the blue," and she's distressed at being the target of his aggressive behavior. All she wanted was a cat who would love her and cuddle with her — but she ended up with an attack cat! At this point, Sid's owner is considering surrendering him to a shelter. Should she?

Daisy, a five-year-old calico, has always been reactive when she sees the gray cat who lives next door. She hisses, puffs up her fur, and yowls whenever she sees the cat from the living room window. Daisy also acts this way when she sees her neighbor walking his little Yorkshire Terrier — who is also gray. Many times, when Daisy has been highly agitated by the sight of one of these gray characters, she has run from the window to seek out her owner and attack her legs — once sending her to the hospital. Daisy's owner is very distressed and confused by her cat's behavior. She wonders, "Why does Daisy seek me out and attack me?"

There isn't a day that goes by that a veterinarian isn't faced with an aggressive cat: ears back, eyes wide, body crouched, tail tucked, hissing and growling. The veterinarian needs to examine the cat and is only trying to help. But how?

Based on their basic survival plan (run and hide first, fight last), cats' aggressive responses are often misunderstood. When given the choice to escape, most cats will. However, when cornered or pushed too far, a cat can inflict significant damage with her teeth and claws. Growling, hissing, yowling, scratching, and biting are normal parts of every cat's behavioral repertoire. Still, just because a behavior is normal doesn't make it acceptable.

In the examples here, the aggressive behaviors of Molly, Sid, and Daisy may look similar, but each cat has their own unique motivation. Molly was likely inadequately socialized and not given clear rules about how to properly interact with humans. What was cute when she was a kitten (biting body parts) is no longer so cute, but she has no idea when or why the rules changed.

Sid is most likely viewing his new owner as his only playmate, not his enemy. Kittens start to play at around three weeks of age, and play mostly in pairs by eight weeks of age. This kind of play is often rough. If denied this pair play, what is a kitten to do but play with the only playmate around — his owner.

Daisy is exhibiting a common type of behavior in cats called redirected aggression. The aroused cat can't interact with a target she perceives as a potential threat (in this case, the cat next door and the Yorkshire Terrier), so her emotional response is redirected to a less appropriate but accessible target — another pet or a human. This type of aggression can be intense, highly emotional, and quite distressing to the one who is being injured.

As for cats at the veterinarian's office, the primary cause of aggression is a perceived threat. Many cats believe their life is in danger — period — and they have no way to run or hide.

Regardless of the motivation, cat bites and scratches can cause local tissue infection and, in some cases, much worse. Approximately 30 to 40 percent of cat bites on the hands become infected due to the deep penetration and small skin opening made by feline fangs. According to the Centers for Disease Control, an estimated twelve thousand outpatients get cat scratch disease, and five hundred inpatients are hospitalized for it each year. Aggression toward their human family may cause cats to lose their homes.

## Facts, Not Fiction

Aggression can be thought of as any behavior that harms — or at least threatens to harm — and is intended to increase the distance between the aggressor and the victim (either by causing the victim to run away or severely injuring or killing her). Neuroscientists call this type of aggression "affective." However, this definition cannot explain all the interactions with a cat that can lead to a bite or scratch, and there are also forms of non-affective aggression that do not have the intention to create distance or harm. For example, Molly's and Sid's biting behavior is not intended to injure their human playmate, but rather to practice and develop play and predatory skills. These are normal behaviors, and understanding that is really important when we think about how to treat the problem.

Of course, if your cat is experiencing any medical problem that makes her feel unwell, such as hormonal imbalances, metabolic changes, pain or discomfort, nausea, or lack of sleep, she may become more irritable and perhaps aggressive. Bottom line: each cat is different, and every cat has a story to tell and a reason she behaves the way she does.

Why would a cat feel the need to show affective aggression? Because the cat herself perceives a threat, even if we do not. While cats may seem like super predators with formidable weapons, they are also prey animals in their natural environment, and are therefore vulnerable. That makes them cautious and sometimes afraid, even if nothing really dangerous has ever happened to them. This perception may be displayed as overt fear (ears back, hissing, crouching), or it may be evident in more offensive body language (stalking, chasing), as in the case of territorial aggression.

## Types of Aggression

There are many types of aggression in cats, including misdirected play behavior, fear-related aggression, redirected aggression, pain-related aggression, and petting-induced aggression. There is also irritable aggression, which is associated with disease; inter-cat aggression, which is directed toward other cats either living in the same home or not (see chapters 4 and 5); and predatory behavior, which is not considered aggression (typically it's directed at food targets, but it may also be a component of play behavior).

**Misdirected play behavior** (also called play-related aggression) is typically seen in kittens and young cats, but it can be seen in cats of any age, because playful behavior is a large part of cats' normal behavioral repertoire. Normal feline pair play involves stalking, crouching, and attacking. Once contact is made, two cats can be very physical, rolling around, nipping, batting, and chasing.

If a cat has no appropriate play outlet (such as stimulating toys or another individual willing to play), this normal behavior is often directed onto other cats who are unwilling to play or to people in the household. In an environment where consistent and appropriate play is not provided, play can become excessive or misdirected.

How do you know when your cat is feeling threatened and when she is just trying to entertain herself? Body language is key. A playful cat approaches her "victim" as she would potential prey such as a mouse or bug creeping around the house. She crouches in wait (often behind an object or around a corner), stalks, chases, and pounces. Her tail is likely twitching and her ears and whiskers are forward as she moves toward the fleeing target.

Olive displays a stalking posture while playing. She stares at a prey object (a toy) with her body low, then slowly moves forward. Cats showing this behavior typically don't vocalize. *Patrizia Porazzi*

A cat experiencing **fear-related aggression** often looks defensive. Her ears are back, her body and tail are lowered, her fur may be standing on end, and her eyes are open wide. You may note that her eyes look big and black. That's because when cats believe they are in danger, the fight-or-flight response kicks in, and the release of adrenaline causes the pupils to dilate.

Fearfully aggressive cats can be quite vocal, hissing, growling, and yowling — even screeching. (By the way, there really is no other motivation for hissing besides fear. If a cat is hissing, she is scared.) In extreme cases of fear, the cat may empty her anal glands, urinate, or defecate.

In **redirected aggression,** a cat is emotionally aroused (experiencing fear or frustration, for example) by a stimulus that she can't directly get to, such as a sudden noise, the sight of an outdoor cat (or dog), or the smell of an unfamiliar animal. When the arousal becomes too great for the cat to control, she may redirect it away from the original stimulus and onto an innocent target.

The resulting aggression is usually directed toward a nearby individual, but sometimes the cat will actively seek out an individual, as in Daisy's case. Depending on the level of provocation, this aggression can be very severe, and the arousal can last hours or even days in some cats. Sometimes the aggressor will continue to associate the victim with the initial frightening trigger for months, and the victim can also be traumatized for a long time.

**Pain-related aggression** looks very similar to fear-related aggression and occurs in situations where there is an overt or underlying cause of pain, discomfort, or irritability. The target is likely to be the veterinarian or anyone attempting to touch or move an injured, pain-afflicted, or sick cat.

**Petting-induced aggression** occurs after a cat has been touched longer than she can tolerate or in places she doesn't like to be touched. She will typically signal her displeasure by pulling her ears back, twitching her tail, and sometimes swatting or vocalizing. Her pupils will often suddenly dilate in this situation.

Cats typically groom each other on their heads and necks, usually for a short time, so petting them in other areas or for longer than they like can trigger this behavior. All cats are very sensitive to touch due to the abundance of touch receptors in their skin. However, some cats may be more sensitive than others and perceive petting as a more intense stimulus. This may be one reason some cats hiss or growl before turning around to bite the person who is petting them.

## What Does That Mean?

**Aggression:** Behavior that harms or threatens to harm another individual. Because aggressive behavior often has a cost for the aggressor (who might get hurt if there's a fight), the function of aggression is often to increase the distance between the aggressor and the target. In cats, distance-increasing behaviors include hissing, growling, swatting, scratching, nipping, and biting. Notable exceptions to the desire to create more distance are play-motivated and predatory behavior.

**Fear-related aggression:** Aggression that is used as self-defense. It may be a last resort for cats who otherwise cannot escape, or it may be preemptive behavior when they anticipate a threat. Cats can learn that certain situations — such as guests coming into the house — cause them to feel afraid. In a proactive manner, then, the best defense becomes a good offense.

**Pain-related aggression:** Aggression that occurs directly as a result of pain or discomfort.

**Irritable aggression:** Aggression that may be associated with a disease or discomfort. For example, a cat who is experiencing malaise or nausea has a lower threshold of aggression, and so things that didn't used to or don't typically bother her suddenly do.

**Petting-induced aggression:** Aggression associated with being petted in an undesired location, or in a desired location but for too long or too intensely.

**Redirected aggression:** Aggression that occurs when a cat is aroused by some trigger (such as another cat outside) but can't get to that trigger. Her emotional response is then redirected to another target.

**Predatory behavior:** Behavior that is motivated by the instinct to detect, pursue, and kill for food; not really an aggressive behavior. Unlike overtly aggressive behaviors, the object of predatory behavior is *not* to increase the distance between the aggressor (cat) and the target (prey). Cats who are being predatory are usually silent, while in other types of aggression there is often hissing, growling, or other vocalizations.

**Misdirected play behavior:** A normal feline play behavior that is directed at an unwilling human or cat. This is not really an aggressive behavior.

## Is That Really True?

*Are hand-reared kittens more likely to become aggressive adult cats?* No. Dr. E. Chon conducted a study looking at the effects of queen-rearing versus hand-rearing on feline aggression and other problematic behaviors. The results showed that hand-reared kittens are no more likely than queen-reared kittens to display fear and aggression toward people or other cats, and are no more likely to develop behavior problems.

However, the study also found that the presence of another cat in the household and the use of a wand-type toy can decrease the likelihood of aggression toward people. This means that kittens need appropriate outlets for play — other cats and toys, not fingers and toes — especially if they were hand-reared.

In the examples at the beginning of this chapter, both Sid and Molly are young cats and have shown this behavior since kittenhood. Kittens have a sensitive socialization period from approximately two to seven weeks of age when they are most open to new experiences. This is a critical time for socialization and learning the rules. If Molly was taught to play a certain way with her humans, that's the way she is likely to continue to play with them. If Sid had his playmate taken from him, he is likely in search of another one.

Fear may also play a role in aggressive behavior displayed by kittens. Studies have shown that kittens who are handled by people during that early sensitive time are more likely to approach people and stay with them than are those who are handled by people only later in kittenhood or not at all. Cats who are fearful when you handle them may hiss, scratch, and bite. Because the defensively aggressive cat fears an attack, the crouched posture, the hissing and growling, and certainly the scratching and biting are attempts to get the scary thing to go away.

*My cat comes up to me for petting and then turns around to bite me! Is she psycho?* No, your cat isn't psycho. When you stop to think about it, one of the biggest problems we have living with cats is communication. Neither of us speaks the other's language. What we believe our cats think or want may not be what they think or want at all.

We all have times when we want to be touched and times when we don't. If we're with a person who speaks our language, we can tell them, "That hurts!" or "That tickles!" In both cases, the touching may have started out as something we wanted, but over time it became annoying — and we said so. Your cat may have told you that she had enough long before she tried to bite you, but you missed the signals. Cat language can be very subtle: ears go back, eyes get big and wide, tail starts to twitch. (See chapter 1 for more on feline body language.) It is during that "conversation" that you need to stop petting your cat, so that she doesn't have to "yell" at you!

*Should I spray my aggressive cat with water?* Keep in mind that most aggressive cats are fearful cats and are trying to protect themselves, not dominate anyone. Any punishment used to interrupt fear-based aggression will feed into the negative emotional loop of fear and may make it worse over time.

Even when the aggression is not motivated by fear, or when fear is a small component, using spray bottles or pistols is not a good idea. The problem with this and most forms of punishment is that it is difficult to do well and can damage the bond between you and your cat. Plus, although it may stop the behavior, it won't help your cat understand what the right behavior would be.

For punishment to work, three conditions must be met.

1. It must be consistent, meaning it has to happen *every* time the behavior occurs. No exceptions.
2. It must be timely — within one or two seconds of the start of the behavior — so the cat relates the punishment with the behavior.
3. It must be aversive enough to stop the behavior.

For most cats, a squirt of water doesn't meet that third requirement (and often the first two requirements are not met either). The problem with implementing something aversive is that cats easily become fearful, and that fear can be transferred to the person administering the punishment. Now that your cat is afraid of you, what started out as misdirected play or petting-induced aggression has become fear-related aggression.

Remember what you learned in chapter 6 about all the other problems with punishment as well. The best way to teach your cat is to show her the behavior you want, not to punish her for behavior you don't want. Toss your cat a toy instead of spraying her with water. Give her a yummy treat for interacting with you calmly rather than aggressively. Stop the interaction when it is clear that she is afraid or uncomfortable. That way, you're teaching your cat what you want her to know: that you're a good, gentle, and safe human being.

## How Do We Begin?

Even though we love our cats and they love us, we need to acknowledge that in certain situations, they may bite or scratch. Is your cat being playful, the way she would be with another cat? Is she afraid because you are trying to put drops in her eyes or ears? Has she had enough of your petting? Are you cuddling her when she wants to be left alone? Remember, what might seem like gestures of comfort to us — hugging, kissing, touching, holding — aren't always perceived that way by our cats. Take time to notice what your cat is saying in all her interactions with you and with others.

- **Know when your cat is likely to exhibit aggressive behavior.**
  Context is important in determining the cause of your cat's behavior and in managing it. Start by understanding the most common causes of aggression in cats.
    * Play: especially common in kittens and young cats
    * Fear/self-defense: when a cat is scared by a stimulus such as a noisy object you are holding
    * Confrontation: when a cat is scolded (this is, ultimately, a form of self-defense)
    * Pain/discomfort: including during grooming (especially long-haired cats) and nail trimming
    * Intolerance of prolonged petting or touching
    * Redirected behavior in response to another trigger inside or outside the home

* Physical manipulation or restraint, such as when you're medicating your cat
* Frustration: the inability to obtain something she desires or to escape to safety

- **Be aware of feline communication and body language.** A cat's body language is much more subtle than a dog's, but we can still tune in to what our cats are saying. However, unlike dogs, who have a wide range of threatening and reconciliation behaviors, cats have fewer options for expressing both aggressive and loving intent. Start watching your cat in various situations. How does she look when it's just you and her? Does this look change when there are others in the room? By learning your cat's language, you can better respond to these changes — even the subtle ones — and get her to a safe place before she needs to "yell" and become aggressive. What's most important to your cat is learning that when she expresses discomfort, you will change the circumstances. When she knows that smaller changes in body language actually enable her to affect outcomes, she no longer has the need to escalate to aggression.

- **Avoid unnecessary provocation.** Your cat doesn't need to meet and love all your friends and family. If she wants to hide, let her. If taking your cat to the veterinary clinic brings out the tiger within her, consider a house call instead. You can also teach your cat to associate certain people — including your veterinarian — with good things because they are always paired with a great outcome (yummy treats or fun games) and they are gentle and respectful toward her.

## Safety First

The best strategy for dealing with aggressive behavior is to avoid it in the first place. But that isn't always possible. If you are faced with a hissing and yowling cat, it is important to remove yourself from the situation quickly. Your movements must be slow and quiet and increase the distance between you and the cat.

Be aware, however, that your movements may trigger an attack. In that case, try to protect yourself. Some cats are easy to distract with high-value treats, but these may not be handy, especially if the attack is unexpected. Always try to put a physical barrier between you and an upset cat (pillows, blankets, flat pieces of cardboard). If your cat is a repeat offender, make sure to keep treats and safeguards handy. Punishment is never the answer, as it will only add fuel to the fire and arouse your cat more.

Once you have removed yourself from the situation, give your cat time to settle down. Depending on the cause of the arousal, the amount of time may vary. If your cat was upset by your attempt to trim her nails, it may take only a few minutes for her to forgive and forget. However, if she has just seen her enemy outside the front window, it may take hours or days for her to calm down. In either case, it's important to give her as much time as she needs.

If there is a pattern to your cat's aggressive behavior, work with her to help her learn how to accept situations that usually cause her to feel nervous and aroused. The goal is to teach your cat new things that will create a positive association with these potentially scary situations. (See chapters 6 and 9 for more information about how to do that.)

## The Cat's Environment

Providing a number and variety of three-dimensional options for your cat to climb on and scratch can help in a number of ways. From the cat's point of view, cat trees and shelves let her get away from a potentially scary individual or situation, while watching it all from a safe space up above.

Smokey Joe and Peanut have safe spots on their cat tree where they can observe the world around them without assuming unnecessary risks. *Brittany Vance*

This staircase just for the cats provides access to a series of high shelves seen in the next photo. *R. Hack*

At the top of the stairs in the previous photo, shelves located high on the wall offer safe vantage points. *R. Hack*

It is important to remember that there are normal feline behaviors we should acknowledge, allow, and respect. These include hunting and feeding. In her book *Feline Behavior: A Guide for Veterinarians,* Dr. Bonnie Beaver, DACVB, says, "If allowed to set their own schedule, cats will eat up to thirteen small, evenly sized meals a day. When fed periodically [that is, scheduled meals], cats tend to be more aggressive and less cooperative than if fed free-choice." In many cases of human-directed aggression that I have seen personally, once the cat is offered food in a way that feels natural to her, the aggressive behavior will improve. In a study by Dr. Leticia Dantas, DACVB, several behavior issues, including aggression, rough play, and obesity, were diminished by making food-dispensing toys available.

Other factors may need to be addressed at the same time, especially if weight gain is an issue, but changing the way food is offered is an easy place to start. In keeping with cats' normal hunting and feeding patterns, the free-fed cat doesn't need to have food in a bowl all day long. There are some food-dispensing toys that dispense kibble as the cat rolls them around and paws at them, and others with doors that slide open to reveal canned food.

Cats are crepuscular, which means they are most active at dawn and dusk. In the wild, this is when they would do most of their hunting. So not only are cats more likely to be hungry and want to be fed at those times, but they are also more likely to be playful then. Understanding these patterns and playing with your cat closer to bedtime and when you wake up may stop her from bothering you while you're sleeping. Automatic feeders can be timed to open before you wake up, so your cat won't start the day by pestering you for food.

## The Playfully Aggressive Cat

Social play among cats is common in their early life, and most kittens play very roughly with one another until eight weeks of age or even later. Therefore, if you have the opportunity to adopt littermates or two (or more) kittens of relatively the same age, do so. A study I participated in found that cats who are related or who have spent most of their time together groom each other more and remain near each other more than unrelated cats or cats who don't know each other well. Two cats who are friends have an outlet for their normal playful behavior. They are the target of each other's exuberant play — not you!

Whether you have two cats or just one, it is important to provide lots of opportunities for appropriate play. After eight weeks of age, cats tend to show more interest in playing with objects rather than just tussling with other kittens. That's why your cat needs toys she can play with on her own, as well as toys both of you can play with together. These interactive toys are especially useful when you're a sitting or standing target: cooking dinner, working at your desk, watching TV.

One idea is to tie a string around your waist with a fuzzy mouse on the other end. That way, when you walk around, your cat can play with you without you having to play with her! Make sure the string is at least five feet long, so the toy is never too close to your body. If you see that this causes the cat to be alert when you move around without the string and toy, it may be wise to choose a different toy and play style, to prevent any inappropriate play directed at your body.

When you do play with your cat, make sure she learns that your hands and feet are *not* toys. As discussed earlier, cute little kittens who learn that fingers are fun to chew on will not understand why these "toys" are off-limits as they get older.

## Redirected Aggression

Redirected behavior occurs when a cat is highly aroused by a target she can't get to (such as another cat she sees outside) and redirects that arousal to another, inappropriate target. This may be another cat, a dog, or a human being. By the time the cat locates a target, her arousal level might be very high, resulting in severe aggression.

If you know your cat responds to specific triggers, such as stray or neighbor-owned cats outside, cutting off access is the first line of defense. Try simply closing the door to certain rooms or applying an opaque film to windows that look out on these cats' territories. To keep outside cats off your property, you can place ultrasonic noise emitters with motion detectors (such as the CatStop Ultrasonic Cat Deterrent) in strategic areas around the perimeter that only cats and some other animals, but not humans, can hear. (The organization Neighborhood Cats lists several humane and effective strategies for keeping stray and feral cats out of gardens and yards on its website. See "Keeping Cats out of Gardens and Yards," www.neighborhoodcats.org/how-to-tnr/colony-care/keeping-cats-out-of-gardens-and-yards-2.) Also remove bird feeders that may attract other cats.

Many cats with redirected aggression get very wound up — howling with a guttural cry as they go looking for a target. If your cat warns you in this way, try to break through the arousal by shaking a bag or can of treats and then tossing some treats toward the cat. This will pair the situation with something positive and yummy and give your cat something else to do instead of attacking you. But also be ready with a pillow or a large, thick comforter to protect yourself if the promise of treats doesn't stop the agitation.

If the arousal is extreme and your cat is in a room with a door, close the door and give her time to calm down. Whatever you do, don't reach for or try to pick up the cat, as she is likely to become more aroused by the perceived threat and act even more aggressively. Don't take it personally: at this moment, your cat is so emotionally and physiologically upset that she doesn't even recognize you.

## The Petting-Intolerant Cat

We don't really understand why some cats like to be petted for long periods of time and others can endure it for only a short time or not at all. Chalk it up to individual preferences, or consider that some cats may feel petting differently than others.

Feline hyperesthesia syndrome (FHS) is a disorder that causes cats to feel pain or abnormal sensations from minimal touch and sometimes without even being touched at all. While most cats who are petting intolerant don't have FHS, it is important to consider that what we intend when we touch cats may not be how our touch is received. Even the gentlest petting may feel uncomfortable to some cats, triggering an aggressive response. Some behaviorists propose that since cats groom each other only on the head and neck, they are more amenable to being touched and petted there.

Cats who have reached the limit of their petting tolerance are typically very clear about it, letting us know when our petting has gone on too long or has hit an area where they don't like to be touched. The cat's ears will swivel back, and her pupils will dilate. The skin along her sides and back may ripple, her whiskers may come forward, and her tail may twitch. When you see any of these signs, respect what your cat is saying and stop petting her. If you notice that these signs of distress tend to appear after a predictable length of time, stop the petting *before* your cat reaches this threshold; keep it short and sweet!

Slowly and gradually, by pairing petting with yummy food or treats, you might be able to increase the length of each petting session by teaching your cat that great things happen when you're petting her. When she understands that you will respect her limits and cease petting when she signals that she's had enough, this may make her more likely to permit and even solicit petting. You also need to respect that your cat may want to be nearby, even on your lap, but not be stroked, scratched, or touched.

---

### Making Nail Trimming Tolerable and Safe for Your Cat and You!

Nail trimming may not be necessary for cats who have appropriate scratching outlets. However, some cats will not use them or may still have some overgrowth of their nails and need to have them trimmed. Although this procedure may be a source of conflict between your cat and you, many cats can be trained to have their nails trimmed in a safe and peaceful way.

- Start by using a pair of nail trimmers that feel good in your hands. Human nail clippers can work just as well as those made especially for cats, and most people find that they are more comfortable to use.
- Don't think you have to complete the manicure/pedicure all at once. Pairing just one trimmed nail with a special treat will slowly teach your cat that this is fun! Having two people involved will make it easier: one person can be giving the cat treats while the other is trimming her nails.
- Find a position that's comfortable for both you and your cat. Often it's easiest is to have your cat sit on your lap. This puts all four paws in one area that's easy to get to — although trimming the nails on the back paws is rarely necessary.
- It's best to start trimming your cat's nails when she is still a kitten. But remember, you can always teach an old cat new tricks!

If your cat doesn't adjust to nail trimming as well as you hoped, you may need to work harder at counterconditioning and desensitization, and to focus on shorter sessions.

Keep in mind, though, that if your cat regularly bites, scratches, and struggles during the procedure, nail trimming may not be the way to go. The aggression may even increase over time and may cause injuries to you and your cat. If necessary, consider having your veterinarian trim the cat's nails periodically.

## The Fearfully Aggressive Cat

They are called scaredy-cats for a reason! If you look at the world from your cat's point of view, there is a lot she might be afraid of: unfamiliar sights, sounds, and smells; new people; loud and unpredictable toddlers; a new dog. We might know that company is coming weeks in advance and still be anxious about their arrival. All your cat knows is that one day it's just you and her, and the next day it's a houseful of strangers — who may never leave!

Avoidance is often the safest management plan, especially when dealing with strangers your cat will meet only occasionally. Teach her to be comfortably secluded in one part of your home — set up with food, water, a litter box, and enrichment (cat tree, scratching post, toys). That's a great option for cats who are afraid of visitors.

Another option is boarding your cat when you have overnight guests who may be at risk. Before choosing this option, visit the boarding facility and make sure the staff has experience handling fear-aggressive cats. The facility should provide appropriate cages or runs with safe hiding places for the cats, preferably in a cats-only area. Spraying synthetic feline cheek pheromones (Feliway Classic) in the boarding cage may also help calm a nervous and fearful cat.

Some cats can learn that new people mean something good. As described in chapter 9, each guest can be paired with a special treat. This will teach your cat that new people are predictable in a good way, instead of being scary and unpredictable.

Many cats absolutely *hate* going to the veterinarian. Again, explore the options that are available in your area for veterinarians who do house calls. That will help you avoid all of the cat carrier business, the car ride, waiting in the lobby with other cats and/or dogs, then waiting again in the exam room. Given all of those different situations to react to, your cat can get more and more anxious before she even sees the veterinarian. A house call will dodge all of that. There is still the handling for the physical exam and any testing, but there is none of the buildup of arousal. A house call will require you to have your cat readily available for the exam, though, not inaccessible under a bed.

What else might help? Recent research conducted by Dr. Charlie Wright and Dr. Stephen Baugh found that providing a cat with a box of some sort at the veterinary clinic will offer her the opportunity to hide, which may help reduce stress. Pairing the experience with a very special and yummy treat can also teach your cat that the veterinary visit is something good — or, at least, not that scary!

It's useful to keep the cat carrier out in your home at all times and to use treats to associate good things with it. This will make putting your cat inside for a visit to the veterinarian less stressful. Using synthetic feline facial pheromones to decrease stress or an attractant such as catnip or silvervine can also help improve the association with the carrier. (See appendix A for more information on acclimating your cat to her carrier.)

## Avoiding Pitfalls and Staying on Track

Some behavior problems are more challenging to treat than others. This is particularly true when the behavior is significantly influenced by the cat's genetics rather than being solely the result of learning.

Not all types of feline aggression follow the patterns described in this chapter. In some cases, changing and managing the environment and attempting to modify your cat's behavior are not enough to significantly reduce the aggression. In those cases, medications, supplements, special diets, and other adjunctive therapies to decrease anxiety and reactivity can be helpful. Their usefulness depends on several factors, including a veterinarian's or veterinary behaviorist's assessment of the individual cat, and the goals and expectations of your family.

First and foremost, remember that only veterinarians, including veterinary behaviorists, are qualified and licensed to recommend and prescribe medications for cats. There are no FDA-approved behavioral medications for cats, so all would have be prescribed off label, meaning the drug has not been licensed or specifically approved to treat aggression. Many of the antianxiety medications prescribed for cats were first developed as antidepressants for people. The use of these drugs in cats is supported by studies on behavior problems other than aggression, but their use for aggression also can be justified in some specific cases.

What are some situations where behavioral medications might help?

- **When there is underlying anxiety or fear.** Anxious and fearful cats are not likely to respond well to behavior modification alone. For example, there are many cats who react aggressively to new people because they are afraid. You can try improving the association with the unknown person through training, but anxiety and fear often inhibit learning and prevent fearful cats from making the positive associations we would like them to have. Just imagine that you were trying to learn how to solve difficult math equations while snakes were crawling on you (or tarantulas and scorpions, if you like snakes). It would be hard to learn anything in that situation. Anxiety and fear can be thought of as forms of pain and suffering, and your cat deserves relief.

- **When it is not possible to control the stimulus that provokes the cat's anxiety or fear.** A cat may show fear and mild aggression toward a crying newborn, for example. Every sound and movement is potentially a scary stimulus, and medication may help the cat better tolerate this type of situation by decreasing the underlying stress.
- **When the cat's aggression appears explosive.** This is often the case with redirected behavior. A cat can go from zero to sixty after seeing the target. In such situations, medication can help regulate the cat's reactivity so that she is able to process the trigger as it really is — not threatening.
- **When the behavior is related to a physical problem.** For example, irritability and aggression can be linked to pain or other medical conditions (such as a thyroid imbalance or feline hyperesthesia syndrome). Appropriate medical treatment of the cat's condition can sometimes help reduce the aggression.
- **When quality of life for either the aggressive cat or the victim is in jeopardy and a major change is needed.**

Medication should be prescribed only after a full physical and behavioral health assessment. Once the problem is diagnosed, medication should be used as part of a comprehensive treatment plan that includes modifications to the environment and behavior modification. Your veterinarian or veterinary behaviorist should discuss all the expected positive effects, as well as all the possible side effects of the medication prescribed so that you know what to expect with your cat. And remember, although medication is always part of a comprehensive treatment plan, a plan is not a guarantee.

Nutraceuticals and nutritional supplements that have an effect on fear and anxiety, such as alpha-casozepine and L-theanine, may be helpful in treating aggression caused or complicated by anxiety and fear. However, these products have not been extensively studied or approved for treating feline aggression. Especially if your cat is showing aggression that is likely to result in physical injuries, you should consult with your veterinarian and not rely on nutritional supplements alone.

## The Declawing Controversy

Cats can scratch human skin in a number of contexts, not all of them aggressive. But certainly, if a cat is feeling threatened — or even playful, as discussed earlier — sharp claws coming into contact with human skin can cause injury. Cat scratches can range from minor soreness to life-threatening infections and bleeding, especially in older people who have thinner skin and may be taking blood thinners.

Onychectomy, or declawing, is an ethically controversial procedure and consists of the amputation of all or part of a cat's third phalanges (the phalanx is the last bone of a cat's toe). Although ethically questionable, declawing does reduce the risk of injury if scratching directed at people is part of a cat's aggressive behavior. However, without concurrent changes in environmental triggers, behavioral interventions, and other treatment options, declawing is unlikely on its own to be curative and should be avoided.

It has been postulated that cats with intact claws who scratch objects or people are at a higher risk for relinquishment to shelters than declawed cats. On the flip side, it has also been suggested that a declawed cat is more likely to exhibit behavior problems other than scratching, such as aggressive biting and house soiling, and is therefore at risk of losing her home. Very recent studies have only perpetuated the controversy.

One study found that declawing cats increases the risk of unwanted behaviors (aggression and house soiling) and may increase the risk of a cat developing back pain. However, suboptimal surgical technique also was found to increase the risk of back pain. Another study looked at whether the type of procedure used to declaw cats — carbon dioxide laser or a nonlaser technique — has any effect on the incidence of house soiling. Overall, declawing was identified as a risk factor for house soiling in cats. Specifically, the cats who had been declawed using a nonlaser technique had a higher risk of house soiling than the ones who had undergone the laser technique. The study also found that declawed cats who lived in multicat households (three to five cats) were more than three times as likely to have soiled their house than single cats with intact claws.

Declawing remains an emotional and controversial subject, and the procedure is now banned in some countries and US states. The American College of Veterinary Behaviorists believes that declawing cats should be the last option considered as a treatment for aggression, and then only when a person's safety is at high risk. The American Veterinary Medical Association believes it is the obligation of veterinarians to provide cat owners with complete information with regard to feline onychectomy. Declawing should never be considered as a solution for destructive behavior associated with scratching.

Inherent in the debate over whether or not to declaw is the fact that declawing doesn't address the *reason* a cat may be scratching. This is a normal feline behavior, and if it is causing problems, the root of the problems should be addressed. Every cat owner should know the facts about the procedure, what it is, and what the options are, along with the alternatives to declawing, before making a decision.

What are the alternatives? As discussed earlier in this chapter (see "Making Nail Trimming Tolerable and Safe for Your Cat and You!"), routinely trimming your cat's nails — and making it a positive experience — can reduce the risk of scratching. Another option is applying nail caps to your cat's nails after they have been cut short. Many cats will allow their owners to apply these caps at home, while others need to be sedated at a veterinary clinic.

## What Did We Say?

- From a cat's point of view, most human-directed aggression is provoked and is a defensive behavior. Misdirected play and predatory behavior are the exceptions.
- Some feline signals of anxiety and fear can be very obvious (ears back, hissing, growling), while others can be very subtle (a look of wariness, avoidance, hiding).
- Pay attention to *your* cat's face, ears, tail, body posture, and vocalizations to understand what she is saying.

- Be vigilant about protecting your cat from situations that will only set her up for fear and failure.
- Kittens have a sensitive period during which handling by humans can be very important in forming attachments in the future. If possible, handle your kitten as early as possible.
- Keep in mind your cat's normal behaviors and patterns, especially regarding hunting, playing, and eating. The more natural outlets for these behaviors you can give her, the less likely she will be to forcefully express them.
- Always talk to your veterinarian or a veterinary behaviorist about any aggressive behavior you've experienced with your cat. A hands-on visit is best to explain the behavior to the veterinarian and allow him to diagnose the problem and formulate a treatment plan tailored just for you and your cat.
- Treatment of any behavior problem — especially aggression — always takes a multipronged approach. Environmental changes, management, and behavior modification can go a long way to ameliorate the problem. In some cases, however, other therapies, including medication, may be warranted and helpful.

# 8

# My House Is Not Your Toilet
## *Feline Elimination Problems*

Sabrina Poggiagliolmi, DVM, MS, DACVB

Stella and her owners came in for an appointment because she was refusing to enter her litter box and was urinating and defecating all around the house. Because of her elimination habits, Stella was confined to the finished basement, which had easy-to-clean tile flooring. She was a healthy young cat; why was she refusing to use the litter box?

The family had adopted Stella after finding her as a stray kitten in a parking lot, and they wanted to offer her a great home. Stella's owners were not what you might call cat people; they'd never had a cat before and didn't really know much beyond the very basics of what a cat needs. Unfortunately for Stella, they were not aware that they had to scoop her litter box at least twice a day so that it would always be clean. They thought just dumping all the contents of the box once a week would be enough.

Fortunately, when they brought her to the veterinarian, she asked them about their litter box hygiene routine as well as Stella's bathroom habits. The veterinarian recommended that they start scooping Stella's box morning and evening, every day, so that Stella always had a clean toilet. This was all it took to solve the problem, and Stella was given full access to the house again. Her time in jail was finally over!

Cats are famously clean creatures, but we sometimes forget that this also applies to their toilet habits. My mother's cat, Margot, used the flowerpots on the balcony whenever my mom got lazy and started scooping the box every other day. To make my clients understand how important it is to keep a cat's litter box clean, I ask them if they would use a public restroom where the toilets had not been flushed. Of course they wouldn't! So why should they expect their cats to use a dirty box?

## Facts, Not Fiction

Cats inherited a natural preference for sandy elimination areas from their desert-dwelling African ancestor, *Felis silvestris lybica*. This explains why it is easy to train any kitten or cat to use a litter box filled with a fine-textured material (usually litter). In fact, many people choose cats as pets because they are known to be clean animals who need little training to use the litter box.

Normally, adult cats urinate two to four times a day and have a bowel movement (defecate) at least once a day (the frequency may vary depending on their diet). During urination, both female and male cats sniff and dig a hole, squat over it (it looks like they are sitting, but their hindquarters are not fully touching the ground), and deposit their urine. Once the bladder has been voided, most cats cover the hole with litter and then leave.

Cats sniff and dig before eliminating in their litter box. *Sabrina Poggiagliolmi*

Once the cat has found a good spot in the box, he digs a shallow hole and then squats to start urinating. After the action is finished, some cats sniff again and cover the spot by raking litter over it. *Sabrina Poggiagliolmi*

When defecating, cats prepare the chosen area the same way they do when urinating. They assume a similar position, too, but their hindquarters are not as close to the ground and their back is more curved. After defecating, cats may or may not cover their feces.

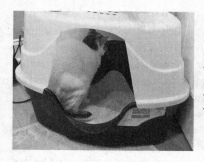

Cats also assume a squatting position to defecate, but their hindquarters are not as close to the ground and their back is more curved than when they are urinating. *Carlo Siracusa*

House soiling (that is, depositing urine and/or feces outside the litter box) is the number one feline behavior problem seen by both veterinarians and veterinary behaviorists in the United States. House soiling, including urine marking, can be a cat's response to issues with the litter box (location, accessibility, cleanliness), changes in the household environment, or other events that he might find stressful.

Many cats soil outside the litter box for the sole purpose of voiding the bladder and bowel in a different location. Also, some cats do not like using the same box for urination and defecation. In these cases, the cats are simply using a toilet other than the one their owner wants them to use. The toileting cat typically eliminates regular amounts of urine or feces in one or several spots around the house, using a squatting posture.

A similar but separate problem is urine marking. When cats mark with urine, they usually spray a vertical surface by backing up toward it. The body posture they assume when they spray is unmistakable and straightforward: They stand erect, hold their tail straight up, and squirt a small amount of urine on the chosen spot. Often the tip of their tail quivers as they squirt. Sometimes cats tread with their back paws while spraying. Usually they sniff the selected spot before marking; some cats also sniff after depositing urine.

Some cats may urine mark on horizontal surfaces. In this case, they usually assume a squatting position, sometimes with their tail up and their feet treading but not always. (Some cats start out squatting and end up standing.) Generally, less urine is expelled in marking and spraying than in urination, so the urine mark is smaller than a full emptying of the bladder, but that is not always the case.

The frequency of urine marking depends on hormonal status, stress factors, and, in some cases, litter box issues. Both male and female cats urine mark, but intact (unneutered) males spray more frequently than neutered males or intact females. They use this behavior to leave a clear message: to define their territory, to make other individuals aware of their presence (particularly important for sexually intact cats), or to make marked areas feel safer and more familiar. It is interesting to note that cats who urine mark still use their litter boxes for both urinating and defecating.

Marking with feces, called middening, is rarely seen in cats. Usually the feces are deposited in visible and socially relevant areas of the house, such as on a couch, also with the goal of delineating territory or leaving a message for another cat.

## Is That Really True?

*Is my cat being spiteful or vengeful when he eliminates outside the litter box?* As offensive as finding cat urine around your house can be, your cat is not deliberately engaging in a feud with you. Try not to take his bathroom habits personally. This is not about you; it is about his individual preferences or his attempts to tell you something.

First and foremost, your cat may be sick. There are many illnesses (discussed later in this chapter) that typically manifest as changes in litter box habits. He also may be unhappy about where the litter box is located or something having to do with the box itself. He may be stressed by and anxious about his environment. Remember, your cat did not decide where, how, and with whom he wanted to live; you decided for him.

It is the responsibility of caregivers (both owners and veterinarians) to understand why a cat is eliminating outside the litter box and to find a solution to the problem that is respectful of the cat's well-being. It is very important for you to avoid anthropomorphizing your cat and to realize instead that he is house soiling out of anxiety, not out of spite or a desire for revenge.

*Is urine marking a sign of dominance?* Your cat is an intriguing and elegant creature who possesses fascinating communication skills. Among these skills, marking plays an important role. You may have noticed that he marks his environment (also known as your home!) in different ways: with his chin, with his head and the sides of his face, with his whole body, with his paws, and . . . with his urine.

Urine marking is one of the many behaviors cats use to convey a message, perhaps *Single tabby male seeks calico female.* Or *Beware: cat on the premises!* Or even *That new baby is stressing me out!*

By contrast, behaviorists define dominance as controlling access to resources. Your cat is not trying to control access to anything by depositing his urine outside the box. Dominance is not the issue (and, more broadly, not an issue in cat-human interactions at all).

*Should I reprimand my cat when he eliminates outside his litter box?* No. Punishment, including verbal reprimands, is unlikely to change your cat's elimination habits. Keep in mind that poor litter box management, fear, anxiety, and stress are among the most frequent causes of feline house soiling. Punishment can actually exacerbate the situation and make the house-soiling problem worse.

As frustrating as it is to find urine or feces on your favorite chair or your brand-new carpet, the best thing you can do is simply clean it up. Showing the urine or feces to your cat or, worse, rubbing his nose in it will only make him afraid of you and more anxious about his eliminations in general.

*To teach my cat to use the litter box, should I lock him in the bathroom with the box?* While you work on the treatment plan for house soiling with your veterinarian, do your best to prevent your cat from eliminating outside the litter box. During the initial stages of treatment, this may include confining the cat to a safe and comfortable room with a large litter box and all the resources he needs (things to eat, drink, scratch on, perch on, and play with) when you cannot actively supervise him.

When you can supervise your cat, allow him to spend time outside the room. If you catch him sniffing around to find a spot to eliminate or getting into position to do so, call him with a happy voice and ask him to come to you. When you get his attention, toss him a treat and then send or bring him to his safe room with the litter box.

Keep in mind that some cats become even more stressed when confined, so confining them is not appropriate. Others will use the litter box when confined but continue to house soil when let out, because the underlying reason for the problem has not been addressed. If this is the case with your cat, thinking about what is different in his safe room will give you clues to what the real problem is.

*Why bother? Nothing will ever change.* Don't despair! Feline house soiling is actually among the behavior problems with the best prognosis for improvement. By choosing the right behavioral and medical treatment plan and, if necessary, the right behavioral drug, house soiling can be cured or, at least, significantly reduced. In a study by Dr. Patricia Pryor, DACVB, and her colleagues, one treatment plan for urine marking (involving the number of boxes, cleaning the boxes, and other factors) decreased house soiling in all of the cats by 90 percent or more. Always consult with your veterinarian or a veterinary behaviorist when your cat is eliminating outside the litter box.

---

### What Does That Mean?

**Urination:** The act of fully emptying the bladder. A healthy, non-marking cat usually squats while urinating.

**Defecation:** The act of eliminating feces.

**Urine marking:** The act of depositing urine, usually by spraying on vertical surfaces, with the intention of leaving a visible and smelly signature (*I was here; please take note*). A cat typically stands and backs up to a vertical surface while keeping his tail straight up, with the tip quivering. Sometimes a cat may squat to mark on a horizontal surface. Whatever position the cat chooses, he typically eliminates a smaller amount of urine than when he totally empties his bladder.

**Middening:** The act of depositing feces with the aim of sending a social message; this is rarely used by cats.

**Aversion:** A strong dislike. The usual aversions that may keep a cat from using the litter box are location of the box, size of the box, cleanliness, and type of litter.

**Preference:** In this context, "preference" refers to the surface a cat prefers to eliminate on or in for safety, cleanliness, privacy, quiet, comfort, or other reasons.

**House soiling:** Depositing urine or feces outside the litter box, but not with the intention of marking.

## How Do We Begin?

When a cat stops using his litter box, he is at risk for abandonment, relinquishment, or, even worse, euthanasia. This is truly heartbreaking, especially because eliminating outside the litter box is often a sign of a medical problem. This is particularly true when cats defecate outside the box. If your cat stops using the box, the first thing he needs is a complete checkup.

To get to the root of the problem, your veterinarian will perform a thorough physical examination, blood work, and possibly X-rays or ultrasound imaging, as well as urine and fecal testing. It's a common misconception that if there's a medical cause of house soiling, it's usually a urinary tract infection. In fact, urinary tract infections are not common in cats, and other urinary tract diseases account for only a portion of the possible causes of house soiling in cats. Any medical problem that causes distress, discomfort, pain, or an increase in the volume or urgency of elimination can cause or contribute to house soiling.

If your cat is senior (over ten years of age) or geriatric (fifteen years or older), a neurological evaluation and an orthopedic examination can help rule out joint, muscle, and nerve conditions that may cause discomfort when climbing in and out of the box or posturing to eliminate. Hair loss on the lower abdomen could be a sign of bladder pain in a cat of any age.

The results of the veterinary exam will determine whether any further testing is needed. If there's a medical cause, it must be addressed and managed, or your cat will not stop house soiling. Even when the medical problem is managed, however, some cats may continue to house soil or mark, because they learned to eliminate elsewhere while they were sick and now have a preference for that spot. In that case, you'll need to combine both a medical and a behavioral approach.

### Medical Causes of House Soiling

Urinating or defecating outside the litter box may be the first and only sign of a serious health problem. That's why a veterinary checkup is always the first step when your cat stops using the box. Medical problems can arise suddenly, so even if your cat received a clean bill of health from his veterinarian just a few months ago, he may have developed an illness since then. Medical problems that commonly lead to feline house soiling include:

- Crystals or stones in the urinary tract
- Feline interstitial cystitis, or FIC (also sometimes called Pandora syndrome)
- Cancer
- Kidney disease
- Diabetes
- Hyperthyroidism
- Intestinal parasites
- Degenerative joint disease (including arthritis)
- Impacted anal glands
- Rectal strictures
- Pelvic or tail fractures
- Diarrhea
- Constipation
- Hormonal disorders
- Bacterial infections

After any medical problem is ruled out, you and your veterinarian will need to determine whether it's a toileting issue or a marking issue. Collect as much information as possible about the elimination problem before visiting your veterinarian. This will help you both figure out what is causing the problem.

Start by thinking about the litter box, and make sure you can answer the following questions. All of these details are important because they matter deeply to your cat.

- How big is the litter box? Is it uncovered or covered? With or without a collar or a liner?
- How many boxes do you have, and where are they?
- What is the litter made of? Is it clumping or not? Scented or unscented? How much litter do you put in the box?

- How often do you scoop the box? How often do you dump all the litter and clean the box? What kind of cleaner do you use?
- Have you recently made any changes to the box or the litter?

Next, think about your household, including its inhabitants and their relationships.

- How many adults and children live in your home? How many cats, dogs, and other pets? How do they get along with the cat who has the problem?
- Does your cat have access to the outdoors?
- What is his daily routine of eating, playing, and socializing?

Gather information about your cat's typical behavior in the litter box.

- How often does he eliminate each day?
- Has he ever strained, vocalized, or seemed startled during or immediately after eliminating?
- Does he sniff and dig before eliminating in the box?
- Does he cover his waste when he's done, or does he seem to jump out as quickly as he can? Do you notice that he scratches the walls, floor, and sides of the litter box, but avoids scratching the litter itself?
- Does he ever perch on the sides of the box to eliminate, rather than standing inside it?

Establish the frequency of the unwanted elimination. This will help you and your veterinarian track improvement.

- How often do you find urine or feces outside the litter box?
- When did it start, and how long has it been going on? Did it start suddenly?
- Was it initially associated with any medical problem? Keep in mind that a single painful event in the litter box can create a long-lasting aversion.

- Did it seem to coincide with a specific event or change in your household? Changes in the cat's environment (change in your work schedule, vacation, new furniture), recent additions to the household (roommate, spouse, baby, new pet), or losses to the household (someone moving out, the death of another pet or person) may be contributing to the current problem.
- Where in the house does the cat eliminate? Cats who urinate on their owner's bed or belongings might suffer from separation anxiety or be at odds with someone in the household.
- Does the urine seem to be in large puddles on the floor (toileting) or smaller amounts on vertical surfaces (marking)?

Make a sketch of the floor plan of your home, noting where the unwanted elimination has occurred and where litter boxes, food and water dishes, feline resting places, perching sites, scratching posts, and play areas are located. Understanding how your cat uses each part of your home will help you and your veterinarian understand what is motivating the cat to eliminate in certain areas.

## What's Going on Here?

If you want to convince your cat to stop using your home as his personal scent canvas and resume using his litter box, you must first figure out why he stopped using the box. As mentioned previously, there are many reasons that a cat might stop using a litter box. Let's take a look at the most common ones.

### Problems with the Box

Size and style matter. The box may be too small, too hard to climb into, or too closed in for your cat. Many cats will avoid a covered box, especially if you forget to scoop it, because all the bad smells are trapped inside — similar to how you might avoid a Porta Potti unless you feel super desperate! They may also avoid a box if they have been ambushed by other cats when exiting the box. With a covered box, or one stuck in a closet or cabinet, they cannot clearly see if anyone is lurking nearby — and can't escape if someone is.

The box may simply not be scooped or cleaned often enough. Just as you would not want to use an unflushed toilet, many cats will avoid using a box containing their own or another cat's excrement. There may also be a liner in the box that the cat finds unpleasant because he doesn't like the feel of plastic under his paws when he scratches in the box, or he may have gotten a claw stuck in the plastic.

## Problems with the Litter

Some cats prefer certain types of litter over others. If the litter is not the fine, sandy texture to which your cat is naturally drawn, he may seek this substrate elsewhere, such as the soil in potted plants or gravel in gas fireplaces. Large, hard pellets or crystals may be less appealing than finer, clumping clay. Nonclumping litter holds on to urine and feces, may remain wet when soiled, and will retain odors unless the entire contents of the box are dumped almost daily.

Some cats have unusual substrate preferences, such as hard surfaces, while others seek out the softest, most absorbable options, such as carpets, towels, and baskets full of laundry. It has been hypothesized that some cats may develop an aversion to typical litter because of a previous painful elimination experience, such as during a bout of constipation or bladder stones.

Cats are also easily offended by strong smells, so your cat may not like a heavily perfumed or scented litter. (Litter is scented to appeal to humans, not cats!) Litter that is too shallow or too deep in the box may also be an issue.

## Problems with the Location

The litter box is not our most attractive household feature, so we humans often choose locations that are far away from our main living space. This requires the cat to navigate through different floors, scale various barriers, and go to darker, more dungeonlike areas of the home. While this may not be a major issue for a young, confident kitty, if an older or more timid cat, or one experiencing pain, is not willing (or able) to work that hard, he will choose alternative areas for toileting.

In some cases, the box may be too close to the cat's food and water bowls, making him less likely to soil in that area. Frightening experiences in a location, such as a furnace or a freezer starting up, an ambush or blocking by another pet, or the loud buzz of a dryer cycle ending, can deter a cat from returning to a certain area.

## Stress and the Litter Box

Stress is one of the main triggers for feline house soiling. Your cat is a creature of habit — just as some humans are — and any change in his environment may trigger anxiety. Anxiety is a reaction of apprehension or uneasiness to an anticipated danger or threat. Any addition or loss to the household, such as a new pet (even if you're only fostering), a newborn child, a new spouse or roommate, or the death or departure of a person or another pet, may be enough to trigger house soiling.

Cats can develop anxiety when they move to a new home or when they are having trouble with other household pets, their human family members, or visitors to the home. New furniture, with its unfamiliar appearance and smell, may trigger anxiety. The proximity of outdoor cats (feral or semi-feral) or wild animals can be perceived as a threat. A change in your work schedule or a prolonged absence when you go on vacation may also trigger anxiety.

In this case, house soiling is just one of the possible signs of anxiety. Others may be:

- Frequently pulling his ears back
- Dilated pupils in well-lit settings
- A crouched body posture
- Tucking his tail
- Avoiding interactions with people or pets in the home when he was social in the past
- Frequent hiding
- Increased vocalization, such as meowing or yowling
- Frequent regurgitation of undigested food
- Poor coat condition or matting

Stress activates a physical response, triggering the release of substances such as hormones, neurotransmitters, and biological regulators of inflammation and pain. Some of these substances increase the vulnerability of the bladder to pain-inducing compounds in the urine. This process causes the pain and discomfort observed in cats affected by a form of bladder disease called feline interstitial cystitis (FIC). Studies have confirmed that stress is the main cause of FIC, no matter how innocuous some of the causes of that stress — new furniture, changes in work hours, visiting friends — may seem to us. Each cat is an individual, and the responses to various stressors will differ from cat to cat.

## Urine Marking

Due to hormonal influences, it is normal — almost expected — that unneutered cats (males more than females) will spray urine to communicate their sexual status. However, if your neutered cat is marking rather than toileting, consider that the most common cause of this behavior is social conflict within the household (with other cats, other pets, or humans) or outside the house (cats or wild animals passing close enough for your cat to see, hear, or smell them).

If your cat has developed the habit of marking surfaces with his urine, you may find his "messages" near windows and doors through which he has spotted animals outside. By leaving these smelly signals in these spots, he is signaling potential intruders to stay away from his space. He may also prefer to leave his messages on appliances, such as microwaves, stereos, and radiators, or on objects carrying your smell, such as dirty laundry, personal items, the sofa, or your bed.

Cats who are stressed about litter box hygiene or other cats using their litter box may spray urine against the walls of the box, rather than squatting to urinate. In rare circumstances, some cats prefer to adopt a standing, spraying posture for toileting in the litter box.

Cats who tend to spray within their own space, rather than along its boundaries, may be experiencing a conflict with individuals living in the house. Or they may be offended by scents on items you have brought into the home — anything from new furniture to grocery bags, new shoes to the shoes you wore to volunteer at your local animal shelter. In this case, the object that brings unknown odors into the home is challenging his comfort and safety, and that scent needs to be replaced with his own familiar smell.

Although it's rare, humans can be targeted as well. We may, in fact, make a cat uncomfortable simply with our presence or smell.

## The Optimal Litter Box

The 2014 *AAFP and ISFM Guidelines for Diagnosing and Solving House-Soiling Behavior in Cats* (https://journals.sagepub.com/doi/pdf/10.1177/1098612X14539092) highlights how important it is to offer what the American Association of Feline Practitioners and the International Society of Feline Medicine call the "optimal litter box" to your beloved kitty. The goal is to make the litter box extremely attractive.

Before we get into what the research tells us about litter box preferences, though, remember that aversions and preferences are individual, and while studies show that most cats tend to dislike or like a specific option, your cat may very well prefer the opposite. So, if your cat regularly uses his very large but covered litter box with scented, pelleted litter, you don't need to replace it. If you have doubts, you can check his preference by adding another litter box with different characteristics to see if he prefers the new one to the old one.

### How Many Litter Boxes?

Generally speaking, the number of the boxes should equal the number of cats in the home, plus one additional box. This means that if you have one cat, he should have at least two boxes. Why? He may not like using the same box for urination and defecation or may prefer not to use a box that already has urine or feces in it (cats are very clean animals, remember).

If you have several cats, the bare minimum number of litter boxes should be equal to the number of groups of cats who get along well together. So, for example, if you have seven cats and two of them are best buddies, another two are always together, and the rest form their own little family of three, then you have three groups and should have a minimum of three litter boxes, but ideally eight. If all the cats live in their own separate areas, especially if they do not move around the home much, you need a box where each cat lives.

## Where Should the Boxes Be Located?

The boxes should be placed in different rooms, to avoid ambushes from bully cats who guard all the resources, and on different levels (if the cats are living in a multistory house), to make them more accessible. Avoid noisy rooms (such as the laundry room, where the washer and dryer are located) or congested areas (for example, near the front or back door). Also keep the boxes away from young children and the rooms where they play. These kinds of locations could scare the cats and force them to look for quieter places to eliminate.

All the boxes should be easy to access. Avoid "hiding" a litter box in a small cabinet or closet that is accessible only through a flap or a crack in the door. Choose well-lit rooms as opposed to dark corners. Avoid rooms whose doors are often closed, where cats may be shut out from the box. Also avoid placing boxes downstairs in the basement or upstairs in the attic, especially if you have senior cats or very young kittens, who may find these locations challenging to reach.

## What Size Box?

A larger box gives the cat the possibility of finding areas in the box that are not soiled. A popular guideline (though not backed by research) is that the box should be one and a half times the length of your adult cat (from the tip of his nose to the end of his rump) in order to give him enough room to dig, posture, and cover his eliminations.

Plastic storage boxes, appropriately modified to provide easy access, make great litter boxes. They are inexpensive, large, deep, and easy to clean. And the high sides help keep everything inside the box.
*Craig Zeichner*

Depending on the size of your cat, you may find the "jumbo" boxes available in stores to be too small. Large plastic storage boxes make perfect alternatives and come in many more sizes. Also consider the cat's age when choosing a litter box. The height of the sides may need to be adjusted for a kitten, an adult, or a senior. An older cat affected by a joint disease or other painful condition may benefit from having a little ramp or one side of the box cut down to make access easier.

## Covered or Uncovered?

Most cats prefer an uncovered box, because a cover traps odors and prevents visual access to their surroundings. But some cats prefer a covered box, and others have no preference at all. Some uncovered boxes have a plastic collar or shield to help keep litter inside. While this type of box may keep the surrounding space tidier, it may also decrease access to the box and reduce the space your cat has to dig, sniff, and squat. Both a box with a collar or shield and an covered box may be problematic if your cat is very large or obese. Regardless of whether the box is covered or uncovered, the most important factor is that you scoop out the urine and feces every day. A study by Dr. Debra F. Horwitz, DACVB, found that not cleaning the litter box daily, as well as using a scented litter, is more commonly associated with house soiling than using a covered litter box.

## What Kind of Litter?

Research has shown that most cats prefer fine-grained, unscented, clumping clay litter. This makes sense, because domestic cats are descended from a desert-dwelling ancestor who eliminated in fine, dry sand and soil. Of course, there will always be exceptions, and it's your cat who should get to choose the litter, not you.

Aside from traditional clay litter, clumping litter is now made from grass, corn, or other materials. These products represent a greener option and are gentler on your cat's paws and nose, as they are usually less dusty and dehydrating than clay litter. However, any litter made from a food item poses the risk that your cat may try to eat it. Monitor closely when first using a food-based litter, and avoid this type of litter if your cat has a history of eating things he shouldn't.

Grass-based clumping litter is natural, nontoxic, biodegradable, and softer and gentler on your cat's feet than traditional clay clumping litter. *Carlo Siracusa*

If your cat has developed a litter aversion (refusing to use the litter box or touch the material inside), offer him different types of substrates (litter, sand, soil) or different kinds of litter to identify one that he will accept. Do this by setting out a litter box "cafeteria": several boxes in the same location filled with different litter materials. How will you know if your cat doesn't like a litter you are offering? A study by ACVB diplomates Dr. Wailani Sung and Dr. Sharon Crowell-Davis found that the time a cat spends digging in the litter box can be used as a way to test litter preference: the less digging, the less he likes the litter.

## How Do You Keep the Box Clean?

This is when it is truly important to remember how clean and particular your cat is. Boxes must be scooped at least once a day, but twice a day is much better. When I am home, I scoop my cats' boxes as soon as they use them (sometimes it's more than twice a day). Any time you remove litter clumps, add a little more litter to the box to maintain the desired depth of at least one and a half inches.

Change the litter completely at least once a month if it's a clumping type, even more frequently if it doesn't clump or if more than one cat uses the same box. Dump out all the litter and wash the box with warm, soapy water. Let it air-dry, preferably in the sun, which is a natural deodorizer.

I do not recommend using detergents or disinfecting cleaners because they contain strong chemicals that can leave behind unwanted and repulsive scents (to your cat's nose). Research by Dr. Nicholas Dodman, DACVB, and his colleagues found that cats show less dissatisfaction with their litter box and fewer house-soiling and marking behaviors when the box is odorless.

---

### Litter Box Guidelines

- Big and roomy — at least one and a half times the length of your cat, with lots of headroom if it's covered
- Easy to enter and exit
- Scooped at least daily
- Filled with at least one and a half inches of clean, dry, soft, fine-grained, unscented litter
- Preferably no liner, collar, or cover
- Smells like nothing at all
- Located away from food and water, but still in the cat's core area
- In a quiet spot, with minimal human and pet traffic
- Not hemmed in, blocked off, or inside a closet or cabinet, so the cat can see who is approaching

---

## Feline Interstitial Cystitis

Feline interstitial cystitis (FIC) is an inflammation of the bladder without any identifiable cause. Affected cats may experience a wide range of symptoms, including increased frequency of urination, pain when they urinate and possibly at other times as well, urination outside the litter box, blood in their urine, personality changes, and excessive grooming of the hair on the abdomen, likely as a result of bladder pain.

Recent studies suggest that FIC appears to be associated with a series of complex interactions between the nervous system, the adrenal glands, and the bladder. There may be a genetic component, meaning some cats may be predisposed to develop FIC, but a cat's environment and stress level clearly play a role as well. The goal of treatment is to relieve pain and reduce stress.

If your cat exhibits any of the signs mentioned here, you should take him to your veterinarian immediately for a full physical examination. These are also signs of numerous treatable medical conditions that can have serious complications if left undiagnosed and untreated.

There is no specific test for FIC, so the diagnosis is made when all other medical problems have been ruled out. That does not mean, however, it is not a real medical condition.

## A Multimodal Approach to Treatment

Studies of cats with FIC have found that it's often triggered by environmental stressors. The most common triggers are conflicts with either humans or other cats in the household, although anything that can stress a cat can trigger the problem. Effective treatment involves addressing the cat's environment, changing his diet, controlling his pain and bladder discomfort, and increasing his water intake. As first described by Dr. C. A. Tony Buffington and colleagues, this multimodal approach addresses the environment and helps prevent recurrence. When only medical therapies are used to treat FIC, symptoms often return.

Stress increases when cats have no control over their environment. This lack of control occurs when cats experience a change in routine or when new pets or humans are introduced to the household. It's always best to keep a consistent routine that includes playtime, feeding, and regular interactions.

Hobbes has a habit of spraying urine when he is stressed out. This elevated perch gives him a safe vantage point away from household stressors and his feline housemates.
*Anne Gallutia*

One good way to give your cat some control over his environment and decrease his stress is to provide him with a few safe areas that he can retreat to. These will allow him to observe his surroundings and have time to himself. If you have many cats in your household, you'll want to increase the amount of three-dimensional safe space by creating perches, ramps, and elevated walkways so the cats can avoid one another when they feel it is necessary.

Environmental enrichment is an important part of this approach. (See chapter 3 to learn more about all the ways you can enrich your cat's environment.) While it may be tempting to make all of these changes at once, it's better to make them gradually to allow your cat time to adapt. Even positive changes to the environment can be overwhelming for a cat.

Avoid punishing your cat if you find him urinating outside the litter box. Yelling or physically hitting him will only increase fear, anxiety, and distress and make the problem worse.

## Encourage Your Cat to Drink

Although it may seem contradictory for a house-soiling cat to increase his water intake, it is an important part of treating FIC. Add more water bowls around the house and wash them daily. Make sure the bowls are wide enough that the cat's whiskers don't touch the sides. This will make the bowls more comfortable for him to drink out of and encourage him to drink more. Whereas some cats will regularly drink out of bowls, others prefer running water. For these cats, and for the freshest water, consider providing a kitty fountain or allowing them to drink from a faucet.

## Avoiding Pitfalls and Staying on Track

First of all, take a deep breath. Feline house soiling is a frustrating and embarrassing problem for many cat owners. There is hope, though, to get your cat back on track for more desirable litter box habits. As you get started, you'll want to keep his needs in mind. After all, the box is for him.

You'll also have to be extremely patient and committed. Your cat will need time to learn that the box is a comfortable place to go when he needs to empty his bladder and bowels. Sometimes, the problem has an easy solution; other times, it may be more complicated to restore regular litter box use.

Be aware that cats may choose to eliminate on soft substrates such beds, pillows, couches, carpets, and rugs. These spots are pleasant to the touch and magically absorb urine — no digging or covering required. In 2002, Dr. Stefanie Schwartz, DACVB, published a retrospective study in which she determined that cats with separation anxiety may urinate on their owners' beds when they are left home alone. It's been theorized that this may be because they take comfort in their owners' scent.

To keep your cat from soiling the same spot over and over, you'll need to clean the places where he has toileted and prevent access to them. Use a product specifically designed to clean cat urine. A study by Dr. Bonnie Beaver, DACVB, and her colleagues evaluated how effective eleven cleaning products were in getting cat urine smell out of carpets and found that many of the products specifically marketed to eliminate cat urine odor are effective and prevent the return of the smell. Avoid products that contain ammonia or chlorine (such as bleach), which will attract the cat back to these spots.

If your cat is marking and targets appliances, you may have to clean each soiled spot more than once. The heat generated when the appliance is turned on may make the smell return, and the cat will feel the need to mark it again.

If your cat has been urinating on a soft substrate, such as carpeting or upholstered furniture, make sure these items are thoroughly cleaned, ideally by a company that specializes in cleaning pet stains and odors. If the substrate can be removed, such as a rug, take it away until your cat's house soiling has completely resolved.

If possible, prevent access to the areas your cat has been soiling. Close doors or put up baby gates to keep him out of those areas. If you can't close an area off, cover the spots where he has been eliminating with aluminum foil or plastic wrap, or use a plastic carpet runner with the nubs turned up. Lemon- or orange-scented potpourri should keep your cat away as well, but make sure to put the potpourri where he can't eat it, because it can be toxic. Or try putting his bedding or his food and water bowls in those areas, because usually cats will not eliminate where they eat, drink, or rest.

Another idea is to try putting a litter box right on the spot, then gradually moving it to a more desired area. ("Gradually" means that after ninety days of consistent use of the box in that spot, you can start moving it one inch a day.)

Be aware that when you remove access to one spot, your cat may just use another one. So you will still need to address the cause of the problem with an optimal litter box and the other suggestions in this chapter. Preventing a return to the "scene of the crime" will only stop the cat from going in that spot out of habit. The goal of any treatment should be to resolve what is triggering your cat's behavior and make his environment as enriching and stress-free as possible. (See chapters 5 and 9 for more information about sources of stress for cats.)

Studies have shown that environmental enrichment can help prevent recurrent house soiling. To keep your cat healthy and comfortable in his environment, make sure there are multiple feeding stations, perches, scratching posts, toys, and resting areas. As we saw in chapters 3 and 6, daily play and interaction with you can reinforce the human-animal bond and make your cat's environment more predictable and pleasant.

### Standing Streams

If your cat loves to spray in his box or urinates standing up, use a plastic storage box with high sides as a litter box. Just cut down one side so that your cat can easily get in and out (see the photo earlier in this chapter).

Or make an L-shaped litter box by placing a large litter box on the floor, then standing another box up on one of its short sides and inserting the horizontal box into it. This arrangement will contain the urine.

If the presence of outdoor pets or wildlife is triggering house soiling, blocking visual access to the outside world may be enough to prevent it. Keep the blinds down or use thick curtains or opaque window film to prevent your cat from seeing outside. There are also many humane ways

An L-shaped litter box, made from two large litter boxes, can accommodate cats who spray in their boxes.

*Debra F. Horwitz*

to keep unwanted visitors out of your yard. The feral cat advocacy group Neighborhood Cats offers a number of solutions that will work just as well for raccoons as they do for cats (see "Keeping Cats out of Gardens and Yards," www.neighborhoodcats.org/how-to-tnr/colony-care/keeping-cats-out-of-gardens-and-yards-2).

## What You Should Never Do

Often our first response to an unwanted behavior in our cats is to punish the culprit — at least by yelling at them. Refrain from reprimanding, scolding, or in any way punishing your cat, even if it is *really* tempting. Punishment will only make the problem worse, because it will add more stress to the situation. Plus, your cat may now feel threatened by you and respond to your aggressiveness with fear-related aggression (see chapter 7).

When you need to change soiling or marking behavior, start by making sure your cat has what he needs — an optimal litter box — and then rewarding him for using it. Rewards (food, praise, affection, toys) reinforce desired behaviors. When you show kindness toward your cat, you will strengthen your bond with him, and everyone will be less stressed — including you.

When you use positive reinforcement, your cat will become more comfortable around you and feel more at ease in his own skin, and thus less prone to display the unwanted behavior. Also, he will retain his new learned behavior for a longer period of time. Not bad!

## Should You Consider Medication for Your Cat?

Unfortunately, there is no magic pill or quick fix to treat any behavior problem. If anxiety plays an important role in your cat's house soiling, you might consider medication, pheromone therapy, or natural supplements. But if the problem is a dirty litter box or access blocked by a bully cat, medication will not change the situation. And medication will never work on its own. The goal of any medication is to lessen your cat's anxiety so that he can be more receptive to all the other recommended solutions. Medication should always be considered an adjunct to behavior and environmental modification, never a replacement for it.

Be aware that not all cats will respond to the same medication in the same way, and that most of the drugs used for this issue will take four to six weeks to reach their full effect. Among the different house-soiling problems, urine marking seems to respond well to medication.

Synthetic feline facial pheromones also can be used to help cats with house-soiling issues. They are available on the market as plug-in diffusers and sprays.

- Diffusers increase comfort in the areas where they are placed and may be of most benefit in rooms with litter boxes, high traffic, or other stressors.
- Sprays can be applied to new items to make them more familiar to your cat.

Natural supplements that contain casein (a milk protein), whey (another milk protein), magnolia (*Magnolia officinalis*), *Phellodendron amurense* (Amur cork tree), and L-theanine (an amino acid) may have a calming effect on cats with house-soiling problems, but there is no scientific evidence to confirm this.

## What Did We Say?
- Take your cat to see his veterinarian as soon as house-soiling problems arise to rule out possible medical conditions and address them.
- House soiling can be treated.

- House soiling is not a result of spite or a display of dominance.
- Offer your cat an optimal litter box.
- Good litter box hygiene is extremely important to your cat.
- Remove all triggers of your cat's anxiety.
- Pay attention to your cat's needs and preferences.
- Medication may be appropriate to help your cat deal with stress, but it should be combined with behavioral and environmental modification.
- Avoid punishment.
- Be patient and consistent in implementing the necessary changes.

DR. AMY L. PIKE, DACVB, and DR. KELLY BALLANTYNE, DACVB, also contributed to this chapter.

# 9

# I'm a Scaredy-Cat
## *Please Keep Quiet and Don't Make Me Meet New People or Go Anywhere — Especially to the Veterinarian!*

Kersti Seksel, BVSc, MRCVS, MA,
FANZCVS, DACVB, DECAWBM, FAVA

Lucy crouches, her body tense, ready to spring into action. Her ears are pricked and alert, pointing forward, listening carefully to every sound. Her eyes are vigilant, pupils dilated, carefully watching; every movement in the room is closely monitored. Her tail rapidly flicks back and forth. She spots the fly, leaps into the air, catches it against the glass with an expertly placed paw. The buzzing stops. She carefully lifts her paw, very slowly. The buzzing resumes, and Lucy is off again, jumping and leaping over chairs and following the fly around the house.

This is the confident Lucy her owner knows and loves.

At other times, Lucy is not so confident, and Taylor struggles to understand her personality change: "Every time my friends come over to play bridge, Lucy disappears. She is such a pretty cat, and my friends want to greet and pet her, but she is nowhere to be seen until two hours after they leave. I just don't understand how she can be so outgoing and confident one minute and so withdrawn the next. Does she hate my friends?"

How can Lucy be so mercurial? You may think your indoor cat has an easy life, just lying on the couch and being pampered. Food, water, beds, and toys are all within easy reach. There's no danger to her. So this change from a confident cat to a timid and withdrawn animal is very confusing. What could she possibly have to worry about?

To a cat, the unknown means danger. Therefore, being cautious and hiding are survival instincts. In addition, cats are creatures of habit; they don't like change. For them, the world should be predictable, because that is what feels safe. Unfortunately, life does change. People have visitors, move to a new house, buy new furniture, add another pet (or person) to the family, and when the cat is unwell, they take her to the veterinarian. Talk about scary unknowns! A trip to the veterinary office can be one of the biggest terrors for cats — just like going to the dentist may be for some people.

## Facts, Not Fiction

Cats are all individuals, just as people are. In separate papers, Dr. Sharon Crowell-Davis, DACVB, Dr. Jacqui Ley, and I have noted that some cats are extroverts and enjoy company, while others are introverts and prefer a more solitary life. Some cats cope with change better than others — again, just like people. But on the whole, cats prefer an unchanging environment and a consistent routine, or at least for both to be predictable.

Cats can live in a variety of social environments, which helps explain how successful they have been living with people. Although they are solitary hunters (they catch prey that is too small to share except with their kittens), they can be found living by themselves or in large social communities, as well as in many variations and combinations in between. New cats are not easily accepted into an established group, which helps explain why your cat may not like the new kitten you have fallen in love with and just brought home.

As with people, some of a cat's personality depends on the personality of her parents. According to a study done by Dr. Ilana Reisner, DACVB, and Dr. Katherine Houpt, DACVB, a cat's father appears to have a greater influence than her mother on whether she is outgoing or timid and whether she is more or less resistant to handling as a kitten. Certainly, a cat needs to have a good mother looking after her to develop into a happy, healthy, well-balanced cat, but the evidence shows that the father has a strong genetic influence on her social development even if he is not there to help raise her. A study done by Dr. Sandra McCune found that early handling and socialization can influence a cat's friendliness toward people and confirmed the positive influence of having a friendly father.

Cats are (or appear to be) very independent and self-sufficient, accepting interaction only when they want it. This leads many people to think that all cats are aloof and independent and do not need much care, which is simply not true. Dr. Julie Feaver and her colleagues at the University of Cambridge describe three types of cat personalities: sociable, confident, and easygoing; timid and nervous; and active/aggressive. Cats can be social, and most enjoy interacting with their caregivers, but their evolutionary past makes them wary of change and new things.

Although all cats are naturally cautious, some are more timid than others. Genetics, early handling and socialization, and life experiences all play a role in how a cat's personality develops. *Craig Zeichner*

## Is That Really True?

*Is it true that dogs have owners and cats have staff?* Cats are an enigma for many people. So what draws someone to share their home with a cat? Anyone who has ever owned a cat cannot help but admire the amazing athleticism and fine grace of the domestic cat. She can climb trees, walk a fence like a tightrope, and get herself into all sorts of clever places. Yet she also can be hidden and withdrawn. Most owners would probably tell you that it is, in fact, a cat's "wildness" — her ability to be self-contained and enigmatic yet still willing to share her life with us — that is at least part of the attraction.

Cats have been human companions for a very long time — more than 9,000 years. The earliest direct evidence of cat domestication is the remains of a kitten who was buried alongside a human 9,500 years ago in

Cyprus. That cat was large and closely resembled the African wildcat (*Felis silvestris lybica*). This discovery, combined with genetic studies, suggests that cats were probably domesticated in the Near East and then were brought to Cyprus and Egypt. Cats evolved in arid areas and are solitary ambush hunters. They do not kill prey next to a water source, for fear of contaminating it and becoming ill.

As cats became domesticated and diverged from their wild relatives, they adapted to hunting mice and other vermin attracted to the food found in human towns and villages. This role for cats created a mutually beneficial relationship, but without much interaction between cats and people. Since then, the relationship has waxed and waned through different times and cultures, with the cat sometimes cherished and sometimes persecuted, until we come to the relationship we have today.

Our cats still retain some of their wild roots, and their response to danger is to flee whenever possible rather than fight — which is what a small animal who is both prey and predator in her natural environment would do. They still prefer not to eat next to where they drink, and to rest up high, away from potential danger. Understanding the evolutionary history and biology of the cat helps us better understand why cats may become anxious when living with us as companions.

## Feline Fear and Anxiety

Almost every cat will experience fear at some time in her life. Fear is a normal response to potentially threatening things in the environment. Anxiety is a state of worry or unease about something that may happen or an outcome that is uncertain, and most cats will have some anxious moments. But when either fear or anxiety begins to take over and affect a cat's quality of life, we should consider whether the cat has an anxiety disorder. A study by Dr. Michelle Bamberger and Dr. Katherine Houpt, DACVB, found that although a low percentage of cats are formally diagnosed with anxiety, many behavior problems in cats (house soiling, fighting, urine marking) are undoubtedly driven by underlying anxiety.

Heightened anxiety may be inherited, meaning that some cats were born with an inclination to react more strongly to anxiety-producing events. However, what your cat has learned from previous experiences (good, bad, and neutral), as well as the environment in which she finds herself at any given time, can also contribute to the way she responds to stress and changes in her environment.

Stress is one of the major causes of anxiety. How cats react to stress, though, depends greatly on their personality, how well they were socialized as kittens, and their genetic predisposition. Stress in and of itself is not harmful if the animal can resolve or escape the stressful situation. But continued stress can cause anxiety and be detrimental to a cat's health and well-being.

An anxious or fearful cat may hide, urinate or defecate in places that you consider unacceptable or inappropriate, spray urine (often near windows and doors if she hears or smells cats outside), overgroom herself, or vocalize more or less. Fear and anxiety also may cause your cat to react with a fight-or-flight response. This is an involuntary, adrenaline-mediated state in which the cat's instinct to survive takes over. If your cat is afraid, she may run and hide (the flight response), but if she is cornered, she may react by hissing, spitting, scratching, or biting (the fight response). Before she is pushed that far, she may show you two other Fs — freeze and fidget (or fiddle).

## The Four Fs

Cats exhibit fear and stress in four ways — what we sometimes call the four Fs. This is very similar to the way humans exhibit fear.

1. **Flight.** A fearful cat will often try to escape a situation by fleeing. This may be an obvious sudden exit from the room, but it can also be more subtle, such as moving behind an owner or under a table.
2. **Fight.** It is a common misconception that a fighting cat is not a fearful cat. Aggression is one of the ways a cat can exhibit fear and communicate that she needs space. It's important for the welfare of your cat to remember that if she is growling, hissing, swatting, or biting, she is likely in a high state of fear and emotional arousal. Her goal in displaying this behavior is to make the threat go away and create distance between herself and danger, not necessarily to fight.

3. **Freeze.** A "frozen" cat is doing her best impression of a statue. She may stand very still, lie down with all her limbs and her tail pulled under her, or move in what appears to be slow motion.

4. **Fidget (Fiddle).** When a cat is conflicted about how to respond, she fidgets. It's one of the most common fear or anxiety responses seen in cats. Conflicted cats seem to be in constant motion and may be excessively licking their lips, yawning, licking themselves, or scanning the room. These behaviors are inappropriate or out of context relative to the cat's situation. This is the cat equivalent of a person chewing their nails, twirling their hair, or laughing inappropriately during a serious meeting.

---

### What Does That Mean?

**Socialization:** The process of learning to accept the close proximity of your own species as well as other species. This does not mean every cat has to like every other cat and be best friends or even second-best friends with another cat — let alone like all people, dogs, rabbits, or other species. We don't like everyone we meet, so why should our cats?

**Habituation:** The process of learning that things the cat regularly comes across in her environment (sights, sounds, smells) are nothing to be worried about, and even learning to ignore them. For example, if you live on a busy street, after a while you do not hear the traffic anymore. That's habituation.

**Resilience:** The ability to bounce back or recover quickly after experiencing change, a new situation, or a potential threat.

---

## What Makes a Cat Anxious?

Anxiety can arise from feeling uncertain about what is going to happen next. If your cat is anxious, it may be because she has trouble predicting the outcomes of events, and because of her anxiety, she perceives many normal events as threatening. Even if the outcome of an event is pleasant, she is so anxious that she cannot take in that information. Anxious cats do not cope well with changes, however insignificant the changes may seem to us.

The environments that cats find themselves in today are different from the ones their wild ancestors inhabited. We adopt a cat and expect her to adapt to the life we have chosen for her. It is not surprising that some cats find it difficult to do so. We, as caregivers, then struggle to understand why our cat does not behave the way we want her to.

One example of an anxiety-producing change is coming into a home with multiple cats, a scenario that has been discussed in previous chapters. This forces the cat to live in a social group she did not choose. The addition of another person to the cat's household also can be disruptive. Imagine a scenario in which you and your cat are living in what appears to be perfect harmony. There's just the two of you, you have a steady job with regular hours, and life has predictability and balance. Then you meet your special someone, and you start dating, staying out late, and staying over at your partner's place.

What seemed like a perfect relationship between you and your cat has changed in a way that seems unpredictable to her. She begins to hide under the bed when your partner comes over, does not approach for petting from you, and hisses when your partner tries to pet her. Things take their course, and your partner moves in. The cat has been forced into a social group that is nothing like the one she initially had or would form naturally. Suddenly she stops using her litter box and is scratching the furniture. Why is this happening?

Most cats (and people, too!) do not like change. They like to remain in control of their environment, or at least have some ability to predict what might change or to find a safe place to ride out the change. Since none of this is under their control, how might they respond? In some situations, a cat may deposit urine or stool outside the litter box, perhaps because she wants to avoid the new person or pet. Or she may spray urine or scratch in areas other than her scratching post, because marking her territory helps her feel more secure. She may hide a lot or become less active, in an effort to save her energy for whatever might happen next. She might vocalize more frequently. Rather than being spiteful, these are all ways that cats show anxiety and stress.

## Anxiety and the Brain

As we've seen, anxiety can be caused by the environment and circumstances in which a cat lives. But cats who are anxious all the time may also have a problem with how their brain processes information, causing them to become worried about things and events that are not truly dangerous or threatening. The brain receives information via chemical messengers called neurotransmitters, which bind to neuroreceptors at the junctions between nerve cells (called synapses). Different neurotransmitters have different effects on thoughts and feelings. Varying levels of neurotransmitters or a problem with them can lead to changes in emotion and create prolonged anxiety and fear.

The rest of the body is not immune to this prolonged anxiety response. This is not surprising when you consider how your own body reacts to prolonged stress. In cats, the bowels and skin may be affected, for example, which may lead to itchy skin or a sensitive stomach. Anxiety can also lead to inflammation in the urinary tract, which can cause pain and result in litter box problems. In the brain, this may lead to difficulty remembering new information. The result is that anxious animals have a hard time learning new things.

Without treatment, anxiety will worsen over time. Each exposure to the situation that is causing the anxiety will make the cat's reaction stronger — unless we intervene to help her cope and change.

## Is It Normal for a Cat to Hide All the Time?

Absolutely not! Be aware of the cat who remains hidden most of the time. An anxious cat may like to hide in dark places where no one can see her, or in inaccessible places that she can easily defend and where she can stay just out of reach. You may often find your anxious cat under the bed or other low-to-the-ground furniture, beneath the stairs, or inside a closet, cupboard, or box.

Both anxious and confident cats may seek out elevated locations, but what distinguishes them is their facial expressions and body postures. A confident cat is relaxed and surveying the land from her elevated perch; a

While it's normal for cats to scoot under furniture when something startles or surprises them, a cat who hides all the time needs help to feel better. *Kersti Seksel*

scared cat may be crouched down near the back of the space to avoid detection and increase safety. (See chapter 1 to learn more about feline body language and chapter 5 to learn what stress and anxiety look like in cats.)

## Why Does My Cat Meow at Me for Food?

Cats with anxiety may vocalize more. Sometimes this can be to increase the distance between themselves and the person or animal upsetting them (that's when you'll hear hisses and growls) or to reduce the distance by soliciting you to interact. Often this activity is thought to be food seeking, but anxious cats just vocalize more; they're not always asking for food.

\* \* \*

It is important to recognize that cats do not display any of these behaviors (hiding, eliminating outside the litter box, or vocalizing more) because they want to get back at you or are spiteful or vindictive. The behaviors are all expressions of anxiety. This book can help you in many situations, but sometimes it may be necessary to seek professional help. Studies have shown that the longer a behavior problem persists, the harder it is to resolve.

## How Do We Begin?

Anxiety and stress can arise from many different sources, so it's important to try to figure out what is stressing your cat and take steps to reduce or eliminate those stressors. First, always consider your cat's physical health. Cats who are physically sick may be anxious. They are very good at hiding illness and may show only subtle signs, if any, of being unwell. For example, a sick cat may hide or become clingy. Common health problems that contribute to anxiety are endocrine disorders, arthritis, and infections. The first step toward helping your cat is a visit to your veterinarian. When you resolve any underlying physical health issues, the anxiety may resolve or be diminished.

To help your cat cope in her environment, it is important to meet her behavioral needs. This means providing lots of resources that offer outlets for typical cat behavior. By looking at what your cat does most of the time, you can make her natural activities even more pleasant and reduce the potential for stress and anxiety.

Everything has the potential to increase stress and anxiety, but environmental changes are high on the list. Some common environmental stressors are limited availability of resources such as food, water, and resting places; sharing a house with people, especially noisy and busy children; and living with other cats.

Look around your home and think about the things cats need in their environment (see chapter 3). Can your anxious cat get to all her resources without being harassed by another cat, a dog, or a person? Is she getting enough play and mental stimulation? Are stray cats coming around, making her feel as if she constantly has to defend her territory? What can you do to resolve these situations for your cat?

### Socialization and Handling

Being handled, especially by strangers, can be very frightening for a cat who is not used to it. Yet handling is not something cat owners generally teach their cats. Puppy owners take their pups to puppy classes and doggy playdates, and as a result dogs learn how to accept being handled all over their body by new people. But while kitten kindergarten classes have been available for some time (see chapter 4), they are still not widely offered, and kitten owners seldom get the same assistance as puppy owners in socializing their cats to handling.

The most important time for a kitten is between two and seven weeks of age, when she is especially sensitive to socialization. During this period, the kitten is (or should be) still with her mother and littermates. This means that whoever is caring for mom and her kittens must provide plenty of opportunities for the kittens to participate in family life and to learn to accept handling, noises, other pets, and other everyday occurrences. It is harder, though possible, to socialize a cat to these things later on.

## Establishing a Routine

Cats are creatures of habit and are very sensitive to changes in their life. To help minimize the stress caused by any changes in the environment, such as new furniture or new people in the home, try to keep your cat's food and mealtimes the same. Set time aside each day for grooming, playing, petting, cuddling, and sleeping, and try to do each activity at about the same time every day.

If you have more than one cat, you will have to set aside time for each activity with each cat, during which she will have your undivided attention. That way, no cat will miss out, everyone will get her fair share of attention, and they can all relax knowing their special time is coming.

The most important thing is to establish a routine for your cat that you can live with. If you plan to change anything, do it gradually, over a number of weeks. If your cat is not going to be allowed in certain areas of the house, such as the nursery (if you are expecting a baby), shut that door now. You may want to set up a special area for your cat to rest and sleep, as well as to receive one-on-one attention.

To help your cat get used to the idea of a new baby's presence, let her sniff and explore the stroller and crib, as well as some of the baby's clothes. Exposing the cat to baby noises and smells also can be helpful.

Before the baby arrives, think about how your routine will change and start implementing those anticipated changes now so that your cat has time to adjust. Preparation is the key if everyone is to live happily ever after — together.

## Sleeping and Resting

Separate studies by Dr. Jane Dards and by Dr. Carol Haspel and Dr. Robert Calhoon have shown that cats spend more than half of their time sleeping or resting, so give your cat lots of places to do so. Having several shelves at different levels and in different rooms will allow her to choose where she wants to be at any given time. She may prefer to be lying in the sun by the window in the morning, snoozing on top of the cat tree in the afternoon, and curled up in a hammock in the evening.

Offering a variety of perching places throughout your home, especially ones that hold only one cat (if you have more than one), will help reduce your cat's stress. Cats tend to stretch and scratch after they wake up, so place scratching surfaces near where your cat rests.

## Feeding to Decrease Stress

Cats spend about between 15 and 46 percent of their time either hunting or eating. Some cats are grazers, so they need to have food available all the time. Restricting food to set mealtimes may increase their anxiety — just as feeling hungry can make us feel stressed. If you have a grazing cat, try hiding dry cat food in a variety of places around your home to help her explore and "hunt" as she wishes.

If your cat is a gobbler (or overweight), having food available all the time is not a good idea. Feeding this kind of cat using food-dispensing toys will help meet her needs. There are many such toys on the market, or you can make your own. (See chapter 3 for more on food-dispensing toys.)

If you have both grazers and gobblers living in your home, consider including feeders controlled by microchips or special collars. Only cats with a matching chip or collar will have access to a particular feeder.

Remember, not all cats will accept changes in their feeding routine right away, so implement them as gradually as you can, and give your cat time to get used to them. Don't try to force her to eat in a way that doesn't work for her, but also make sure to monitor her food intake and health.

## Play and Exploration to Increase Activity

Play and exploration mimic hunting behavior for cats. These activities may reduce stress because they allow cats to exhibit more of their natural behaviors. Cats in the wild tend to have short bursts of activity, so keep the play sessions short and sweet. Because cats are crepuscular (more active at dusk and dawn), early mornings and early evenings are the best times to schedule play. But if you can only play with your cat late at night or in the middle of the day, she will adjust. The most important thing is to schedule daily playtime.

Never play in a way that involves human hands or feet. This can lead to problems with your cat attacking body parts even when you're not playing, because she will think they are toys. Toys attached to the end of a fishing pole that move around erratically are sure to get her attention and keep her teeth and claws away from you.

Don't be discouraged if your cat tires of certain toys. Dr. Sagi Denenberg, DACVB, found that if you give your cat a five-minute rest and switch toys, she will be ready to play again. You may notice that your cat gets bored with a particular toy after a few days. The excitement of a new toy or one she hasn't seen in a while will likely reignite her zest for play, so rotate her toys and toss in something new every once in a while.

## Climbing and Scratching

Cats love to climb and to sit up high and observe the world. This is part of their natural instinct to feel safe and secure. Cats live in three-dimensional space (unlike humans, who concentrate on floor plans), so vertical space is important to them. Having lots of appealing perching places — on top of cupboards or specially constructed shelves or cat trees — can give them much pleasure and keep them off areas you would prefer they not use (like tabletops or kitchen counters).

Cats are usually attached to their territory and may use scent marking to denote the boundaries. When a cat becomes frightened or anxious, territorial marking with both urine and claws may increase. If scratching posts are not in convenient and accessible locations, the cat may begin unwanted scratching on furniture and other objects. Think carefully about where you place scratching posts so that your cat can easily access them. (See chapter 11 for more on scratching behavior.)

Much as with human children, providing opportunities for your cat to engage in acceptable activities works better than punishing her for unacceptable behaviors. In fact, sometimes punishing unacceptable behaviors just teaches the cat not to do those things in front of you!

## Respect Your Cat's Individuality

Every cat is different, and you are the one who knows your cat best. She may be cuddly, or she may just want to sit nearby but not be touched. When she solicits attention, it does not necessarily mean she wants to be petted or picked up. Even if she jumps onto your lap, she may just want that close contact and warm sleeping spot, not a hug or a cuddle.

Learning her personality and respecting her needs will help decrease her stress and anxiety. And remember, if she does become upset or stressed, cuddling may actually increase her stress rather than decrease it, especially if she wants (or her natural instinct is) to flee.

## Building Resilience

Cats are naturally cautious and can startle easily, because they're both a predator and a prey species. But their resilience and their ability to recover from being startled will vary from cat to cat. If your cat has an inherited tendency to be anxious, she may not be predisposed to be resilient when faced with novelty. Cats who are more resilient may still jump at a sudden noise or movement or hide when guests arrive, but after a very short time they'll recover or come out of hiding. More anxious cats take a lot longer to adjust to even small changes in the household. Some may hide the entire time you have guests and even take a while to come out after they have left.

You can work on increasing your cat's resilience by carefully exposing her to guests and make meeting new people a positive experience for her. This may mean getting her accustomed to a knock on the door or the sound of the doorbell when no one is actually arriving. When she hears this sound of "impending doom," give her a small, tasty treat or get out her favorite toy. You can then progress to having just one person visit. When she is comfortable with one person, try introducing her to small groups of people. Remember, "comfortable" does not mean she will come over for a pat; it may just mean staying in the same room and not running away and hiding.

Ideally, when a visitor arrives, your preliminary work in getting your cat accustomed to receiving a treat when someone knocks or rings the doorbell will bring her to a central location in your home, and she will be eating something when the person enters the room. A high-value food such as tuna is a good choice for this situation, as it will motivate her to stay in the room to receive the special snack. The visitor should be very quiet and not move around too much. He shouldn't approach the cat or speak loudly. Instead, have him sit still and let the cat investigate him in her own time. Spraying a synthetic feline facial pheromone (Feliway Classic) on the person's clothing or a blanket that he can put on his lap may be helpful.

If your cat approaches the guest, he can gently drop treats on the floor for her. All interactions will depend on the cat. If she is feeling confident, curious, and friendly, she may approach and solicit attention from the visitor. If she is more cautious, she may take more time before she approaches him. Never try to force interactions on your cat; she will approach someone new if and when she feels comfortable.

Building resilience can also involve exposing your cat to low levels of novel noises and objects. (See chapter 6 for more on habituation and how cats learn.) Knowing your cat's body language will be very important in helping you successfully socialize her and increase her resilience. Being able to identify the subtle signs of fear or stress, as well as the body language cues telling you that your cat is feeling confident and comfortable, will help you know when to progress and when to take a step back. (See chapter 1 for more on being able to read your cat.)

If, despite your best efforts, your cat still remains anxious, fearful, and stressed, a visit to your veterinarian or a veterinary behaviorist may be necessary to help her overcome her anxiety and fear and to improve her quality of life.

## Avoiding Pitfalls and Staying on Track

Anna worked long hours and was worried about leaving her cat, Sooty, alone all day, so she went to the shelter and adopted Fergus. He had been friendly with other cats in the shelter, and she assumed that he and Sooty would become fast friends, too. But when she brought Fergus home, Sooty started hissing, spitting, and growling as soon as she put Fergus's carrier on the living room floor. Then Sooty ran off and hid in the bedroom closet and wouldn't come out.

Hoping it would just take some time, Anna let Fergus out of his carrier, and he began exploring the house. A few days later, Sooty was still hiding from Fergus and spitting and hissing whenever he came near. Anna couldn't understand why Sooty was so afraid of Fergus and wasn't sure what to do to improve the situation.

*Does my cat need another cat for company?* There is nothing more engaging than to watch two kittens play, and it is a great idea to adopt two kittens to keep each other entertained, particularly if you spend long periods of time away from home during the day. However, most cats, once they reach adulthood, spend much of their time sleeping, and they tolerate solitude very well. Combine this with the fact that some cats are less social than others, and your cat could well view any newcomer as an intruder rather than a new brother or sister. Even if she has lived with another cat before, she might not accept a newcomer to your home. Adding another cat is often stressful.

If you really want to add a second cat to your household, the integration should be done slowly and carefully (see chapter 5). The resident cat will probably not like the newcomer and may even attack her. Cats need to be introduced over a long period of time. And that means they should be kept in separate rooms initially so they can hear and smell each other but do not have direct visual contact. Using a plug-in diffuser with a synthetic maternal appeasing pheromone can help the cats settle down, but it is no substitute for a careful, gradual introduction.

This situation can be even more difficult if you're introducing a kitten to an older cat. Mabel was a three-year-old cat when her owners brought home eight-week-old Missie. They took to each other immediately, and Mabel cleaned Missie and looked after her like her mom. When Mabel died unexpectedly five years later, Missie looked lonely, so they thought she needed a new companion. They got her a new friend, Percy, who was twelve weeks old. The cats hissed at each other immediately, Missie swiped at Percy, and he ran away, which led to a chase. They have been separated ever since.

Owners with a happy, trouble-free cat should think long and hard before introducing a new feline family member. I've seen some very sad cases where a family has two cats who get along very well. When one dies, the other grieves, and the human family members, facing their own grief, decide to get a new kitten to keep the resident cat company. The trouble is, the older cat doesn't want a new companion; she wants her old friend back.

Choosing a cat of similar age and activity level may help both cats adjust. But if, despite a gradual introduction, one cat is still very fearful of the other cat, the fearful cat may be suffering from anxiety and need veterinary help to build up her confidence and resilience. In some cases, it's the owner who needs to accept that even if the cats learn to tolerate each other, they will never be friends. And sometimes the best alternative is to rehome one of the cats.

Cats may learn to tolerate each other but never really become friends.
*Kersti Seksel*

Here are some tips for keeping two (or more) cats happy. (See chapter 5 for more information.)

- Using pheromones can help reduce some of the anxiety associated with bringing in a new cat. Place a plug-in diffuser with a synthetic maternal appeasing pheromone (Feliway MultiCat) in the house a week before the new feline family member is due to arrive.
- A cat-friendly environment will contain plenty of resources spread throughout the home and provide ample opportunities for the cats to be cats.
- A good basic rule is one of everything for each cat, plus one extra. This means lots of litter boxes, sleeping places, resting places (up high), scratching surfaces, food and water stations, and opportunities for play and exploration.

*Why are trips to the veterinarian so stressful?* Veterinary clinics can be very stressful places for pets. The scents there are strong, and often the products that are used to keep clinics clean and hygienic can be overpowering for sensitive cat noses. Additionally, the other animals visiting the clinic will be secreting stress pheromones, which will signal to your cat that there is something to worry about.

Following are some tips to help your cat have a less stressful visit to the veterinarian.

- Ideally, there should be two areas in the waiting room with a visual barrier between them to prevent dogs and cats from coming into close contact. Unfortunately, not all clinics have a large enough waiting area to be able to separate dogs and cats. If your veterinary office doesn't have this setup, arrange an appointment for a quiet time of the day, and wait in the car with your cat until there is an available consulting room. This strategy will avoid the stress caused by waiting in a noisy environment.
- Encourage your cat to get in the carrier voluntarily, with treats or other goodies if possible (see the next section). Try to prevent her from becoming stressed before you leave the house.
- Covering your cat's carrier with a towel will prevent her from com-

ing face-to-face with a dog or another cat. Spray the towel with a synthetic feline facial pheromone thirty minutes before you leave home so that the alcohol in the spray will have time to evaporate, leaving behind the calming scent of the pheromone.

- When moving the carrier around, make sure to support the base with your hands and wrap your arms around the carrier. This will prevent excessive shaking that may scare the cat.

*Is there any way to teach my cat to be less stressed in her carrier?* Kelly and Gillian moved into a new apartment last year and decided to adopt a puppy and a kitten from an animal shelter. Neither had owned a dog or cat before, and they were determined to be model owners. On the veterinarian's advice, they enrolled in a puppy class with their puppy, Ben. The veterinary technician taught them how to handle Ben gently so that he would be comfortable when he needed to come back for vaccinations. She advised them to buy a crate and gave them a handout about crate training. She also suggested that they bring Ben in for nonmedical visits, when the staff would give him lots of treats. As a result, Ben loves his crate and sees veterinarian visits as a great opportunity for treats and cuddles.

Unfortunately, the same opportunity wasn't available for their kitten, Whiskers. The veterinarian did not offer kitten kindergarten classes. And since Kelly and Gillian were not planning on taking Whiskers out walking every day, they did not realize that she needed to be socialized.

Whiskers loved being petted but did not like being picked up, so they didn't pick her up. They brought her home from the shelter in a carrier, but when they got home, they put the carrier in the closet and forgot about it until it was time for Whiskers to be revaccinated. It was a busy Saturday morning and they were running late, so they called Whiskers over for a treat, grabbed her, and stuffed her into the cat carrier.

By the time they arrived at the veterinarian's office, she was *very* upset. The veterinarian was gentle, but the technician eventually had to wrap Whiskers in a towel so that she could be vaccinated. She was very happy to get back into her carrier. When they got home and let her out of the carrier, she bolted behind the couch and wouldn't come out for the rest of the day. Kelly and Gillian now had a kitten who didn't trust them and who disappeared as soon as she saw the carrier. How much easier for everyone it would have been if only they'd done the same training with Whiskers as they had with Ben!

A frightened cat like this one may prefer to remain in her carrier at the veterinarian's office, but she's not likely to want to get in it again. *Kersti Seksel*

We often tuck our cat carriers away in storage until we need them to take our cats somewhere. As a result, when we take them out, the cats run and hide. At first, it's because it is a scary object they do not see very often. But after a few veterinarian visits, they come to associate the carrier with a scary and sometimes painful trip.

To help accustom your cat to her carrier, keep the carrier out in the house, in a place where she likes to spend her time. Put comfortable bedding and toys inside the carrier to help induce your cat to go in and, hopefully, use it as a bed. Cats like hiding under chairs and desks, so you might tuck the carrier in such a place, where it will become a safe space for your cat to retreat to and rest. Spraying a synthetic feline facial pheromone (Feliway Classic) on the bedding at first, as well as scattering treats or catnip inside, may help get her to explore the carrier.

Once your cat is happy in the carrier and goes in willingly to rest, you can progress to closing the door and moving the carrier to another room before reopening the door. This will help her adjust to the sensation of being carried inside the carrier.

You can then advance to taking her on short car trips, which will help you determine if she suffers from motion sickness. If she does, seek advice from your veterinarian about using a medication to help reduce her nausea. (See appendix A for more carrier training tips.)

## What About Antianxiety Medication?

Pheromones on their own are often not enough to ease moderate to severe anxiety. If your cat is very anxious, fearful, and skittish, and she takes longer than is typical to recover from stressors, she may need medication to reduce her anxiety and help her cope better with the world. The cat's individual symptoms will help your veterinarian determine what medication may be best for her.

Situational medications may be useful to help her tolerate car travel, veterinary visits, moving to a new home, or other short-term stressors. These medications can reduce your cat's anxiety and at higher doses provide a degree of sedation that may be helpful in situations where, for example, the veterinarian needs to do something that you know will scare her.

If your cat is suffering from an anxiety disorder and needs long-term relief, the veterinarian may prescribe a daily medication to help reduce her overall anxiety so that she can deal with everyday situations and stressors. These medications can be used in conjunction with situational medications if more help is needed for more stressful events. Your veterinarian also may refer you to a veterinary behaviorist.

## What Did We Say?

- All cats are anxious or fearful in some situations, but some cats have especially high levels of anxiety and stress due to differences in their neurochemistry.
- Cats like routines; it's all about *same, same, same.*
- Even small changes in the environment can increase a cat's stress.
- Making sure cats have ways to display their natural behaviors will help reduce stress.
- Perceived lack of choice or control is a stressor for cats.
- Do not force cats to interact with people or pets.
- Start early to get your cat used to the cat carrier and to novel situations and people.

- Not all cats want a companion. Being an only child may be a preference for many.
- You cannot cuddle cats to calm them. Rather, a stressed cat may regard cuddling as restraint — preventing her from fleeing a scary situation.
- Respect the individuality of your cat. Some like cuddling; others just want to sit nearby but not be picked up.
- Medication may help reduce your cat's stress.

# 10

# Oral Obsessions
## *Compulsive Grooming and Eating Behaviors*

Leslie Sinn, DVM, DACVB

Sara worried about Joey, her four-year-old domestic shorthair. He was a friendly, well-behaved cat who enjoyed their evening cuddles and play sessions with toys, but something had changed. Off and on for the past few months, he had been chewing on household items, and recently he had been doing it almost compulsively. He no longer chewed only on toys or items left on the floor. Now he was actively pulling stuff off the counter — plastic bags and cell phone cords — and destroying them. His new habit was getting expensive and dangerous!

Sara didn't think Joey was actually eating any of this stuff, but she had seen him spit up bits of plastic and was sure he was eventually going to hurt himself. Nothing she tried made a difference — yelling, spraying water, clapping her hands, booby traps. Joey just slunk away and then found something else to chew on.

What did change was Joey's attitude toward Sara. He now ran away when she approached, and Sara was devastated. Friends and family told her that Joey was being spiteful because she worked long hours and left him alone for a good part of the day. But Sara really wondered whether maybe there was something more to Joey's behavior. She reached out to her veterinarian for help.

The veterinarian checked Joey over from nose to tail, and the cat passed his hands-on exam with flying colors. Being thorough, the veterinarian also did some blood work. The good news was that Joey's blood work was normal. His kidneys, liver, thyroid, and other organs seemed to be working just fine. The bad news was that there was no obvious cause for his behavior change. The veterinarian referred Sara and Joey to a veterinary behaviorist because the veterinarian was very concerned that Joey was showing signs of a compulsive disorder.

The diagnosis of a compulsive disorder is often a diagnosis of exclusion, meaning that all other possible causes must first be ruled out. There is no single test that will determine whether the problem is medical or behavioral. In fact, often the two go hand in hand.

During the behavioral consultation, the veterinary behaviorist reviewed Joey's physical exam, laboratory findings, and history. He explained to Sara that sudden changes in behavior in adult cats are often due to a medical cause or a combination of a medical condition and unwanted behaviors that have become problematic. The big challenge is finding that underlying medical condition. In Joey's case, further testing was needed.

---

### What Is a Diagnosis of Exclusion?

A diagnosis of exclusion is often necessary when there isn't a specific test for a suspected disorder. Changes in behavior are symptoms that can be caused by a physical illness or other changes or problems in an animal's health, management, or environment. To make this kind of diagnosis, a medical professional must eliminate all the other possible causes of a symptom or set of symptoms.

---

When we think about compulsive behaviors, we tend to think about familiar problems in people, such as obsessive worrying, handwashing, or twirling or pulling of hair, as well as other repetitive behaviors. Cats can exhibit similar behaviors.

These behaviors are often symptoms of a physical illness or other issues surrounding a cat's health, management, or environment. Before a medical professional can make a diagnosis of a compulsive disorder, she must rule out all the other possibilities (see "What Is a Diagnosis of Exclusion?" above). Screening tests such as blood work, X-rays, ultrasound imaging, and even biopsies are needed to figure out what is going on and whether there is a medical component.

Not all repetitive behaviors are compulsive disorders. Behaviors can also increase in frequency due to learning (the behavior was rewarded, so it is repeated), association with stress (your cat is anxious and worried, so he grooms himself excessively), or an underlying medical disorder (see "Possible Medical Causes of Repetitive Behaviors" later in this chapter).

A diagnosis of a compulsive disorder is made when a cat cannot seem to control his behavior and often cannot be interrupted or distracted. The behavior may be in response to some sort of trigger (such as cuddling or snuggling) but not always. It can have a dramatic effect on both the cat's and the owner's quality of life, interfering with normal interactions and day-to-day activities. Unfortunately, compulsive behaviors can lead to medical problems. Chronic licking and hair pulling can result in sores and infections. Ingesting objects and a subsequent blockage of the intestinal tract can result in stomach upset, vomiting, diarrhea, or even death.

Research into the causes of compulsive disorders in cats is limited, so we are still unsure what causes these disorders. We do know that compulsive behaviors often begin in young adulthood (between one and two years of age), or spontaneously throughout a cat's life, depending on the underlying cause. We also know that the sex of the cat might be a factor. In a retrospective study by Dr. Michelle Bamberger and Dr. Katherine Houpt, DACVB, male cats were overrepresented in compulsive behavior cases presented to veterinary behaviorists. Oriental breeds, especially Birmans and Siamese, appear to be more at risk for compulsive disorders than other breeds. We aren't sure why that might be, but we suspect that genetics play a role in cats' compulsive behaviors, just as they often do in people's. In one study, Dr. Stephanie Borns-Weil, DACVB, found that early life development may be a risk factor, with small litter size and a weaning age of less than seven weeks associated with an increased risk of wool sucking in Birmans. In the same study, the presence of a medical condition increased the risk of wool sucking in Siamese.

## What Does That Mean?

**Compulsive disorder:** A diagnosis made when a behavior occurs at a high rate, nearly to the exclusion of typical feline behaviors, and interferes with the normal functioning of the cat. It may or may not have an underlying medical component.

**Repetitive behavior:** Any behavior that is repeated over and over again at a frequency, intensity, or duration beyond what is normal for cats. Not all repetitive behaviors become compulsive disorders, and some repetitive behaviors have an underlying medical cause.

**Attention-seeking behavior:** A behavior that's intended to attract the owner's attention. Common examples include yowling, scratching, and jumping on forbidden surfaces. Other behaviors may be more complex, such as tail chasing or eating nonfood items.

**Seizure:** A period of unusual behavior, loss of awareness, or even involuntary movements that cannot be interrupted. Seizures are caused by abnormal electrical activity in the brain, which can have several underlying causes; they vary in their severity.

## Facts, Not Fiction

The kinds of repetitive behaviors we see in cats with compulsive disorders include chewing and sucking on items such as wool or fabric, chewing and sucking on themselves, eating nonfood items (a condition known as pica), repeatedly licking surfaces or people, shaking or scratching the head and face, and chasing the tail. These behaviors often begin as repetitive behaviors that arise from normal activities but are directed at abnormal targets (chewing on plastic) or are excessive (grooming to the point of pulling out hair); are purposeless (sucking on fabric); or are repeated at a high frequency. Your cat may perform these behaviors so intensely and so often that he ignores you and won't engage in normal activities, such as playing or eating. He may continue the repetitive behaviors even though he is physically hurting himself.

Compulsive disorders can be caused by many things, and they are not always clearly understood. Remember, a behavior is a symptom of an underlying problem, such as a medical condition. Attention seeking, frustration, and conflict may also play a role. True compulsive behaviors are caused by changes in neurotransmitters, the chemical messengers of the brain. Endorphins, dopamine, glutamate, and serotonin have all been identified as contributors to compulsive disorders.

*Are all repetitive behaviors signs of a compulsive disorder?* The short answer is no. Not all repetitive behaviors are abnormal, so not all are considered signs of a disorder. If a cat is rewarded for a behavior, he will increase the frequency and even the intensity of the behavior. Our attention is often very rewarding to our cats. If you praise your cat and pet him for bringing you his mouse toy, he will be more likely to bring it to you in the future — all very normal!

When you give your cat attention for any behavior (wool sucking, for example), that behavior could increase in frequency and possibly become repetitive. Yet it is unlikely that your attention alone will result in a compulsive disorder, because the behavior problem is usually more complex than that.

Repetitive behaviors are considered problematic when they occur frequently for long periods of time, when they put your cat's health at risk, or when they begin to interfere with his normal functioning or interactions — in other words, when they begin to affect his quality of life and yours. At that point, they are labeled compulsive disorders. Owners of cats with repetitive behaviors often spend large amounts of time and money, as well as many sleepless nights, worrying about and trying to change their cat's behaviors. Mounting frustration and stress over a seemingly unsolvable problem can erode the bond and personal connection they have with their cat.

## Is That Really True?

What myths stand in our way of understanding this problem?

*Can cats really be obsessive?* That is actually a question we veterinary behaviorists ask ourselves all the time! We have no way of knowing whether cats obsess about things, since we can't ask them what they are feeling or why they are doing certain things. As a result, there is a lot of discussion and disagreement about what to call repetitive behaviors.

In human medicine, compulsive repetitive behaviors are commonly labeled obsessive-compulsive disorder (OCD), because the behaviors are preceded by recurrent thoughts or images that drive the person to perform the behaviors. But since we don't know what cats are thinking, many veterinarians simply refer to these behaviors as repetitive, and the diagnosis is a compulsive disorder.

*Does my cat just need more activities and exercise?* Lack of attention and exercise, though not usually the cause of a compulsive disorder, often contribute to it. A bored, stressed, under-exercised, environmentally deprived cat doesn't have many options, and some may choose to engage in repetitive behaviors. Honestly evaluating the amount of attention and exercise your cat is receiving is an important part of a comprehensive treatment plan.

By making sure your cat has many ways to spend his time, you can provide him with healthy alternatives to his unwanted repetitive behaviors. Generally, this is referred to as enrichment, a concept that has been widely embraced by animal behaviorists worldwide.

Cats in the United States are commonly kept indoors and have limited choices about how to spend their time. Providing them with perches, resting spots, hiding boxes, novel toys, food-dispensing toys, things to look at, playtime, and other ways to fill their days may help diminish behaviors such as compulsive fabric sucking. Providing exercise opportunities in the form of harness training and subsequent time outdoors on walks, fishing-pole toys or crinkle balls, an outdoor enclosure or catio, or even trick training are all wonderful ways to keep your cat engaged in positive interactions with you and his environment. (See chapter 3 for more information on providing the ideal environment for your cat. The Indoor Pet Initiative at The Ohio State University College of Veterinary Medicine website, https://indoorpet. osu.edu, is also a great place to learn about enriching your cat's environment).

*Is my cat being spiteful?* No. Repetitive behaviors are often due to an underlying medical condition, especially when they involve overgrooming or the cat chewing on himself. Your cat may be responding to pain and discomfort and cannot stop these behaviors. He may even be doing so to try to make himself more comfortable. He deserves your tolerance and patience, as well as a visit to your veterinarian.

Remember, some of these medical problems can be hard to diagnose and include dental problems, gastrointestinal issues, arthritis, and bladder pain, to name just a few. The process may entail multiple visits to your veterinarian and a team approach to finding a diagnosis, treatment, and, hopefully, a cure. It may also include seeking out veterinary specialists. In a case series by Dr. Stephen Waisglass and Dr. Gary Landsberg, DACVB, for example, eighteen of twenty-one cats who were thought to be pulling out their hair due to abnormal behavior were actually found to have underlying medical problems when additional laboratory tests were performed.

*Is my cat doing these things to get my attention?* Maybe, but it's unlikely. Certainly, a repetitive behavior is a plea for help. Your cat is not eating plastic because it is fun. He is most likely engaging in this abnormal behavior because his stomach hurts or he lacks appropriate items to chew on. Remember, a behavior can be reinforced by repetition — often accidentally — causing the cat to do it more frequently.

---

### How Can I Prevent My Cat from Developing Compulsive Behaviors?

We can't give very effective advice on preventing compulsive behaviors because we don't always know what causes them in the first place. Avoiding early weaning (before seven weeks of age), providing an enriched home environment, and trying to eliminate sources of stress for your cat may help. Even with these proactive measures, some cats might begin to perform repetitive behaviors that may at some time become compulsive due to abnormal brain chemistry or other health disorders.

---

## How Do We Begin?

Repetitive behaviors call for prompt veterinary intervention. Do not assume that your cat will get better on his own or with time. And don't assume that the cat will get better if you just ignore the behavior. Get help as soon as you possibly can. The longer a repetitive behavior continues, the more difficult it can be to successfully treat it.

Your veterinarian and any specialists he may refer you to will be able to rule out medical causes for your cat's behavior changes. Be especially suspicious if it is a problem, as with Joey, that appears suddenly in middle age, with no apparent underlying trigger.

Before you talk to your veterinarian, sit down and make some notes about the behavior. When did it start? Have there been any changes in your cat's environment? Can you develop a timeline? When does your cat perform the behavior now? How often? For how long? Can you identify a trigger? What have you tried to do to help his behavior? What made it better, and what made it worse? All of this information will provide vital clues to determining the underlying cause.

Be aware that many of the medical causes of repetitive behaviors can be hard to find and may require the help of a veterinary specialist and advanced testing to uncover. If you are referred to a veterinary behaviorist, she will need a detailed history to help your cat. Journaling is an excellent way to keep track of pertinent information. In addition, once a treatment plan is put in place, continued journaling will help you and your cat's medical team track the success of the plan.

In Joey's situation, the veterinary behaviorist carefully reviewed his physical examination, laboratory results, history, and behavior with Sara. She shared the fact that Joey had a sensitive stomach. He vomited once or twice a week, often just liquid with no food or hair in what he threw up. With this important piece of information, the veterinary behaviorist asked for help from an internal medicine colleague. They decided to do an ultrasound of Joey's belly. Fortunately, they didn't see any plastic or other foreign objects there, but they did find thickened intestinal walls, which can be a sign of irritation of the intestinal tract. Inflammatory bowel disease was the likely cause of Joey's behavior.

Joey was started on antinausea medication and a hypoallergenic diet. The veterinary behaviorist also developed a management, environmental enrichment, and behavior modification plan tailored to Joey and his home environment. Thankfully, Joey responded well to this comprehensive combination of medical care and other interventions.

What a lucky cat Joey was to have an owner like Sara, who didn't give up in her search for a solution to his behavior problem!

### Possible Medical Causes of Repetitive Behaviors

- Overgrooming and hair pulling: inhaled and food allergies, fungal disease, gastrointestinal disease, pain, altered sensation (paresthesia)
- Fabric sucking: gastrointestinal disease
- Pica (eating nonfood objects): gastrointestinal disease, endocrine disease, neurological disease

- Excessive licking: gastrointestinal disease
- Circling or pacing: pain, neurological disease, endocrine or metabolic problems, ophthalmologic problems, cognitive decline
- Nighttime waking and excessive vocalization: pain, cognitive decline, arthritis, hyperthyroidism, other endocrine or metabolic problems

Source: Adapted from Karen L. Overall, "Medical Differentials with Potential Behavioral Manifestations," *Veterinary Clinics of North America: Small Animal Practice* 33, no. 2 (2003): 213–29.

## Managing Compulsive Disorders

What can you do to control, change, or work through a compulsive disorder? What results can you expect, and how quickly?

If your cat has a true compulsive disorder, it must be actively managed, and that management must be ongoing. This section addresses some key points, but your cat's situation is unique, so be sure to work with your veterinarian or veterinary behaviorist to develop a plan that offers the best possible fit for you and your cat.

### Avoid the Trigger

The first step with any behavior problem, no matter what the cause, is to prevent your cat from repeating the same behavior over and over again. This is key. If your cat sucks wool blankets, put away the blankets. If he chews and eats plastic, put away the plastic bags and cords. Can't put everything away? Create a hazard-proof safe room where your cat can go when you can't supervise him.

Some things are hard to prevent. For example, how do you keep your cat from licking himself or pulling out his hair? In some situations, a physical barrier may be necessary, such as a soft collar or a cat onesie that will make it impossible for him to overgroom. But don't fool yourself; this is only a stopgap measure for your cat's safety. It is most definitely *not* a cure! And it can backfire if it increases your cat's anxiety and distress.

If you know your cat's compulsive behavior has a specific trigger, do everything you can to avoid that trigger. It's important to prevent your cat from practicing and getting better at performing his compulsive behavior. For example, if your cat's hair pulling and licking is set off by the presence of outside cats, block visual access by covering the patio door with opaque window film, or block his access to the ground-level window wells by closing the basement door.

## Desensitization and Classical Counterconditioning

If your cat's repetitive behaviors are set off by a specific trigger and you can identify it but not eliminate it, gradual exposure to the trigger while offering the cat something he enjoys, such as food or play, may help. This is called desensitization and classical counterconditioning. (See chapter 6 for more information on this process.)

For example, this technique could be used with a cat who frantically begins to pluck his hair whenever the grandchildren run screeching through your house. Provide your cat with a safe room so that he can avoid the kids in most situations. Under supervision, you might engage your cat in some pleasant way, such as with gentle petting or by feeding him a meal, while your grandchildren play quietly nearby, then return him to his safe room before the kids resume their rambunctious games.

## Response Substitution

Teaching an alternative behavior that is more appropriate, especially a behavior that is likely to prevent the undesired one, is a very successful strategy. For example, your cat can't yowl if you encourage him to pick up and retrieve a toy in a situation that would normally trigger him. (See "Putting It All Together" later in this chapter for an example of how this might work.)

## Redirection (Avoid Accidental Reinforcement)

Regardless of the cause, redirecting your cat away from his repetitive behavior is a critical part of management. You can do this in a number of

222 • DECODING YOUR CAT

ways by interrupting or distracting him. Examples include calling his name, throwing a toy, rustling a treat bag, getting up and walking away, using a birdcall whistle, or otherwise distracting his attention away from himself and directing it toward you.

Timing is very important. You don't want to accidentally make a link between the unwanted behavior and a reward. That is, you want to avoid teaching your cat to make the association *When I do X behavior, I get something good.* Preferably, have your cat do something else first, such as sit or come, then reward him with a treat, a toy, or some one-on-one time.

## Interrupt the Unwanted Behavior

You may have heard that you can interrupt your cat with a loud noise or some other action, such as using a spray bottle, that will startle him and cause him to stop his unwanted behavior long enough to direct him to another, more desirable activity, such as chasing a tossed toy. There are problems with this approach, though, because it can cause a fear reaction in him. In some situations, rather than stopping the unwanted behavior, your cat will simply associate you with the scary noise.

Remember Sara's cat, Joey, and how he started to avoid her when she clapped her hands or used a spray bottle to stop his chewing? Proceed cautiously, and if anything you try seems to make the situation worse, stop and seek help from a veterinarian or veterinary behaviorist.

## Enrichment

We have already discussed how your cat's environment can contribute to repetitive behaviors, especially if he experiences it as stressful. Make a careful assessment of your home and be sure your cat has an abundance of resources, such as water, food, perches, hiding boxes, resting places, scratching posts, litter boxes, toys, food-dispensing toys, playtime, and anything else you can think of. His environment should be peaceful and cat-centered, addressing his particular feline needs (see chapter 3).

It's important for your cat to remain active. Indoor cats in particular may not get enough exercise and may begin to fill their time with repetitive behaviors. Inactivity may contribute to boredom, and boredom may make a repetitive behavior worse. One way to combat this common problem is to set aside fifteen minutes twice a day to play, groom, exercise, and train your cat. (See chapter 6 for more on training.)

## Identify and Treat Other Behavior Problems

If your cat has multiple problems, all of them need to be addressed at the same time. This includes both behavioral and medical issues. Cats can experience a variety of health problems linked to stress, including inflammatory bowel disease, chronic cystitis, and dental disease, among others.

Many of these medical conditions have behavioral signs, such as eliminating outside the litter box, pica, increased aggression associated with pain, and decreased interest in play and human companions. All medical and behavioral conditions must be identified and addressed simultaneously.

## Putting It All Together

Sally was a cute, tiny domestic shorthair. She had been found as a kitten and bottle-fed by her owners. She never really thrived and had difficulty leaping on and off elevated surfaces. She was evaluated by her veterinarian, and X-rays revealed that her growth plates (areas of tissue near the ends of bones that normally fuse as the cat matures) had never closed. She was diagnosed with a rare condition, congenital hypothyroidism, and treated successfully with an oral thyroid hormone.

Around one year of age, she began chasing her tail, sometimes catching it and chewing on it until it bled. Pain medication seemed to help some, but the tail chasing and self-injury continued.

Sally's veterinarian referred her owners to a veterinary behaviorist. The veterinary behaviorist completed a physical exam and found that Sally was sensitive over her pelvis, where her tail met her back. Whenever that area was touched, her skin would ripple and she would try to move away. The veterinary behaviorist suspected pinched nerves due to Sally's skeletal abnormalities and recommended long-term treatment with a medication designed to help with nerve pain.

The behaviorist also recommended interrupting Sally if she started chasing her tail and rewarding a more appropriate behavior instead. Her owners discovered that gently swaddling her in a thick blanket was the best way to interrupt her inappropriate behavior. Anything else they tried only made the behavior worse.

In addition, the veterinary behaviorist suggested using targeting — having Sally touch her nose to one of the owners' fingers for a treat — as a competing appropriate behavior that could be rewarded. Sally enjoyed the new game and the activity it created for her. She became a targeting champ! Whenever her owners felt that she might be likely to chase her tail, they would ask her to target their finger and reward her with a treat and lots of attention.

By starting Sally on a more effective pain medication and rewarding a competing and more appropriate behavior, her owners were able to stop her self-mutilation and reduce her tail chasing from multiple times a day to once every few weeks.

## When Can Medication Help?

Medication can help cats with compulsive disorders. The choice of drugs can be limited, though, as little research has been done on cats (most studies involve dogs). The two most commonly used psychoactive drugs for compulsive disorders affect the production and effect of serotonin, a neurotransmitter within the brain that regulates mood. Individual studies by Dr. Kersti Seksel, DACVB, and Dr. Karen Overall, DACVB, have shown that this class of drugs is effective in treating compulsive disorders in cats.

If your cat is diagnosed with a compulsive disorder, he may need medication for months or even for life, depending on his situation. Psychoactive medication must be withdrawn slowly and only under direct veterinary supervision. Side effects of these drugs are, thankfully, rare, but carefully following safety protocols will help minimize the likelihood of an adverse response.

If your cat doesn't respond to medication, it may indicate that there is an underlying medical problem that has not yet been identified. To help make a diagnosis, your veterinarian may suggest trying different medications that treat suspected physical problems for a period of two to three weeks each and seeing whether your cat responds.

Response to treatment acts as a real-life test. For example, if your veterinarian suspects that pain is playing a role in your cat's behavior but cannot identify the source of the pain, she may ask you to give him pain medication for two to three weeks and report back about any changes in his behavior. If his behavior has improved, it suggests that he is uncomfortable or in pain, and the medication is helping reduce his discomfort.

---

### Key Points for Dealing with Compulsive Behaviors

- Avoid triggers.
- If a trigger can be identified, desensitize and countercondition your cat.
- Redirect your cat's behavior to a more appropriate alternative.
- Avoid accidentally reinforcing the behavior.
- Enrich your cat's environment.
- Use medications, if needed.
- Keep in close contact with your veterinarian and other members of your cat's health care team.

---

## Avoiding Pitfalls and Staying on Track

Having a cat who behaves oddly can be an isolating experience. Well-meaning family and friends are always ready to provide free advice. One of the common themes is blaming the owner, meaning that somehow you caused your cat to behave this way. Frequently, owners blame themselves. But, as discussed in this chapter, most of these behaviors have a medical basis, so it's unlikely that you caused the behavior.

Communicating with your cat's health care team is vital. That means sharing information and asking questions. Dealing with repetitive behaviors is a process of discovery that often involves multiple steps and many visits to your veterinarian or one or more veterinary specialists. A clear and open exchange of information is critical to be able to determine the underlying cause of your cat's behavior and to address all of his issues, as well as your concerns. Work with your cat's veterinary team to determine the best course of action for you and your cat.

Keep a record of your cat's behavior and his response to your interventions. Start with the baseline assessment you made when you first spoke to your veterinarian. Has anything changed about when your cat performs the behavior, how often, or for how long? What interventions have worked? What has made the behavior worse? Charting your cat's behavior will help you discover the best strategies for successfully dealing with the problem.

Frustration is common and understandable. One way to combat frustration is to have an action plan. Another is to use journaling to remind yourself that things are getting better.

As frustrated as you may get, avoid yelling, reprimanding, or otherwise punishing your cat. Remember that he is doing these things because he cannot help himself. Do you bite your nails when you are nervous? Do you twirl your hair before you have to speak in public? Would it help you to be more at ease if someone yelled at you or even hit you?

Punishment is never a good choice. It only increases fear and anxiety and will not resolve the behavior. Instead, your cat may start to fear and avoid you. See chapter 6 for more on the fallout associated with using punishment. The American Veterinary Society of Animal Behavior also has an excellent position statement on punishment (https://avsab.org/wp-content/uploads/2019/01/Punishment-Position-Statement_bleeds-10-2018-updated.pdf).

Similarly, you may feel or be told that your cat is being defiant or getting back at you by performing this behavior. As discussed earlier in this chapter, such behaviors are caused by underlying medical or psychological conditions, not feelings of revenge. Your cat would stop if he could, but he cannot.

Finally, be patient. Figuring out what is causing a compulsive behavior can be challenging and may involve trial and error and multiple medical tests. This process can be time-consuming and sometimes expensive. Once a treatment plan is set, actually changing the behavior may take some time as well. Behavior change doesn't happen quickly in any species, so it's best to embrace a long-term outlook that will involve months rather than days of work to see improvement.

## What Did We Say?

- A compulsive behavior is often due to an underlying medical condition.
- Compulsive behaviors may be exacerbated by stress or a poor environment.

- It is important to treat the whole cat and address the overall environment and all the enrichment options.
- Treatment focuses on management, avoiding triggers, providing an enriched environment, uncovering any underlying medical problems, redirecting your cat, and reinforcing appropriate behaviors, as well as classical counterconditioning and desensitization if a trigger can be identified.
- Medications can be very helpful in decreasing the intensity and frequency of compulsive behaviors.
- Compulsive behaviors can take time to address, so patience, celebrating small victories, and ongoing communication with your veterinary team is critical in helping your cat.

# 11

# I Know It's Normal, but How Do I Make It Stop?

*Normal Feline Behaviors That Drive People Crazy*

Beth Groetzinger Strickler, MS, DVM, DACVB, CDBC, and Wailani Sung, MS, PhD, DVM, DACVB

Craig adopted a kitten at an adoption event and was really excited — she was so adorable! He decided to name her Strudel. On the way home with her, he stopped at the pet supply store and picked up a litter box, litter, food and water bowls, cat food, a tall scratching post, and the cutest toys he could find. He set up all her new things and went right back to his regular routine.

Over the next few days, Strudel repeatedly jumped up on the dinner table, counters, and dressers, sampling Craig's dinner and knocking his belongings all over the floor. He came home one day to find her hanging from the curtains while looking out the window. She began to turn his sofa into shreds. Strudel seemed to start to wind up just as the sun was setting. She would meow and jump on Craig from behind corners and doors. Craig wondered, "What have I done wrong? What have I gotten myself into?"

Many people get a cat because they like the idea of a low-maintenance companion, but that is simply not the reality of owning a cat. Cats are an intelligent, highly social species. A cat's needs are more complicated than you might imagine. Part of living successfully with a new feline companion is learning what is normal for cats, as well as your cat's specific likes, needs, and interests.

Strudel's behaviors, for example, were all quite normal. Cats love to climb, rest in high places, search for their food, and mark areas with their claws. They love to play by hunting and pouncing. Unfortunately, these behaviors are annoying to us, and may even make some people consider giving up their cat. When you know what is and is not normal, what to expect from your cat, when and how to intervene, and when to seek help, the bond between you and her will grow stronger, and you can give her the best possible life.

In some situations, it may be necessary to consult with your veterinarian or a professional knowledgeable in cat behavior to determine whether an undesirable behavior is abnormal. Sometimes, more serious behaviors (such as aggression, anxiety, or compulsive behaviors) need to be ruled out or addressed. A qualified professional can help you get through this process.

---

### What Does That Mean?

**Species-specific behavior:** A behavior that is specific to members of a species and is unlearned; the animal knows how to do it without specific training. In cats, these behaviors include cheek rubbing, scratching, and hunting small prey.

**Motivation:** The reason an animal behaves in a particular way.

**Crepuscular:** More active at dusk and dawn.

**Nocturnal:** More active at night.

---

## Facts, Not Fiction

Cats are naturally curious animals with complex behaviors and behavioral needs. If left to their own devices, they often express normal cat behaviors in ways that people may not appreciate. Usually that happens because we are not fulfilling some of our cats' basic needs (see chapter 3), so they find other ways to display species-specific behaviors. When you understand what your cat needs and provide more appropriate ways for her to express her innate behaviors, everyone in the family will be happier.

In this chapter, we'll explore why your cat may scratch your furniture, ambush you, jump on the counters, leave you a pile of dead rodents, keep you up at night, and eat your houseplants. To start, we'll take a closer look at some of the most common problems you may encounter by walking through a typical day in Strudel and Craig's life.

*Craig is lying peacefully in bed thinking about the day ahead.* Scritch, scritch, scritch. *He hears the sounds of eight little nails digging into the side of the couch. Craig contemplates racing into the room to yell at Strudel or chase her away — as he has done many times before. Not only does the sound drive him crazy, but the couch is now hopelessly damaged.*

Why does Strudel do this? Scratching is a normal and essential cat behavior. All cats must scratch. First of all, it is necessary to remove the outer layers of their nails. It also keeps the nails razor sharp. When cats are unable to scratch, those outer layers thicken, and the nails can curve under and dig into the paw pads, causing pain and infection. Cats use their sharp claws to help them climb to high places and anchor themselves as they jump, so keeping them in good condition is important.

Scratching also stretches the spine and helps keep cats limber. Some cats scratch as a displacement behavior — a way to blow off excess energy. Scratching leaves a message behind as well — both in scent and visually. Scent marking is part of normal cat behavior, and scratching, like cheek rubbing, leaves the cat's scent on objects. Cats have scent glands between their paw pads (and on their cheeks and several other places) that deposit chemicals called pheromones to communicate with other cats.

For cats who spends all or some of their time outside, scent marking is a way of letting other cats know they are in the area and conveying details about their mood. Outside cats scratch on wooden fence posts, logs, and trees, but indoor cats like Strudel scratch on couches and other furniture, leaving gouges in the wood and small holes or tears in the fabric. All cats have an instinct to leave these marks, even if a cat is the only one in a home. It's like a cat's own personal billboard. Scent and visual marking makes cats feel more secure in their territory.

*As Craig walks sleepily down the hallway, thinking only of his morning coffee, Strudel ambushes him. Suddenly, out of nowhere, she is attached to his leg, hits him a few times with her back paws, and — poof — she is gone! Why would she do that?*

Most likely, she's just an exuberant young cat playing — although this could also be a sign of a serious aggression problem. This is a situation where Craig might want to have a discussion with a behavior professional to help figure out what is going on. Playful stalking behaviors are common in young cats. When cats engage in hunting behavior, it is to their advantage to sneak up on their prey. This does not mean that Strudel views Craig as food. Rather, play is a ritualized display of hunting behavior in cats, and silent, sneaky attacks are part of normal feline play. Other cats and other pets in the home may be targets as well.

Cats are great climbers and jumpers, and they love to explore new places and view the world from elevated spaces. Often this means they jump up on places like the kitchen counters. In Strudel's case, she may also have been enticed by fascinating smells as Craig prepared his meals, or a desire to be closer to Craig. As for clinging to the curtains, she had probably found a spot where the sun comes in the window, and it felt good to be right there. All those positive experiences made her want to visit those places again.

*When Craig comes into the kitchen, he finds Strudel on the countertop. He yells, "Get off!" and uses his arm to sweep her to the floor. As she lands, she's confused. Why can't she visit the countertop? It has so many exciting things to investigate!*

Chester demonstrates how much cats love to explore high places.
*Carolyn Phillips*

*Craig finishes his coffee, takes a deep breath, and starts back toward the bedroom. Strudel intercepts him in the hallway to deposit a large, dead insect at his feet.*

Cats are natural predators. This is likely how they were domesticated thousands of years ago. When humans started farming crops, they also started storing grain. And that attracted rodents — which attracted cats.

Hunting behavior, also known as predatory behavior, is instinctive. All cats are born with the hunting instinct, although some display this behavior more than others, and the hunting skills of cats can vary depending on their experience. When your cat sees any prey animal (often a toy or a moving person), she will immediately exhibit typical hunting body posture, crouching down and staring at the prey. She will begin to stalk the prey, approach, and then leap or pounce, catching her prey in her mouth or paws. The hunt will end as the cat bites the back of the prey's neck, killing the small animal.

*Craig disposes of the dead insect and thinks his day is back on track. Then he notices Strudel chewing on a houseplant. He thinks, "Hey, cats are carnivores; they eat meat. Why is she even doing that?"*

No one knows for sure why cats chew on plants, but there are many theories. Eating grass and other greens may be a normal, innate behavior in cats. Even though they do not need to eat grass or other plant material regularly as part of their diet, they must obtain some benefit from this behavior. It's not limited to domestic felines either. Fecal material recovered from wild relatives of cats, such as cougars, may contain up to 5 to 10 percent of grassy material.

*After a day at work, Craig comes home for a relaxing evening. Just as he's settling on the couch with his favorite movie, Strudel starts running around the house, jumping on and off the furniture. Craig decides to ignore her and go to bed. But in the middle of the night, Strudel wakes him up, meowing and knocking things on the floor.*

Nocturnal activities are a common complaint of cat owners. They are especially annoying for people who spend all day at work and want to come home to some peace and quiet. Cats are naturally crepuscular (active at dawn and dusk), because that's when their most common prey is out and about. The average cat spends a significant amount of time sleeping and resting. An outdoor farm cat may sleep or rest between seven and eleven hours a day, while an indoor laboratory cat (whose light and dark cycle is controlled) may sleep or rest ten to sixteen hours.

Unfortunately, some indoor pet cats have been reported to sleep or rest up to twenty hours per day — typically because they have nothing else to do. It's no wonder they are awake in the evening when their owners get home from work. Their human companions are the only thing happening in their day!

## Is That Really True?

*What myths stand in our way as we try to cope with cats' annoying behaviors?* The first is probably that cats are being spiteful or are just plain naughty when they behave the way Strudel does. Whether your cat is jumping on your counter, eating your plants, or scratching your furniture, these activities are natural behaviors for all cats. Cats of all sizes, ages, and breeds scratch, vocalize, climb, and hunt. Your cat is not out to get you. It's just what she does.

*Will cats hunt even if no one teaches them?* Even if you got her as a young kitten without any exposure to the great outdoors? Even if she has never seen another cat do it?

Yes.

Hunting is an instinctive behavior in cats. They will hunt when there is an opportunity to do so. Your kitten does not need a role model to teach her. When your cat sees a small, furry creature scamper across the floor, she will go after it. Cats have receptors in their eyes that are immediately drawn to fast-moving objects. Hunting is part of a sequence of predatory behaviors triggered by the sound or sight of the prey animal.

*Why does my cat hunt if she's not hungry, and why does she bring the things she kills to me?* The underlying motivation for capturing and killing prey is not necessarily hunger. In the wild, cats hunt and eat multiple prey items throughout the day. They never know when the next meal will show up, so they do not let any opportunity pass. In other words, your cat may not be able to help herself. If she is truly hungry, she will eat the prey after killing it. When she leaves the dead bodies behind, it may very well be because she is full. Your cat may leave the prey item where she lost interest in it (because it stopped moving), bring it into the house (if she's allowed outdoors) to possibly snack on it later, or bring it to you as a request for play (*Please make this toy move again*).

*I use a squirt bottle when I'm home to keep the cat off the counter, but I see evidence that she gets up there when I'm not home. What can I do?* We know that cats associate behaviors with consequences (see chapter 6). Some cats might associate the presence of the water bottle with the consequence of getting squirted rather than the action of getting on the counter. Those cats may not learn to stay off the counter; instead, they may learn that water bottles predict bad things. When you are home, you need to reward your cat for walking over to the counter, looking up at it, and walking away. She made the right choice. If you play with her and engage her in training games, she may be too tired to jump on the counter when you leave for the day. Alternatively, your cat may just want a high perch in the kitchen, so providing a high vantage point that is not the counter may do the trick.

*Why do cats like to knock things on the floor?* Cats are curious and interested in whatever is in their environment. Many cats like to use their paws and mouth to engage with items in their world. Sometimes that may mean your cat will inadvertently knock an item on the floor while she is using her paws to manipulate it. Sometimes she may be trying to pick the item up, and it falls down. Other times she may find the item fun to bat around and play with, or enjoy watching the motion as it falls, or like the interesting sound it makes when it hits the floor. Or she may knock things over to get your attention. If your cat knocks something on the floor and you respond by engaging with her in any way, she is likely to do it again.

Cats will examine whatever is in their world. One of Porter's favorite pastimes is investigating shoes. *Debra F. Horwitz*

*Why does my cat continue to scratch my sofa even when I have bought her a scratching post and a scratching pad and placed them right next to the sofa?* Sometimes a cat needs to stand on her hind legs and really stretch when she scratches. If your sofa is taller than the scratching post, she may prefer the longer length. If you have just a scratching pad on the floor next to the sofa, she may prefer to scratch on a vertical surface. If you have just a post, she may also want a horizontal surface and end up scratching the top of the sofa or the seat cushion. An easy solution is to provide her with a tall scratching post that also has a horizontal surface for her to scratch. That way, you will satisfy both her needs without sacrificing your sofa. If your sofa still carries the wounds inflicted by your cat, she may go back to it because of the visual and scent marks on it. If this is the case, you may need to protect the sofa with a plastic throw or a slipcover.

## How Do We Begin?

If it is in a cat's nature to perform a certain behavior, is all hope lost? Absolutely not! Cats can be trained, and behaviors can be changed. (See chapter 6 to learn how.) Understanding the underlying motivations behind the behavior is an important first step. Deterring your cat from performing a natural behavior in a way you find unacceptable also involves a degree of human behavior modification. In other words, you'll need to change what you offer your cat and how you interact with her. These strategies typically include:

- Providing plenty of physical and mental stimulation
- Using management techniques to prevent or discourage the behavior you don't want
- Offering more appropriate outlets for your cat to express the behavior in a way that's okay with you

Providing an enriching environment where cats can hunt and explore is often all it takes to satisfy most of their basic needs. For example, feeding cats several meals a day mimics their natural eating habits, and offering food-dispensing toys or hiding little food bowls around the house encourages them to hunt for their food and provides appropriate physical and mental outlets for their energy.

Scheduling ten to twenty minutes of playtime with appropriate toys every day affords additional physical and mental stimulation. Engaging your cat in routine, scheduled training sessions will help her find an outlet for her energy and her need to be mentally active. The training sessions will give her the attention she craves and allow her to work off any excess energy she has accumulated during the day — while at the same time giving you a positive way to interact with her.

Do your best to limit temptations and set your cat up for success — that's what we mean by management techniques. Cover your furniture to prevent her from scratching, put your plants out of reach, do not leave food out on the kitchen counters, and do not allow her outside if you don't want her to hunt small critters.

Whenever possible, distract your cat either before she starts or while she is performing a behavior you don't like. When you have her attention, redirect her to other behaviors you would prefer. For example, if you see her approaching the side of the couch, don't wait for her to scratch it. She doesn't know it's the wrong thing to do. Get her attention by calling her name, then direct her to a scratching post (maybe even scratch it a few times yourself) and reward her for scratching there. Instead of allowing your cat to ambush you in the hallway, call her to come to you and then toss a few toys for her to chase in the opposite direction, so you can walk down the hallway unscathed.

## Getting on the Counter and Other High Spots

We have already discussed why cats like to be up high. This is one of those situations where changing your cat's behavior may need to start with a change in your own behavior — along with a change in the cat's environment.

Keep the counters clear of anything of interest to your cat, such as food or plants or even a sun-warmed place to rest. Any of these things will intermittently reward her for jumping up on the counter, even if she only gets access to them every once in a while.

Deterrents may be helpful in the short term to keep your cat off a particular area, but they will not address the underlying motivation for her to go to that location. The problem is that deterrents may cause anxiety and stress, especially if your cat is unable to express her normal climbing and perching behavior elsewhere. If she's very scared by something that makes a loud noise or sprays air, she may injure herself when attempting to run away. Plus, if the deterrent is associated with you, there is the risk of damaging your precious bond — and of teaching your kitty that she can jump up on anything when you are not around. (See the next section for detailed information about deterrents.)

Ultimately, if your cat loves to climb and to rest on high perches, placing a deterrent in one spot will just motivate her to find another elevated area to explore or rest on. So the best answer is to provide her with places where she is allowed to climb. Cat trees (both homemade and purchased) are great options. Even a simple box or paper bag on a high shelf may be of interest to her. Place these new elevated options in areas where your cat already climbs up high.

A good cat tree can offer high perching areas, hiding areas, and a tall, sturdy scratching post. *Craig Zeichner*

Cats typically like to rest on soft surfaces. Place a blanket, thermal mat, or cat bed in an acceptable elevated area, and reward your cat when she is resting there. To make these areas even more attractive, hide small morsels of food there. Not only will this entice your cat to the new spot, but she will be hunting as well — accomplishing two enrichment tasks at once. To keep things interesting, remember to vary the rewards she finds in the areas you want her to explore.

Cats are also attracted to warm areas. Offering a heated bed or thermal mat specifically designed for cats will make a resting space even more appealing.

## Scratching and Destroying the Furniture

Let's take a step back and examine your home. Are you providing your cat with enough scratching posts? Some cats prefer to scratch in more than one location, so make sure to offer your cat at least two options for scratching in different rooms of the house.

Are you providing your cat with a choice of scratching posts made from different materials? Some cats have a preference for certain materials. Commercial cat trees come in a variety of materials, ranging from carpet to sisal to cardboard to natural wood. Offer your cat a choice. For example, provide an inexpensive cardboard scratcher laced with catnip alongside a tall one wound with sisal. When you find out which one she scratches on more frequently, offer more scratchers made of that material. If she has picked your favorite chair and refuses any other substitute, it may be worth your time to get a piece of the upholstery and affix it to one side of a scratching post. Reward her when she scratches on the material.

Keep in mind that some cats may prefer to scratch on horizontal surfaces, such as your carpeting or stair treads. If your cat seems to prefer this, it's very important to provide scratchers that fulfill her horizontal scratching desires. You can easily figure out if your cat has a horizontal versus a vertical scratching preference by providing two scratchers made from her preferred material. Place one in a horizontal position on the floor, and stand the other one up vertically. Then see which one she uses more.

---

### Make Your Own Scratching Post

If you are handy, you can make your own sturdy scratching post. Nail two pieces of untreated wood together at a ninety-degree angle. Make sure the piece of wood you use for the base is big and heavy, so the scratcher doesn't wobble when your cat uses it. The upright piece should be tall enough that your cat has to stretch to reach the top when she's standing on her back legs.

Cut a two-by-four to make a diagonal scratching surface extending from the upright piece to the base, completing a triangle. Wrap the two-by-four with sisal or a rough fabric. Nail it securely to the base and the top of the upright, making sure the nails do not stick out. Another good option is to use a wooden log as the angled piece. Wood is the natural choice for most cats living in the wild. Do not use a chemically treated log intended for your fireplace, however.

Is the scratching post located in an area where the cat spends most of her time? Cats living outdoors tend to scratch on objects within their home territory more often than on objects around the periphery. They leave marks on prominent objects to create a visual signal to other cats in the area. That's why some cats at home prefer to scratch on furniture in a prominent location in one room. After all, what good is it to leave a message that no one will see? Also, just as you may want to stretch your arms out after a good nap, some cats may prefer to scratch close to where they nap.

Provide scratching posts in areas frequented by your cat instead of hiding them behind the sofa or in a back room or the basement. Place one close to where your cat prefers to sleep. Typically, she will tell you where the best spot is — right next to the piece of furniture she is currently scratching. When she starts to scratch her post instead of the furniture, praise and reward her. Then, over the next several weeks, slowly move the scratching post (inches a day) to your desired location, but still within the area preferred by your cat.

Some cats adjust to these changes right away. It may take time for others to learn to like the new options. Be patient and encourage your cat to use the scratching post. While you are retraining her, deter her from scratching on furniture by placing a plastic cover or double-sided sticky tape over the scratched areas. Tape made to deter cats (such as Sticky Paws) is sticky enough to stay on your furniture without leaving behind a gummy residue. Many cats find the stickiness of the tape unpleasant, which provides extra motivation for them to switch from the furniture to the new scratching post.

Sometimes you can entice your cat to scratch on the post by rubbing catnip on it or by playing with a toy that you make move up and down the post. A pheromone product called Feliscratch by Feliway promotes scratching on objects to which it has been applied. Feliscratch contains an artificial version of the pheromone that cats release from the scent glands on their paws when they scratch. By applying the product to the desired surface, you can encourage your cat to scratch there. Over a few weeks, she will learn to consistently scratch on that surface, and the product will no longer be needed.

Pavlov's Cat Scratch Feeder is a feeder that looks like a big scratching post. When your cat scratches and pulls down on the post, it releases food at the bottom. This helps reinforce using the item. She learns *I scratch here, I eat. The more I scratch, the more I get to eat.*

Plastic nail caps glued over your cat's nails can limit the damage caused to your furniture. You can apply them yourself or have a groomer or veterinary technician do it. The nail caps will need to be replaced every six to eight weeks, and some will often fall off or be chewed off within two to three weeks. And you will still need to give your cat plenty of attractive scratching options.

Both the American College of Veterinary Behaviorists and the American Veterinary Medical Association believe that declawing should not be a routine procedure performed on nearly every cat (as it once was). (See chapter 7 for a discussion of this position.) Although ethically questionable, declawing does reduce the risk of injury if scratching directed toward people is part of a cat's aggressive behavior. However, without behavioral interventions, concurrent changes in environmental triggers, and other treatment options, it is unlikely on its own to be curative and should be avoided in nearly all cases.

---

### Make Scratching Posts User-Friendly

Scratching is an essential part of being a cat. With patience and persistence — and the right scratching posts in the right places — you can train your cat to scratch on the surfaces you want her to scratch on.

- Place a scratching post right next to the furniture your cat is currently scratching.
- Offer a variety of scratching surfaces, sizes, and shapes instead of just one option.
- Always offer praise and food rewards or pats whenever your cat scratches on her scratching post.

---

## Hunting

Our domestic cats may be small compared with their larger, more powerful wild cousins, but they are also very successful hunters. If your cat hunts away from home, you may never realize what a mighty hunter she is. Successful feline hunters can have an impact on the wildlife in their yard or the immediate neighborhood. Cats are often blamed for a reduction in the number of songbirds in an area, for example, and that should be a consideration when they are allowed outside.

The easiest way to protect local wildlife from your cat is not to let her outside. Cats who stay indoors live longer, healthier lives and avoid the risk of infections and devastating interactions with automobiles, predators, and malicious humans.

Alternatively, you can limit and supervise the time your cat spends outside. Consider installing cat-safe fencing to keep her in your yard. Buy or build a window box or catio (a patio for your cat) so that she can enjoy some outside time but not hunt small creatures. Train her to wear a harness and leash so that you can hold on to her when you go out together. But never leave your cat outside alone on a leash or tether!

You can reduce your cat's urge to hunt by providing plenty of food so she's not hungry. A well-fed cat may still stalk, chase, and kill prey, but she may be less likely to eat it. And some cats may be less motivated to pursue those little prey animals on a full stomach. Your cat may prefer to take a nap after a satisfying meal.

You can also satisfy your cat's hunting instinct and keep her entertained indoors by using food-dispensing toys. Choose different types of toys to keep this activity interesting and challenging. You can make a multitude of toys using simple household items such as toilet paper rolls, empty yogurt containers, and small cardboard boxes. These toys can provide endless minutes or hours of amusement for your cat. You can also find plenty of food-dispensing toys at the pet supply store, as well as feeding stations (some of which look like space stations), which will require your cat to stick her paw through the opening, bat at the dry food to knock it down to a lower level, and then fish it out.

## The Three-Minute Food-Dispensing Toy

Place your cat's dry food in an empty cardboard toilet paper or paper towel roll, fold the ends in, punch holes in the cylinder, and let the good times roll. You may need to roll the toy around several times

> and let your cat see the kibble falling out of it to entice her to work for her food.

If your cat is not interested in playing with food-dispensing toys, you can still make her hunt for her food. Buy several small food dishes or soy sauce dishes and divide your cat's meal between three to five dishes; place them around the house. Initially, you can put one dish in her normal feeding area, then place the others in areas she is likely to walk past or visit, such as the windowsill or her favorite napping spot. You must make sure your cat is getting enough to eat every day, though, so begin slowly. If she's having trouble "hunting" at first, call her attention to the dishes as you put them down.

It's easier to change the behavior of cats who have never experienced true hunting in the outside world. Cats who have practiced outdoor hunting need patient owners. The fact that they've been able to practice this instinctive behavior makes it difficult to change. It takes people several weeks, even months, to change a behavior, and cats are no different. Bells or ultrasonic devices may limit their hunting success by warning prey of their approach. There is also a product called the CatBib, which inhibits the cat's ability to kill birds (it's literally a bib), but it may also cause frustration and fear. Not all cats will be deterred by these products, and some wily cats will still be able to hunt.

## Waking You Up at Night

Why do cats get the crazies at night? A young, energetic cat like Strudel who has been lying around the house all day may be craving interaction and engagement when you return in the evening. If you don't play with her before you go to bed, she'll still be wound up. A short play session in the early evening and another one just before bedtime may help satisfy her need for activity.

Engaging your cat in activities during the day — when you are typically not at home — may require some strategic planning. Opportunities for her to interact with her environment need to be interesting to her and offer her a reward that is motivating enough to keep her at it. Food-dispensing toys can certainly be a part of keeping your cat moving while you're at work. It may require some trial and error to determine what play objects will keep her active enough during the day that she will sleep well at night.

Another option is to provide a playmate for your cat. This can be a cat or kitten who has a similar activity level and play style. (See chapter 5 for advice about how to avoid problems when introducing a new cat.) A friend of another species may also be a great companion. Many cats develop wonderful friendships with dogs, although many others always remain terrified of canines. Remember that each pet will need individual attention, resources, veterinary care, and more.

Cats who wake up during the night may be responding to noises they hear outside the home, including wildlife and street noises. They also may be reacting to noises they hear inside the home, such as alarms beeping, owners snoring, or even the rustling of mice or other critters in the walls.

Some breeds (such as Siamese and other Oriental breeds) are just naturally chatty and may simply be attempting to communicate with you. If you don't want your cat to talk to you during the night, don't answer her when she starts a midnight conversation.

Like many Siamese, Squeak is quite talkative. *Wailani Sung*

If your cat cries or yowls throughout the night, make sure she has been spayed (or he has been neutered) and is not responding to hormones. Some hormonal or endocrine disorders also can cause excessive vocalization. So can pain and discomfort, as well as illnesses such as high blood pressure and hyperthyroidism. To rule out these problems, you need to take your cat to the veterinarian.

An older cat who has slept well during the night for most of her life may begin to have disrupted sleep as she ages. She may have difficulty falling asleep, or she may wake up periodically throughout the night. She may even be a bit disoriented and call out. These changes in behavior could be due to pain or another medical condition, such as cognitive dysfunction syndrome (a disease similar to Alzheimer's disease in people), so a visit to your veterinarian is in order. (See chapter 13 for more about senior and geriatric cats.)

Some cats like to get up early and eat early, and will persistently pester their owners until breakfast (or a two a.m. snack) is provided. Remember, cats are very smart and learn quickly. Many enjoy any type of attention from us, whether it's food, play, or even yelling at them. Make sure you do not accidentally reward your cat for waking you up in the night.

Most cats prefer to stick to a routine. Your cat may have established a routine of waking up early for breakfast (even on Sunday). Food-dispensing toys left out overnight will help satisfy cats who get hungry at all hours. A feeder with a timer that automatically dispenses food may appease cats who wake up their owners early in the morning for their breakfast. Set the timer to go off a few minutes *before* the time the cat typically starts meowing. This will take you out of the sequence of events.

Insecurity can be another cause of nighttime waking. Think about whether something has changed in the cat's routine — or yours. One of our feline patients began waking up at night after a move to a new home. After some sleuthing, the owners realized that the cat's treasured afghan had not been unpacked and placed on her favorite sleeping spot. Once the afghan was set out, she returned to her usual sleeping routine. Problem solved!

## Pouncing on People

The first step in helping your cat learn how to play appropriately is to engage in daily structured play sessions using toys that are far away from your body (such as fishing-pole or wand toys), items you toss, or items that move on their own. Kittens tend to outgrow pouncing behaviors if they are redirected to appropriate toys and not reinforced for pouncing. If there's a time of day when your cat typically likes to engage in these playful behaviors, schedule the play session shortly *before* she is usually ready to play.

Never play with your cat using your hands or feet. Make the initial play sessions short, then extend to fifteen minutes at a time once or twice a day. Use toys that move, flutter, and bounce to allow your cat to engage in her natural stalking, running, and attacking behaviors. Be sure the toys are safe and can't be swallowed, and put away string toys when you are not playing with your cat.

To avoid boredom and keep your cat fully engaged, rotate and change the toys she plays with. If she loves a laser pointer, be sure that you allow her to "catch" the light by settling it on a treat or toy she can pounce on and catch. Otherwise, the game may become frustrating and just get her more wound up.

Clicker training is a good way to help cats burn off excess energy. You can use it to teach your cat a behavior that is incompatible with pouncing on you, such as "go to your perch" or "sit on your mat." If you both enjoy clicker training, you can also teach her cool tricks, such as "high five" and "roll over." (You'll find excellent ideas for kitty training at PositiveCattitudes, www.youtube.com/user/PositiveCattitudes/videos and www.clickertraining.com.)

Some cats may benefit from outdoor exploration in a safe environment. (See "Hunting" earlier in this chapter.) Training your cat to wear a harness and leash is not very difficult. Walking her will allow her to engage in a continuously changing, structured activity. There are many commercially available outdoor cat tunnels and playpens, as well as innovative cat-safe fencing options, all of which may allow your cat to explore the outdoors safely (see, for example, Purr...fect Fence, www.purrfectfence.com; Coyote Roller, https://coyoteroller.com; and Oscillot, https://oscillot.com.au).

Many cats can learn to wear a harness especially designed for cats and walk nicely on a leash. *Debra F. Horwitz*

Consider adding a feline playmate to your home. A good playmate is one who will interact well with your cat, has a similar energy level, and is interested in playing in a similar way. Remember that introducing a new cat to a resident cat may take time and patience and may not work out (see chapter 5). This strategy typically works best with playful kittens and may not be as helpful with adult cats.

It may be helpful to hang bells on your cat's collar so that you know when she is approaching and can remove yourself from the area or have a toy ready to play with. Be sure to use a safe, quick-release collar that will not get hung up or tangled in items in the environment. Some cats find wearing a bell a fun challenge. We have had feline patients who have been able to quietly stalk without jingling up to ten tiny bells on their collar!

## Eating Houseplants

Eating plant matter is a natural behavior for cats. The easiest way to prevent your cat from eating your houseplants is to give her a pot of cat grass or some other safe plant she can chew on. Many pet supply stores carry seeds or grass appropriate for cats to eat. Trim the grass weekly to promote growth of the tips. If your cat tends to vomit after eating grass, try leafy kitchen herbs instead, such as dill, mint, basil, thyme, parsley, or rosemary.

Feral cats have been observed eating greens, and your cat may appreciate some grass grown just for her. *Carlo Siracusa*

---

### Plant Safety

Make sure all the plants you have are nontoxic. Even if you place the plants out of reach, your cat may figure out a way to reach them. When consumed, plants from the lily family cause fatal kidney failure in cats, and other plants pose dangers to kitties as well.

To see if your plants are safe for cats, check out the Pet Poison Helpline (www.petpoisonhelpline.com). And to find a list of cat-safe plants, see "Poisonous Plants" at the ASPCA's website (www.aspca. org/pet-care/animal-poison-control/toxic-and-non-toxic-plants).

---

Meanwhile, place your houseplants out of reach — perhaps on tall shelves or hanging from ceiling hooks. If you cannot keep your plants out of your cat's reach, you can apply a bitter-tasting substance that is available at pet supply stores or spray the plants with white vinegar (if you don't mind the smell). Apply either substance to the underside of the plant's leaves so that when your cat chews on them, she may be deterred by the taste. Keep in mind that some cats may not mind the taste and will keep chewing, only to vomit up what they have eaten on your nice carpet.

Some cats just like to chew on things, especially if their diet is almost all soft foods. Provide your cat with appropriate items to satisfy her chewing needs, such as dental treats or food just for cats that may provide a different texture for chewing. This might prevent them from eating your plants.

If your cat seems to be chewing on your plants only in your presence, she may have learned that you will give her attention when she does this — even if it's negative attention like shouting. When you see her moving toward a plant, head her off. Get her attention by calling her name and having her come to you for interaction, rather than attacking your plant. Do not let her repeat the cycle of "chew on plant, get my person's attention." Instead, preemptively distract her and provide her with positive, more appropriate activities.

If you catch your cat in the act, distract and redirect her to perform other behaviors or focus on other activities. First, get her attention by making a novel noise. Once she has stopped chewing on the plant, immediately redirect her to another, more acceptable behavior, such as chasing after a crinkle ball that you just threw or trying to catch a fishing-pole toy that you are dangling. Clicker training can be useful to teach her to perform some simple tricks and take her mind off of chewing your plants. You can also use clicker training to reinforce more appropriate behaviors, such as playing with other toys or chewing on her cat grass.

Roses are nontoxic to cats—although some felines do not appreciate the prickly thorns. *Wailani Sung*

## Avoiding Pitfalls and Staying on Track

Cat owners tend to default to punishment (such as squirt bottles, booby traps, and loud noises) to change a cat's behavior. While this may work in the short term, it will not change who your cat is and the natural behaviors she needs and wants to express. If you are tempted to use a punishment for a quick fix, remember that your actions may result in an aggressive response from your cat. It may also increase your cat's anxiety and damage the bond between you. And your cat will likely be smart enough to learn not to do certain things in your presence, but to continue to do them when you are not watching.

The more positive solution is to embrace your cat's natural behaviors and provide ways for her to express them that work for both her and you. Then use positive reinforcement to teach her where and how she can perform these behaviors. Treats and praise can be surprisingly powerful motivators for your cat to climb on the cat tree instead of your curtains, or scratch on the scratching post instead of your couch. Clicker training can be used to reinforce appropriate behaviors, redirect your cat to alternative behaviors, and teach her fun new tricks that stimulate her brain.

One of the most common errors is to accidentally reward your cat, whether it's chasing her after she has pounced on you, petting or feeding her when she wakes you up in the middle of the night, or giving in to her cries to be let outside. Some cats can learn from just a single interaction or midnight snack that a particular behavior brings them the desired reward, and then they become persistent.

When you try to ignore the behavior, often the cat will persist and perhaps even increase her efforts to get a reward by engaging in the same behavior over and over again. This is called an extinction burst, where the behavior appears to get worse and increases in frequency. But if you remain consistent and persistent, give your cat appropriate outlets, and don't reward the undesirable behavior, it will eventually fade away.

Eliminate temptation by restricting your cat's access to certain areas or items. If you can't get her to stop chewing your plants or scratching one particular chair, for example, keep them in a room she's not allowed in. If she won't stay out of the trash, get a trash can with a secure cover. If she insists on cruising for food on the countertops, don't leave food out. If she gets up on your dresser and knocks your watch on the floor, put it away.

Be sure to reinforce appropriate behaviors and not fixate on your cat when she is doing the wrong thing. When a talkative cat is quiet, pay attention to her at that moment. When your cat walks up to a plant, sniffs it, and walks away, praise and toss treats toward her. Tell her what a good girl she is every time she uses her scratching post. Teach her where *to* go instead of where *not* to go. Teach her what she *can* do instead of punishing her for what she should *not* do.

And finally, be patient with your cat. Most of what we call nuisance behaviors are normal cat behaviors. Your cat is not doing these things out of spite. It takes time to change an annoying behavior. Understand this, and you will be more successful in the long run.

## What Did We Say?

- Many of the behaviors we find undesirable are natural feline behaviors that your cat is hardwired to do. You can't make her not do them, but you can redirect her to more appropriate outlets for them.
- Cats like to explore and interact with their environment. They especially like to be in elevated areas. Provide your cat with raised

perches she is allowed to use, and encourage her to explore and rest in those areas.

- Cats like to use their claws for scratching. Provide your cat with scratching posts that are tall and sturdy, covered with a material she likes, and in a location she likes, and reward her when you see her using them.
- There are many alternatives to declawing, a procedure that is not endorsed or recommended by the American College of Veterinary Behaviorists or the American Veterinary Medical Association.
- Hunting is a natural feline behavior. Many cats can satisfy their desire to hunt through play and alternative ways of being fed at home.
- Cats who wake owners early in the morning or keep them up at night may benefit from physical and mental engagement throughout the daylight hours, to help them reset their internal clock.
- Many cats are very playful but don't know how to play well with you. You can teach your cat how to play with you in ways you both enjoy.
- Cats and houseplants are sometimes a risky mix. Cats eat plants for many reasons, both medical and behavioral. You can redirect your cat by providing her with safe plants to eat, giving her other items to chew on, or engaging her in other activities.
- Be proactive by teaching your cat what you want her to do rather than only responding to her misbehaviors. Cats are trainable and enjoy our attention. Have fun helping your cat learn how to live well in your home.

# 12

## The Cat Outside: So Close but So Scared

*Getting to Know That Cat You*
*Just Can't Seem to Touch*

Sara Bennett, MS, DVM, DACVB

A beautiful orange and white cat had been hanging around Susan's house for weeks. He looked thin but alert. He was skittish and would not let her get close. She began leaving him food, and he would creep up to eat as soon as she left the area. After several weeks of feeding him, Susan could get closer and closer to him.

One very cold night, he decided he would come into the safety and warmth of the garage. Feeling bad for him, Susan eventually let him into the house. Things went downhill from there. He hid all the time, hissed when she came near, and did not use a litter box. Her good deed became a disaster.

Cats who live outdoors without much human intervention are free to express their normal behaviors, but that freedom comes with risks. They can suffer injuries from cars and trucks, attacks and possible death from dogs or other animals, hostility from some humans, parasites, and other medical problems. They also may endanger other species through their prodigious hunting ability.

Often these cats come into our homes, but because of their lack of prior exposure to a home environment and what it entails, they are fearful and may have difficulty adjusting. Many require specific interventions (including medication) to make them comfortable with indoor life and human companionship.

In this chapter, you will learn how to help and understand feral cats

— whether it is just one cat or a large group — and find up-to-date information on trap-neuter-return programs and feral cat colony management strategies and sanctuaries.

The subject of outdoor cats can be a volatile one. There are many different points of view, including those of cat lovers, veterinarians, and wildlife advocates. It is no secret that cats living outside have a higher risk of disease and injury and that they prey on wildlife such as small rodents, lizards, and birds. Some suggested solutions to the "problem" of outdoor cats include keeping cats strictly indoors; bringing all free-roaming cats to an animal shelter or euthanizing them; or trapping, neutering, and releasing or relocating all free-roaming cats.

While all of these ideas could be viable options for individual cats, none of them works well as a "one size fits all" solution.

## Facts, Not Fiction

Are all outdoor cats the same? Definitely not. A cat found outside may belong to someone who lets him go outside. An outdoor cat might also be someone's indoor cat who got lost after accidentally getting outside. Worst case, an outdoor cat may be a socialized cat who was dumped outside. And some outdoor cats may truly be feral cats.

What's the difference between an indoor-outdoor cat and a feral cat? The answer lies in socialization. A feral cat is the offspring of domestic cats but has had little or no contact with people, especially during his sensitive developmental socialization period as a kitten. This cat will behave essentially like a wild animal, even though he still belongs to a domesticated species. He will fear people and do everything he can to avoid them. If he can't, he will defend himself against them, just as he will if he encounters any predator.

### What Does That Mean?

**Socialization:** A learning process that occurs only during the sensitive socialization period when kittens are especially receptive to being exposed to different environments, situations, and individuals of their own and other species. If they're exposed in a positive manner to people, other cats, dogs and other animals, handling, and a variety of different environments and situations, they will be less likely to be fearful of them later in life. In cats, this period is generally accepted to be between two and seven weeks of age for prime socialization to people. The term "socialization" is often incorrectly used when what is really meant is exposure, since socialization occurs only during a specific period of time in early life.

**Domestic cat:** *Felis catus,* a small, typically furry, carnivorous mammal. Feral, semi-feral, stray, and pet cats are all domestic cats. They are all the same species; the difference between them is the level of social experience they have had with people.

**Stray cat:** A domestic cat who is unowned. Typically, these cats live outside and work to gain the necessary resources — such as food, water, and hiding and resting places — on their own, without the help of the people living in their territory. A stray cat may have a variable level of socialization. He could previously have been an owned cat who escaped outside or got lost, been abandoned, or been born and lived his entire life outside. The biggest difference between a stray cat and a feral cat is the level of social experience with people. Stray cats have some experience with people; feral cats have none.

**Feral cat:** An offspring of domestic cats who has had little or no contact with people. This cat will behave essentially like a wild animal for his entire life, even though he belongs to a domesticated species. He will avoid and be afraid of people.

**Community cat colony:** A stable group of cats living together in a neighborhood and managed by the people living in the area. These cats share food sources, might have preferred associates (cats who like one another and choose to spend time together), and might help raise one another's offspring. Ideally, if the colony is managed by one or more human caretakers, most of the cats in the group will have already been spayed or neutered, so breeding will be minimized.

**Colony caregiver:** A person or group of people who act as caregivers for a colony of cats. These people help monitor the cats' health, supplement feeding as needed, and identify newcomers to the colony who need to be captured and spayed or neutered, and who may have a disease or injury that needs to be treated.

**Trap-neuter-return (TNR):** A program in which feral cats are trapped, spayed or neutered, and then returned to the colony where they were trapped. This process also includes examination by a veterinarian, treatment for whatever health issues are treatable, and vaccinations.

**Classical conditioning:** A process whereby an individual makes an involuntary emotional association with something that had no previous meaning to them, because that thing has now been paired with something inherently pleasant or unpleasant. Also called Pavlovian conditioning. An example is a cat learning that the sound made by a clicker means a treat is coming, and so the cat begins to show more positive responses when he hears the click. Alternatively, a cat might learn that his carrier comes out only when he has to go to the veterinarian, a frightening experience, so he begins to hide whenever he sees the carrier. (See chapter 6 for more on this topic.)

**Capturing:** A training method that uses positive reinforcement (see chapter 6) to reward desired behaviors that are spontaneously displayed by an animal. This can be done at a distance by using a reward marker such as a clicker and then tossing treats to the animal when he shows the desired behavior. This method is particularly suited to training fearful or aggressive animals.

## Is That Really True?

*What would happen if all outdoor cats were captured and taken to a shelter?* For owned cats whose owners let them outside, owned cats who have become lost, and possibly even cats who were intentionally dumped outside, this might not be a bad thing. They all have a chance to be reunited with their owners — if those owners decide to go looking for them. But sadly, most cats brought to shelters as strays, even friendly cats who are clearly not feral, are never claimed by an owner. Some do get adopted by other families, but they will usually only be chosen if they look and act like an enjoyable companion.

Deciding which cats to put up for adoption isn't as simple as choosing those cats who look like friendly house pets for the adoption floor and putting back outside (or euthanizing) the rest. Even the best-run shelter is a stressful place for a cat, which translates to fearful behavior. That means most cats in shelters are probably not showing you their true personality because they are so stressed. Of course, a truly feral cat will be highly stressed in a shelter. But so will a shy owned cat or an older house cat who is used to being pampered.

All kinds of cats who might make great pets can be seen hiding in the corner of their shelter enclosures, or even acting aggressively when approached, since they are afraid and cannot get away. Cats who are stressed also are much more likely to get sick, further reducing their chances of being adopted. Fear-related behavior does not tell us anything about a cat's level of socialization. How can we reliably tell fearful and feral cats apart? It's a question all shelters struggle with.

*What would happen if all feral cats were trapped, neutered, and returned?* Known as TNR, this is a process whereby outdoor cats are trapped, spayed or neutered, and then returned to the outdoors. Typically, this process also includes examination by a veterinarian, treatment for medical problems, vaccinations, and humane euthanasia if a cat is too ill or injured to survive outside.

The "R" in TNR can be a little controversial. It can mean *returning* the cat to the environment where he was trapped, *releasing* him either back to the place where he was found or somewhere else, or *relocating* him to a different location.

The current standard of care emphasizes returning the cat to the environment from which he came, if at all possible. Cats are very bonded to their home territory and will go to extreme lengths to get back there if they find themselves in a different place. This can be quite perilous for a cat, especially if he has to travel across busy streets and highways, where the risk of being hit by a car is high. Cats within an existing colony are usually not welcoming to newcomers, so an unfamiliar cat dropped off at another cat colony might be chased off or injured in a fight.

Relocation might be necessary if a cat comes from an area where he is at great risk of injury, if the area where he lives is somehow changing (for example, a building is being put up on a formerly empty lot), or if he is living in an environmentally sensitive area, such as a wetland refuge. The best way to relocate cats, however, is as a colony, so that at least they do not have the stress of trying to establish new social bonds. The cats should be supervised by the colony caregiver for the first few days to ensure that they become used to their new location and can find plenty of food and shelter — factors that are critical to them considering it their new home.

TNR is most effective as a way to control feral cat populations if most of the cats in a colony are trapped and treated in a short amount of time. Dr. Julie Levy and her team at the University of Florida found that trapping, neutering, vaccinating, and returning 75 percent of the cats in a targeted neighborhood led to a significant decrease in the size of the feral cat population in that area and also reduced the number of cats brought in to the local shelter. This approach essentially creates a stable nonbreeding colony of cats. The resident cats will chase off other cats who might want to settle down there (and breed), and eventually, as the cats become older and die, the colony will disappear on its own.

Generally, a colony of TNR cats is managed, meaning it has a person or group of people who act as caregivers. These people help monitor the cats' health, supplement feeding as needed, and identify newcomers to the colony who need to be trapped and spayed or neutered, or who need to be treated for a disease or injury. The goal in managing a colony is to make sure that the number of cats doesn't exceed the population the environment can support (food and other resources), and also that the caregivers and the surrounding community aren't overwhelmed. TNR programs help caregivers meet this goal in a humane manner.

If the environment cannot sustain the number of free-roaming cats and keep them safe, what is the best option for the cats, the wildlife sharing the area, and the people the cats live among? Often a combination of strategies ends up being the solution. That means targeted TNR; adopting out friendly and well-socialized cats and kittens; and educating the community about the importance of spaying or neutering and vaccinating their cats, keeping their cats on their property and not letting them roam the neighborhood, and not dumping them outside.

When a plan like this is implemented, the cats will have less competition for food and less disease, the wildlife will be subject to less predation, and the people in the community will have less public health risk and nuisance from feral cats. It is important to remind residents that allowing feral cats to stay in their community and also spaying or neutering them costs less for the community and the organizations trying to help manage the cats than keeping them all in a shelter of any kind, including an enclosed sanctuary.

Community involvement is key to the success of such a program, because people in the neighborhood play a crucial role in monitoring the cat colony and educating their neighbors about humane care. There is a deep bond between colony caregivers and the cats they care for, and many consider the cats their pets, even if they cannot touch them.

## How Do We Begin?

When outdoor cats are trapped as part of a TNR program, the cats who are friendly to people, as well as young kittens, can be taken to a shelter and offered for adoption. The TNR team working in the community can help educate the people who live there and those who care for the cats about why it is important to get the cats spayed or neutered and vaccinated, and offer resources to help them do so. This is a more effective approach than just coming in and taking control of the situation.

Cats taken from a high-risk area will be candidates for strategic relocation to an area that's safer for them and the local wildlife and where a colony caregiver can help acclimate and monitor them. These cats might also be considered for a working cat program, such as pest control in barns, warehouses, or other places where their keen skills as hunters will be valued.

*What should we do with shelter cats?* Remember, even the best-run shelters are stressful for cats. The cats are away from their home territory, possibly separated from their beloved people, out of their routine, and out of their element. There are so many novel sights, sounds, and smells. Because cats' senses are much more acute than ours, if we think something is loud or strong-smelling, you better believe the cats are even more offended by it. In addition, everything is unfamiliar and out of their control, and they may not have adequate places where they can hide and feel safe. Cats are hardwired to hide when they're frightened, and if they can't, they become very distressed.

It is important to be able to identify cats who have some level of socialization with people, so that they can be moved to the adoption floor or to foster homes. Cats with no positive social experience — feral cats — should not be housed in the shelter any longer than is absolutely necessary, because the shelter environment is even more stressful and frightening for them. Ideally, they should be quickly identified, spayed or neutered, vaccinated, and returned to their colony.

It is inhumane to keep feral cats housed in a shelter without adequate facilities specifically for them (some shelters have a safe outdoor enclosure where cats can live with minimal handling and supervision) or to try to adopt out a feral cat as a house pet. Attempting to tame and acclimate such a cat to an indoor-only home would be extremely stressful for the cat and have a low chance of success. These cats are easily frightened and can become defensively aggressive very quickly, because they perceive any attempted human interaction as a life-threatening situation.

*How do we determine which cats are socialized and which are feral?* There is a difference between a socialized cat found outdoors and a truly feral cat. A socialized cat may begin to show some social behaviors around people after he has had a few days to acclimate. A truly feral cat will never show any social behaviors, no matter how much time has passed.

That is why it is so important to give cats time to acclimate when they first enter the shelter. A sweet house cat may seem like a terrified feral cat when he first comes in. Ideally, acclimation means one to three days in a quiet room away from the hustle and bustle of the shelter, especially somewhere the cat won't hear any barking dogs. Each cat should be given somewhere to hide inside his enclosure, and his food should be placed near the back of his cage so that he doesn't have to go to the front — where he will feel more vulnerable — to eat.

A quiet, calm, pleasant, patient caregiver should look after the cat on a fixed schedule. This person can spot clean the cage for a few days, rather than deep clean it every day. The cat should be monitored for signs of potential interest in social interaction with the caregiver. The ASPCA has developed a series of behaviors to watch for, called the Feline Spectrum Assessment (www.aspcapro.org/research/feline-spectrum-assessment), that might suggest some level of previous socialization. If the caregiver sees any of these behaviors, the cat can be placed on the path to being adopted.

| Name:<br>**SEYMOUR** | | | |
| Color:<br>**ORANGE & WHITE** | | | |
| Breed:<br>**DOMESTIC SH \ MIX** | | | |
| Sex:<br>**MALE** | Age:<br>**4y 1m** | | |
| Collar Color: | Collar Type: | Tag/Microchip: | |
| Markings: | | Alternate ID: | |

| Intake Date:<br>01/07/2016 | Review Date:<br>01/13/2016 | Intake Type:<br>**STRAY / FIELD** | Intake By:<br>**CB** |
| Comments:<br>Sweet | | | |

This shelter review form shows Seymour in a humane trap when he was taken in to the shelter. You can see his fearful aggressive body language in the photo. *Sara Bennett*

Look at the change in Seymour after he became acclimated to his cage at the shelter. He is lowering his head for a pat. *Sara Bennett*

*What about kittens of feral cats?* The socialization period for kittens is the developmental stage when they are especially receptive to being exposed to different environments, situations, and individuals of their own and other species. If they're exposed in a positive manner to people, other cats, dogs and other animals, handling, and a variety of different environments and situations, they are less likely to be fearful of them later in life.

The most sensitive socialization period is between two and seven weeks of age. When kittens of feral mothers are exposed to people during that time, they usually become acclimated to regular human contact and can make good pets. Kittens who are not exposed to people in a positive manner before three to four months of age will most likely always be afraid of people and should be considered feral.

This exposure must be done slowly, by a patient, friendly, positive person. Give them a day or two to acclimate to the environment, then handle them for very short periods three to four times a day. They can be separated from one another during this time but otherwise should be kept together for their emotional well-being and social development.

Start with the least fearful kitten, to avoid getting the other kittens scared and upset if the one you handle reacts with fear.

Begin the handling exercise by gently picking the kitten up in a towel, then softly stroking him on the head. He can be hand-fed now, too. Remember, if you do it slowly and gently enough, the kitten should not react with fear, but rather become more relaxed over time and even start to enjoy some of the handling and stroking. If the kitten shows fear, slow down.

*How do you acclimate a feral cat to a new environment?* If you have to relocate an adult feral cat, you can try to help him learn about his new home. For example, if the cat is placed in a barn, at first keep him in a large crate or a small room, such as a tack room, with his food, water, bed, scratching and hiding areas, and litter box inside. He can have regular visits from his new caregiver for meals and spot cleaning. After several days, he can start to have more space, such as being let loose in the tack room or barn when his caregiver is present, but he should be returned to the crate or tack room when the caregiver leaves. If you let him out at mealtimes, he'll stick around for the food, which will help create the association that this is now home.

After about three weeks, the cat can be let loose in the barn for longer periods. It is possible that he might still disappear for a day or two, but if the caregiver keeps putting out food at mealtimes, most likely he will eventually turn up for dinner.

## How Can We Help a Fearful Cat Who Has Been Adopted?

Hopefully, the fearful but social cat has been either adopted into a quiet home or placed in a foster home. That's great, because he is out of the stressful shelter environment. But now what? There are many things you can do to try to help this kitty feel more comfortable and less fearful in his new home.

### Limit the Environment

One of the most common mistakes we make when bringing a fearful, shy cat home is to make his world too big, too fast. Rather than give him immediate access to your entire home and pushing him to meet all the family, two-legged or four, on that first day, take it slow.

First, set up a room just for him in your home. It should be a quiet, comfortable room that is not used frequently by the rest of the family. He should have his litter box, food and water, a comfortable resting area, a place to hide, a scratching surface, and something to play with in this space. (See chapters 2 and 3 for some ideas about the best way to set up litter boxes, feeding stations, and resting areas.) The addition of a plug-in diffuser with synthetic feline facial pheromone (Feliway Classic) can help some cats feel more relaxed.

Even in his own quiet room, kitty will need a hiding spot. A box, crate, or carrier will do — anything that he can climb into so that he can feel hidden and secure. He'll be more likely to use his safe space if you put it up off the floor somewhere — on a shelf or the top of a bookcase, for example. It's okay to block off access to places where you don't want him to hide, such as underneath a sofa, but only if you have provided him with another suitable option.

The hiding spot will be more appealing if you line it with a blanket or towel and cover it with another one. You can spot clean this bedding to remove large amounts of hair, but don't wash it frequently. This will help ensure that the space smells like the cat and is familiar and comforting. If you need to wash it, put a new piece of bedding in with the old for a day or two before you remove the old bedding to wash.

If you think your cat would enjoy sitting by the window, try putting a hiding spot at window level. The opening should not face the window, but look off to the side. That way, he can go in the hiding spot, poke out his head to look outside if he wishes, then immediately retreat inside if he wants to hide.

## Give the New Cat Time

The next most important thing you can give a shy kitty is time — quiet time alone to acclimate. Just as cats in the shelter need a day or two to begin to get used to their surroundings, your shy cat will need the same thing in your home. Remember, this is an unfamiliar environment for him. Put him in his room and do not disturb him or allow people or other pets to visit him for the first few days. You can go in quietly to refresh his food and water and scoop his litter box, but do not try to interact with him when you are there. Just take care of his housekeeping and leave.

On the third day, try sitting quietly in his room for several minutes. This is a good time to read a magazine, check your email, or even meditate. The goal is for him to get used to you being there, so ignore him if he ventures out of his hiding spot. Let him control how much distance there is between you.

After a few days of this, if he is venturing out while you are in his room, you can begin to add some short, neutral interactions. These can be as simple as reading aloud from your favorite book, talking softly to him, or even rolling a toy around a little. If he ventures near, toss a small morsel of yummy food in his general direction. Do this using a low, underhand toss, so you don't have to move your arm too much and it doesn't seem as if you're throwing something at him.

Don't be offended if he scurries back to his hiding spot or doesn't eat it right away. You've just changed the game, so he needs time to figure it out. Remember, if he eats the food treat, even if it takes him several minutes, he can still learn through classical conditioning to associate you with good things (see chapter 6).

Favored treat flavors for kitties include cheese, sardines, anchovy paste, meat baby food, and yogurt. Many commercial treats contain these ingredients. Or you can freeze these foods in small ice cube trays to facilitate delivery. Another idea is to make a small food-dispensing toy so that you can roll the treat to him. One half of a plastic Easter egg works great to send a little anchovy paste across the room to him in a nonthreatening way.

You can use food-dispensing toys to offer your new cat some enrichment that doesn't force him to interact with you. They will give him an opportunity to seek out and work for his food. You can buy toys made for cats, or you can make them yourself out of small plastic containers or cardboard toilet paper rolls. (See "The Three-Minute Food-Dispensing Toy" in chapter 11.) Fill a toy with food and put it in the cat's room before you go to bed so that he will have access to it throughout the night.

You can also add short play sessions using a fishing-pole toy or a string toy. (Never leave a cat alone with string or yarn, however, to avoid accidental ingestion.) These toys will create positive interactions that feel safe to the cat (far enough away that they do not involve touch) and will help him learn to trust you.

Don't despair if it takes several weeks to see improvement. A survey done by Dr. Sheila Segurson, DACVB, the research director of Maddie's Fund, found that most foster caretakers and new owners reported it took at least two weeks for a fearful cat to begin to come out of his shell and interact. Remember to keep to a regular schedule for his feeding, cleaning, and visits, so that he knows what to expect throughout the day. This can be very helpful in reducing anxiety.

Here is Seymour, calm, relaxed, and happy in his new home. *Sara Bennett*

## Expand His Social Interactions

After a few weeks, you can begin to try some more social interactions. Start by asking for a nose touch as a way to initiate an interaction. Hold out your index finger near his nose and let him choose to touch your fingertip (or not). If he does, you can then stroke him between his ears, on his cheeks, or under his chin. Do this using only one hand, and for no more than three seconds, then pause and ask for another nose touch. If he offers his nose again, you can pet him for another three seconds. If he doesn't offer his nose, just leave him alone. You can also try this with brushing rather than petting.

Watch your cat's body language closely during all of these interactions to see if he is interested in interacting or would prefer to be left alone. Signs that he is more relaxed and interested include a leg stretched away from his body, his tail loose behind his body, or his whiskers or ears forward. Signs that he is more worried or would prefer to be left alone include his head and neck tucked close to his body, his legs or tail wrapped or tucked close to his body, his whiskers back flat against his face, or his ears to the side or back.

If your cat shows signs that he would prefer to be left alone, respect this and do not force an interaction. The more you honor his preferences, the more he will begin to trust you. (See chapter 1 for more information on reading cat body language.)

You can also incorporate short, fun training sessions into your cat's daily routine using positive reinforcement training (see chapter 6). This is a great way to help teach a shy cat that interactions with people are safe. During these training sessions, use a clicker or a word, such as "good" or "yes," to mark the moment he does something you like, then follow it with a food treat.

For example, if he touches his nose to your finger, say "good" with a happy tone of voice and give him a tiny morsel of food. Repeat and repeat and repeat. When you know he is likely to do this behavior whenever you hold out your finger, you can start to use a word to cue the behavior. For example, a common cue for a nose touch is "touch." Say "touch," then hold out your finger. When he touches it, click or say "good," then give him a treat.

If your cat is too fearful to approach your finger, you might try using a target stick rather than your finger. The stick can be any long, thin object, such as a pen or pencil, a chopstick, or an extendable pointer.

The cat approaches for a nose-to-finger touch, a friendly greeting. This is a natural behavior. *Rebecca Gast*

You can easily capture the nose-to-finger touch behavior by using a target stick instead of your finger. *Lisa White/Courtesy of Karen Pryor Academy's Better Veterinary Visits Course*

You can also teach your cat to come on cue by saying his name, then picking up his food scoop or opening the food bag. As soon as he gets to you, give him a morsel of food.

These training exercises use a technique called capturing, where you simply wait for the cat to offer the desired behavior, then reward it, rather than trying to lure, prompt, or force him into doing it. This technique is especially great for shy or fearful animals and is used frequently when training exotic or zoo animals.

## Make His World Bigger

Once your cat has begun to come out and investigate when you enter his room, or at least doesn't run away immediately when you enter or move around, you can begin to offer him some freedom to leave the room. Give him access to another room or two. Do this at quiet times and for short periods, but make sure he has appropriate hiding spots in those rooms and can also get back to his safe room if he feels he needs to.

You can begin to introduce him to other people, too. Have another person accompany you into his room during housekeeping or interaction time. Initially, they should stay quiet and still. Once he starts venturing out and taking treats, they can begin to participate in the same kinds of positive interactions you've been having.

You can gradually introduce other pets of any species by putting up a baby gate or a screen door in the doorway to your cat's room. (Don't bring other pets into the safe room.) Dogs should be on a leash so they don't rush the gate and can be moved away quickly and safely if they bark or frighten the cat. The best response is for both parties to ignore each other through the gate. Use food rewards for both pets when they show appropriate behavior during a session.

## Have Realistic Expectations

It is important to realize that your fearful cat may always have some limitations. Though he might warm up to you and your family, newcomers and visitors may always be a problem. We see this behavior in feral cat colonies with regular caregivers, too. The cats might learn to accept and perhaps even allow brief periods of touching by one or two very familiar people, but the same luxury is not afforded to other people, even if they are quiet, calm, and patient, and bear good things such as food.

In your home, don't be surprised if your guests never meet your cat, because he runs off to hide as soon as he hears them at the door. That is okay. As long as he has a safe place to hide and nobody bothers him, he will recover and come back out within a few hours of the guests leaving. This is an appropriate coping strategy for him.

Be his advocate and advise guests not to seek him out or try to touch him or interact with him if he does venture out. Guests can toss a yummy food treat or a favorite toy in his direction but should otherwise ignore him. Remember that shy cats are easily frightened and can become defensively aggressive very quickly, because they perceive any unwanted human interaction as a life-threatening event. If a visitor pushes your cat's limits and goes looking for him, this extreme fear response could result in a significant setback for him and potentially undo much of the hard work you've patiently put into gaining his trust.

Another possibility is that your cat may be willing to be around you and even enjoy your company, but he doesn't want you to touch or pet him. That is also okay. You can interact with him through play — using toys you can toss or objects on fishing poles or strings — or even through training. Over time, some cats will learn to tolerate and perhaps even appreciate brief touching or petting. But remember to always respect your cat's boundaries and limitations. You and your cat can have a healthy and fulfilling relationship without cuddling.

## Avoiding Pitfalls and Staying on Track

What if your cat doesn't start to come out of hiding in his room? After at least two weeks of quiet with no interactions, it might be time to consider whether you can make some adjustments to help him feel more secure, or whether a medication or supplement might help reduce his anxiety and fear.

Remember, this is not just about you not being able to interact with him; it is also about his well-being. It is not healthy for him to be so frightened all the time that he never feels comfortable enough to leave his safe place.

Look at the hiding spots he has available. Can he truly feel hidden and secure in all of them? If not, perhaps you can reinforce them. Some cats feel better when they have a bed in a box inside an even bigger box, with a blanket placed over half the opening.

Sit quietly in the room and listen for a few minutes. Are there sounds your kitty can hear that might be frightening? Can he hear your dog barking in the next room, or the TV or video games downstairs? If so, think of ways you can reduce those noises. Cover the windows so the dog can't see things outside to bark at, move the dog crate, or ask the kids to play video games in a different room. Or perhaps add some white noise or relaxing music to the cat's room. (Two possibilities created especially for cats are the website Music for Cats, www.musicforcats.com, and Through a Cat's Ear, a CD/MP3 series available from various outlets.) Remember that if you do this, you don't want the volume to be higher than normal conversation. It doesn't help to try to drown out loud noise with more loud noise.

If these steps don't help reduce your cat's fear in a few weeks, or if he starts to get so frightened that he reacts with hissing, swatting, growling, charging, or biting when you enter his safe room or when guests come over, it's time to speak to your veterinarian about the possibility of adding a medication or supplement. There are many options that are appropriate and safe for cats. This is where a good relationship with a veterinarian who is knowledgeable about animal behavior is crucial. She can help guide you through the steps of reviewing your environment, management, and interactions to make the best choices for your cat.

One of the most important factors to consider and discuss with your veterinarian is how you will get the medication or supplement into your cat. He is already so fearful that trying to catch him and forcibly give him a medication will likely make things worse rather than better, and could even push him to show more aggression toward you. Finding a way to offer the medication in an appetizing fashion so that you don't have to touch him to administer it will result in much less stress than trying to give him a medication forcibly by mouth, by applying it transdermally (to the skin), or even by injection.

The good news is that there are some name-brand formulations of behavior medications that come in highly palatable, chewable tablets and can be given to cats as a treat. Additionally, several generic formulations can be mixed with a special food that your cat enjoys. Some supplements are very tasty, too, and often cats will eat them like treats. (See appendix B for more information on giving meds to your cat.)

For some situations, there are veterinary prescription diets that may diminish anxiety and are quite palatable to cats. Again, talk to your veterinarian about this option.

## The Indoor-Outdoor Debate

The debate about whether it's always best to keep cats strictly indoors is part of a larger debate about the best ways to keep cats as pets. Ultimately, you need to strike a balance between a cat's physical and behavioral health needs.

This decision can be influenced by many variables. One is cultural. In some parts of the world, including some developed countries, people view it as irresponsible to let cats outdoors. In other areas, it is considered irresponsible to keep cats indoors all the time. While the decision to keep a cat indoors may be intended as a way to increase his life span and protect his health, doing so might not always be in the best interest of the cat if his environmental needs cannot be met.

### Can Indoor-Only Cats Be Happy?

Many socialized house cats are fine with staying indoors. They can be pampered with readily available food, water, resting spots, and indoor toilets (litter boxes). From some cats' perspective, this is truly the lap of luxury. Ideally, these cats are well taken care of by the family veterinarian, including regular checkups, appropriate vaccinations, deworming, parasite control, and spaying or neutering. Their risk of injuries from fighting, predation, or being hit by a car is exceedingly low. But this is ideal only as long as their owner can provide for all of their basic needs, which go far beyond access to food, water, and a clean litter box.

Indoor cats also need regular positive social interaction — play, petting, grooming, and training. They need to satisfy their feline urges to hunt, climb, hide, and scratch. These needs can be met with food-dispensing toys, vertically placed resting options such as shelves and cat towers, and appropriate scratching surfaces. But for some cats, all that is still not enough.

Some cats require more enrichment than their owners are able to provide, and they become stressed or frustrated with the limitations of always staying indoors. Behavior problems can result, including aggression during play, inappropriate predatory behavior, destructive scratching, and house soiling.

## Outdoors, but Not Free-Roaming

Outdoor (or indoor-outdoor) cats, while they can enjoy a more fully enriched and varied environment, are exposed to risks that indoor-only cats do not encounter. They are at greater risk of infectious diseases, internal and external parasites, poisoning (intentional and unintentional), and injury due to trauma, such as being hit by a car or attacks from other animals or humans. Anyone with an outdoor space, however, can create a safe outdoor environment that will meet the needs of an active cat with a drive for a high level of novelty and variety.

The first step to letting your cat outdoors safely is teaching him to come when he is called. This is really quite simple, if you think about what a cat does when he hears his food bag or can opened at mealtime. Before opening the food, you can simply say your cat's name and a cue such as "here, kitty." He will come running in anticipation of being fed. Over several repetitions, he will learn that his name plus "here, kitty" means come to you, because a reward (food) awaits.

If you have an outdoor space, the next step is to put up specialized cat fencing or create an enclosed cat space, so that he can come and go as he

Spike can enjoy his neighborhood safely on a harness and leash. *Craig Zeichner*

pleases in this designated space and also be safe from the risks of wandering or intruders. In this way, you will not only minimize the chances of your cat getting hurt but also ensure that he will not bother your neighbors or any wildlife in your yard. (See chapters 3 and 5 for some ideas about creating an outdoor space for your cat.)

If you don't have an outdoor space, you can train your cat to wear a harness and leash. Leash walks are not just for dogs anymore! This is another way to offer safe outdoor time to active cats.

Of course, all cats should have appropriate identification (ideally a microchip), updated vaccinations, and parasite management, but these are even more important for a cat who enjoys outdoor time.

## What Did We Say?

- Feral cats should be considered wild animals. People should not attempt to make them house pets. This is extremely stressful to the cats and can be dangerous.
- Trap-neuter-return programs that target a specific area and catch as many cats as possible in a short amount of time, along with community involvement to help manage a cat colony, is one of the most humane, economical, wildlife-sparing, and effective strategies to manage outdoor cats.
- How fearful a cat in an unfamiliar situation is does not tell us whether the cat is socialized to people. Feral cats and socialized cats can both show extreme fear in a shelter.
- One of the biggest mistakes people make when adopting shy or fearful cats is making their world too big too fast. Slow and steady wins the race.
- Start small when bringing a shy or fearful cat into your home. Remember to give him a quiet safe room where he can acclimate, and allow him to be in charge of the pace and intensity of his interactions. This will empower him to feel more confident and safe.
- Never underestimate the power of a good hiding spot. Every single cat in every single housing situation — whether in a cage in a shelter, a group room in a rescue, or our own homes — should have easy access to a hiding spot. This can save a cat's life and definitely improve his welfare by giving him the chance to perform a highly mo-

tivated species-specific behavior. Not being able to hide can lead to tremendous emotional and physical stress for a cat.

- All cats should have enrichment in their daily lives. This is not optional! Enrichment includes core resources such as food, water, litter boxes, resting spots, and hiding spots. Physical activities such as play and hunting for food are also important. Don't forget training, a great way to add to social and physical activity and also to strengthen the relationship between you and your cat.
- Some cats will become social with their human family but will never be comfortable with visitors. Don't force the issue or let people seek out your cat when he wants to be left alone.
- Above all, respect who your cat is. Remember that his personality is molded by genetics, his previous experiences, and learning, much of which we cannot control. But we can allow him to be the cat he is, whether that's the life of the party, the shy wallflower, or the untouchable. All cats are beautiful and enrich our lives in their own ways.

# 13

# Growing Old with Grace
## *Old Cats Should Learn New Tricks*

Julia Albright, MA, DVM, DACVB,
and Margaret Gruen, DVM, PhD, DACVB

Ursa was Suzanne's first companion when she began her career as a nurse, still finding her way in a new city. Ursa was a ten-day-old ball of gray fluff who looked more like a fuzzy bear than a kitten, which is how she got her name: *ursa* means "bear" in Latin. Ursa was with Suzanne through most of her major life events, including further schooling, marriage, children, and several moves across the country. She was a strong kitten with a will to survive, and a patient and loving cat who tolerated the exuberant adoration of two lively kids.

As Ursa aged and became a senior cat, it became clear she was having some trouble moving around. She walked differently on the stairs, and while she still jumped up to be near Suzanne on the couch or bed, she usually hit her back paws on the furniture as she landed. She also began to wake up in the middle of the night and wander around the house meowing, as though looking for someone. When Suzanne called her, she would come and seem to settle, only to repeat the same behavior the next night. Suzanne wondered what had happened to her loving, adaptable, and comforting friend.

Suzanne didn't know it, but Ursa had many of the afflictions of older cats: arthritis in her hips, hyperthyroidism (overactive thyroid), hypertension (high blood pressure), kidney disease, and mild cognitive dysfunction (dementia). And yet she remained the most loving companion and would greet every guest and friend with her loud meow.

Her welcoming spirit, however, extended only to human companions. She met any attempts to add other pets to the home with stern resistance. Never a cat who would run away from a challenge, Ursa would go after any animal who tried to encroach on her space — even friends' rather large dogs. At one point, when Suzanne tried to foster a litter of kittens for a local rescue group, Ursa was agitated and aggressive with them, and Suzanne had to return them. It became clear that Ursa was happier as an only cat.

Suzanne was worried that Ursa might not be enjoying her senior years and consulted her veterinarian for advice.

## Facts, Not Fiction

Thanks to advances in veterinary medicine, our feline companions live longer and healthier lives. However, with longevity can come behavior changes caused by physical and medical problems. Sometimes owners dismiss these changes as just normal aging when they are really signs of discomfort or medical disorders.

Like most animals, cats try to hide their illnesses and physical decline to avoid looking vulnerable to predators. As a result, we don't always notice when they are sick. We know that aging can be difficult for some cats, but if we give them preventive and necessary medical care, manage and modify their environment, and understand their special needs, older cats can thrive in their golden years.

## Is That Really True?

*How old is a senior cat?* According to the *American Association of Feline Practitioners Senior Care Guidelines* (https://journals.sagepub.com/doi/pdf/10.1016/j.jfms.2009.07.011), there is no specific age at which a cat becomes a "senior." Individual animals and body systems age at different rates. But one convenient way to view older cats is to classify them as "mature or middle-aged" (seven to ten years), "senior" (eleven to fourteen years), and "geriatric" (fifteen years or older).

While the aging process affects different cats in different ways, there are some typical changes that are indicative of advancing age. Among these is a loss of muscle mass and a change in the way the cat carries herself. Cats may begin to lose muscle tone over their backs, with muscle atrophy and loss also apparent around painful joints — perhaps hips affected by arthritis. They may slow down some, but most cats should remain active in their golden years.

It's important to understand that these kinds of physical changes are not reflected in blood work. As you begin to notice various behavioral signs, however, you need to make adjustments in your cat's environment and manage her needs medically to keep her well.

*My cat seems fine, so why does she need regular veterinary visits?* Often the early stages of a disease are diagnosed during preventive veterinary visits — long before there are any physical signs. Many of these diseases are treatable, and the earlier you start treatment, the better. That is why feline medicine experts strongly recommend checkups every six months for cats over the age of seven years.

A thorough physical exam by your veterinarian should include a hands-on assessment of your cat's whole body and blood work to check her body systems. You should also tell your veterinarian as much as you can about any changes, no matter how subtle, in your cat's behavior, appetite, thirst, litter box habits, stool and urine, social interactions, sleeping patterns, vocalizations, desire to play, and mobility. Don't forget to mention any medications and supplements you are giving her. This is all useful information about your cat's health and well-being.

*If my cat is still eating and moving, she's fine, right?* Not necessarily. Changes in a cat's weight, activity, and sleep-wake cycle often indicate a medical concern. Don't wait until your cat's next regular checkup to discuss these changes with your veterinarian. In cats, such changes often occur slowly, over a long period of time, making them hard to spot. It's really helpful if you and your veterinarian keep track of your cat's abilities over the years, especially as she passes age seven, so that you can detect subtle changes in her needs and health status.

---

### What Does That Mean?

**Cognitive dysfunction syndrome (CDS):** A kind of feline dementia caused by a degeneration of the part of the nervous system that is responsible for cognition. It results in a steady decline in the cat's basic decision-making capabilities and general awareness.

**Off-label use:** The use of a drug for an unapproved indication or in an unapproved age group, dosage, or route of administration. Both prescription drugs and over-the-counter drugs can be used in off-label ways, although most studies of off-label use focus on prescription drugs.

**Sensory decline:** The gradual loss of sensory capacities such as vision, hearing, smell, taste, and peripheral sensation. This is a normal part of aging.

**Senior cat:** A cat who is over ten years of age.

**Geriatric cat:** A cat who is over fifteen years of age.

**Sleep-wake cycle:** The biological pattern of alternating sleep and wakefulness, which becomes altered in cats with dementia.

## Medical Conditions and Their Behavioral Signs

In just about every species, certain diseases are more likely to occur with age. In fact, cats are more likely to develop multiple chronic diseases as they age. The good news is that lifestyle changes, such as consistent exercise, appropriate diet, and mental stimulation, can go a long way in reducing the pain and distress associated with many of these diseases and, in some cases, prevent the problems altogether.

In this section, we'll discuss some of the most common chronic diseases in older cats. But first, there are some behavioral signs that are not specific to any one disease. If you see any of these signs, take your cat to the veterinarian right away.

- Vomiting
- Respiratory distress
- Lethargy
- Lack of appetite; refusing to eat
- Abrupt changes in activity
- Lack of grooming

We understand that taking your feline friend to the veterinarian can be stressful. Simple steps, such as getting your cat accustomed to the carrier, can make the process much more pleasant for everyone. See appendix A for more information about carrier training and appendix B to learn about medicating your cat, should that be required.

## Degenerative Joint Disease (Osteoarthritis)

Degenerative joint disease (osteoarthritis) is among the most prevalent diseases associated with old age in cats. More than 80 percent of cats over the age of ten have some arthritis, but only about half of those show clinical signs of associated pain. That means your cat may have arthritis but not show any symptoms.

Although you may notice changes in your cat's gait (the way she walks or runs), cat owners more often notice the signs of painful arthritis when their cat is climbing stairs or jumping. They also report changes in social behavior and find that their cat will not tolerate as much petting. Which abilities are more affected depends, in part, on which joints are affected by the disease. Pain toward the rear leads to more difficulty jumping up and climbing stairs, while pain in the forelimbs manifests as difficulty jumping down or going down stairs. Arthritis can also affect the cat's whole body, as well as her mood.

The pain associated with arthritis is not an inevitable consequence of old age; often it can be treated. Your veterinarian is the best person to decide how. You can also change things in your home to make getting around easier for your cat. Our recommendations later in this chapter, in the section "Managing the Environment for Senior Cats," are applicable to all senior cats, those with and without arthritis. But making these kinds of changes is especially important for those who suffer from arthritis, so that they can continue to do what they enjoy.

## Hyperthyroidism

Hyperthyroidism is most commonly seen in older cats; the average age at the time of diagnosis is twelve years. Thyroid hormones are produced by the thyroid gland, a butterfly-shaped gland just below the Adam's apple at the base of the neck. These hormones are responsible for regulating the metabolism of proteins, carbohydrates, and fats. They are also involved in maintaining body temperature and in the sympathetic nervous system (the fight-or-flight system).

Cats with hyperthyroidism produce too much of the thyroid hormones. The reasons are not well understood, but may be related to the environment, the immune system, nutrition, genetics, or a combination of these factors. Unlike in people, cancer is rarely the cause of an overactive thyroid in cats.

Hyperthyroidism essentially puts a cat's metabolism into overdrive. The owner may see a diverse range of behaviors and health changes, such as hyperactivity, weight loss despite increased hunger, increased drinking and urination, vomiting, rapid heartbeat, and unkempt fur. In addition to these obvious external signs, damage to the heart and kidneys often occurs if hyperthyroidism is not treated.

Hyperthyroidism can be successfully managed in many cats with a special diet or daily oral medication that reduces the production of the thyroid hormones and their damage to the body. Surgery and radioactive iodine treatments are options to permanently knock down the thyroid's activity.

## Chronic Kidney Disease

Chronic kidney disease (CKD) is estimated to affect up to 80 percent of cats over the age of twelve, and it becomes more common as a cat gets older. The kidneys perform many important functions, including filtering out toxins in the body, regulating fluid levels, balancing electrolytes, and producing hormones that are critical for regulating other activities, such as maintaining blood pressure and blood oxygenation.

"Chronic kidney disease" is a general term that describes damage to the kidneys' filtering apparatus or blood supply, resulting in permanent, mild to moderate loss of function. The exact cause of CKD usually cannot be identified, because the cat's body is excellent at compensating for a slow loss of kidney structures — up to about 66 percent. If the disease is identified and medical and dietary interventions are started early, moderate kidney damage can be well managed for years.

Signs that a cat may have kidney disease include excessive drinking and urination, loss of appetite, weight loss, and decreased energy. CKD may make a cat prone to bacterial infections, so frequent trips to the litter box, urinating outside the box, vocalization while urinating, or blood in the urine are other signs. Straining to urinate (due to infection or blockage) can be mistaken for constipation.

## High Blood Pressure

Hyperthyroidism and kidney disease are common causes of high blood pressure (hypertension) in cats. If left untreated, hypertension can speed the progression of kidney disease. It can also cause serious eye, heart, and brain damage. Cats with hypertension often vocalize excessively, pace, and are unsettled; some cats also lose their vision and run into things. Medication to treat high blood pressure can be prescribed by your veterinarian after an examination, blood pressure readings, and other assessments.

## Heart Disease

The most common heart disease in cats is hypertrophic cardiomyopathy (HCM), a thickening of the heart wall. HCM is diagnosed in about 25 percent of cats older than nine years of age. Certain breeds, including Maine Coon, Ragdoll, British Shorthair, and Sphynx cats, are genetically prone to HCM. A thickened heart wall doesn't contract well, and stiffness makes the heart work harder to pump blood throughout the body. The heart muscles, as well as the lungs and blood vessels anywhere in the body, may eventually be damaged.

Cats with mild HCM may live without any noticeable effects for years. Nonspecific signs include lethargy and decreased appetite, but difficulty breathing and panting are among the more common signs that first alert a cat owner to a problem. These signs usually follow a stressful event, such as travel, boarding, or a trip to the veterinary clinic. Your veterinarian may recommend that your cat avoid stressful events and overexertion. Medications to help her heart work more efficiently are also available.

### Heartworm Disease

Heartworm disease is caused by the parasite *Dirofilaria immitis* and is spread by infected mosquitoes. It is not just a problem for cats (and dogs) who go outdoors, because mosquitoes can live indoors even in cold weather. An infected mosquito injects the cat with heartworm larvae, which then mature and migrate to her heart and lungs over the next few months. Any age cat is susceptible to heartworm disease.

The cat's immune system is superior to the dog's in killing off these larvae, but some do mature into adults. Just one or two adult worms can result in serious obstruction and damage to the heart and lungs. At first, coughing may be the only sign. But respiratory distress, lethargy, vomiting, and even sudden death are possible with heartworm infections. The disease is diagnosed via laboratory testing.

Preventive medication is available to keep cats from being infected. This medication is recommended for all cats, because the disease is easy to prevent but difficult to treat.

## Diabetes

Diabetes (the specific medical term is diabetes mellitus) is the most common disease in overweight and aging cats (as well as people). Insulin is a hormone produced by the pancreas that allows the body's main energy source, glucose, to enter the cells. Cats with diabetes do not properly produce or respond to insulin, leading to excess glucose in the blood, which can then cause damage to many bodily systems.

Owners typically note excessive urination and drinking, poor fur quality, lethargy, and hind limb weakness in a diabetic cat. Obesity is a risk factor for diabetes because it directly contributes to the cells' resistance to insulin. Insulin resistance also seems to increase with age.

Some cats' insulin and glucose levels can be controlled with weight loss and a switch to a low-carbohydrate, high-protein diet. Other cats need a diet change plus an oral medication — although oral medications are not effective in all cases. In still other cats, the cells that produce insulin are so damaged that long-term insulin injections are needed. The sooner the disease is diagnosed and lifestyle changes are started, the less likely it is that there will be permanent damage.

## Weight Loss

Excessive loss of weight and muscle mass is very common in older cats. It may be related to other diseases, such as hyperthyroidism, or to conditions that cause poor appetite, such as poor dental health or a gradual decline in the sense of smell.

Regardless of the underlying cause, excessively low body mass is associated with higher mortality in older cats and should be addressed as a disease itself, requiring a specific treatment plan. Offering small, frequent, warm meals; adding flavoring to water; and appetite-enhancing medications available by prescription from your veterinarian can help keep your skinny cat healthy and well hydrated.

## Dental and Oral Disease

Most senior cats have some degree of periodontal (gum) disease. Over time, bacteria interacting with minerals in the saliva causes plaque to build up both above and below the gumline. This damages tooth roots and supporting tissues. The body's immune response can cause even greater inflammation, pain, and damage to tooth and mouth structures.

Dental disease may not be apparent to a cat owner, as signs can be subtle. Often poor appetite, drooling, and dropping food out of the mouth are some of the signs that a cat is experiencing oral pain. In other cases, cats may show sensitivity when handled around the face, head, and neck. After proper treatment, including a dental cleaning and extracting diseased teeth, cats and their owners usually see a dramatic change in mood, activity, and appetite.

Every cat owner should discuss with their veterinarian annual dental cleanings and in-home oral care to potentially reduce the need for more extensive dental work. Nonanesthetic cleanings, such as those offered at grooming salons, are never recommended, because they are too stressful for the cat and a thorough procedure is not possible.

## Sensory Decline and Loss

Behavior changes may be a result of a decline in one or more of a cat's senses. A cat may respond differently to people, other pets, and things in the world if her perception of these things has changed due to loss of vision, smell, or hearing. Some cats may seem less reactive and more placid because their senses are not as keen, but others may become fearful or anxious because the things around them seem different.

A cat who is losing her sight may startle more easily and occasionally bump into things. Some cats become quite distressed when they are blind and vocalize more than before. A cat who is losing her hearing may not react when you enter the room and may be startled when touched, perhaps even hissing or lashing out. A cat who is losing her sense of smell may lose her appetite because she finds her food less appealing.

## Cognitive Dysfunction Syndrome

Some cats may have behavior changes, such as nighttime waking, that cannot be ascribed to any underlying disease. The cause may be cognitive dysfunction syndrome (CDS) — a kind of feline dementia that is a degeneration of the part of the nervous system responsible for cognition. CDS results in a steady decline in the cat's basic decision-making capabilities and general awareness.

*How do I know if my cat has CDS?* In dogs, we describe the behavior changes associated with CDS using the acronym DISHA:

- **D**isorientation
- **I**nteraction changes
- **S**leep-wake cycle changes
- **H**ouse soiling
- **A**ctivity changes and/or Anxiety

Although we don't have many research studies about aging cats, we see enough parallels between geriatric dogs and geriatric cats to assume that this acronym also applies to cats.

A study conducted by Dr. Kelly Moffat, DACVB, and her colleagues, suggests that 28 percent of pet cats ages eleven to fourteen develop at least one behavior problem as they become seniors, and this increases to over 50 percent for cats of fifteen years of age or older. CDS may be one of the reasons for changes in behavior and awareness.

It is very important to have your veterinarian fully assess your cat if you see any of the DISHA signs, because many medical conditions can also cause those symptoms. CDS is diagnosed when the DISHA signs are seen in the absence of medical causes, or when concurrent medical conditions appear to be well controlled.

Advanced imaging, such as magnetic resonance imaging (MRI) and computed tomography (CT) or computerized axial tomography (CAT) scans, can help rule out other brain issues that may be the root cause of cognitive decline, but they cannot diagnose CDS. Behavior changes in your cat are the best diagnostic tool we currently have, which is why it is so important that you discuss these changes with your veterinarian.

*What causes CDS?* In dogs and people, learning impairments and other behavior changes have been shown to be directly related to the degree of degenerative damage to the brain. Researchers assume that the same is true for cats, and limited cognitive testing has verified this. Not surprisingly, cognitive studies have shown that older cats do not perform as well as younger cats in many learning tasks.

In addition to loss of brain neurons, cats (and dogs) suffering from cognitive decline often have changes in the brain tissue, specifically an accumulation of beta-amyloid plaques. This is remarkably similar to what happens to humans with Alzheimer's disease. As cells make energy and perform other basic functions, they produce waste products that, over time, damage various cells in the body, including those in the brain. Brain tissue seems to be particularly vulnerable to oxidative damage, and beta-amyloid plaques around neurons and blood vessels lead to a loss of function in these structures.

Cognitive changes result because neurons responsible for cognition are damaged and no longer release important neurotransmitters, such as dopamine and acetylcholine, which transmit nerve impulses from one neuron to another. Additionally, there are changes in how the brain cells age and remove cellular waste.

## Medications That May Help

Very few treatments have been evaluated in cats, and we often have to extrapolate from canine and human research studies. Many of the treatments for cognitive decline help to prolong the life span of the remaining functioning neurons and neurotransmitters. While we cannot yet cure or reverse the effects of this disease, we can slow its progression and mitigate some of the associated signs.

Your veterinarian may prescribe a medication to decrease anxiety or increase sedation, depending on the nature of your cat's cognitive signs and any other health issues. The following prescription drugs are sometimes used in cats with CDS. They should be used only with veterinary guidance; that includes both reducing or increasing the dosage and stopping the drug entirely.

- Selegiline is the only medication approved for treating CDS in dogs, and it is used off label in cats. It is one of a group of medications called MAO-B inhibitors. These drugs work by increasing the amount of dopamine (a natural substance that is needed to control movement) in the brain. Selegiline may also decrease free-radical production and enhance free-radical scavenging (free radicals are toxic reactive molecules), although this has not been evaluated in clinical trials in cats. Improvement or stabilization of symptoms may take six to eight weeks.
- Benzodiazepines are a class of drugs that are prescribed to treat anxiety and insomnia in humans. They may be beneficial for some cats if night waking is a problem. Side effects may include lethargy or idiosyncratic increases in activity or vocalization. Some of the drugs in this class may cause changes in liver function.

## Nutritional Supplements

Some nutritional supplements are thought to slow the progression of CDS, increase cognitive function in mildly impaired cats, and help calm cats. Often they come in the form of chews or powders that you mix with a cat's food. Although these supplements do not require a prescription, it's still a good idea to discuss them with your veterinarian. She will be aware of the latest studies and recommended uses and dosages.

- Supplements such as Senilife contain phosphatidylserine (an amino acid), the plant compounds ginkgo biloba and resveratrol, and vitamins B6 and E. These compounds may improve membrane functioning and decrease oxidative damage caused by free radicals.
- The amino acid SAMe may help maintain cell membranes and regulate cellular function. SAMe has been evaluated for use in depression, arthritis, and liver disease. Dr. Gary Landsberg, DACVB, was part of a study that found that a SAMe supplement can increase cognitive executive function in mildly impaired senior cats. Treatment was most successful in cats in the earlier, rather than later, stages of cognitive decline.
- Alpha-casozepine (brand name Zylkene) is a chain of amino acids derived from the alpha-S1-casein protein in milk. Though the mechanism of action is not fully understood, alpha-casozepine appears to be structurally similar to GABA, a neurotransmitter that blocks impulses between nerve cells in the brain. It has been proven to be effective in treating anxiety in cats, and while it has not been evaluated for use in CDS, it may be useful as a mild calming therapy.

## How Do We Begin?

Start by keeping your older cat fit, both physically and mentally. We sometimes assume that older cats are no longer interested in playing. However, while they may not initiate play with you or play on their own as much, many older cats, if encouraged, will still play. Physical activity can be an important part of keeping your cat at a healthy weight, which will prevent some diseases and decrease pressure on her aging joints.

Wand toys, laser pointers, and small balls or other toys can all be used to engage cats. Your cat will have her own favorites, so make sure to try several types of toys before giving up on play. Some cats will even engage in solitary play if you introduce new toys or rotate the ones she already has. And remember that short play sessions are still great for interacting with your cat. To decrease her physical effort, have her play while lying on her side or back.

Food-dispensing toys are an important way for cats to stay busy and engaged during the day. As discussed in other chapters, these are easy to make yourself and also available commercially. While these types of toys have not been shown to increase overall activity compared with bowl feeding, they do provide mental enrichment.

Other forms of visual and tactile stimulation can provide enrichment for older cats. Bird feeders and butterfly bushes attract flying critters for visual enrichment and may even encourage cats to reach for their elevated resting spots.

Place scratching posts and other nail-conditioning items in areas near your cat's resting spots so she can scratch and groom when she wakes up. As discussed in chapters 3 and 11, scratchers come in different types and materials, including sisal and cardboard, so offer a few shapes, sizes, and configurations. Older cats may prefer scratching on horizontal surfaces, which are easier for them to use than vertical posts. Giving your cat a variety of options can accommodate her changing preferences, particularly if you have more than one cat.

## Managing the Environment for Senior Cats

One of the best things you can do for your senior cat is set up her space to facilitate continued access, even as her mobility changes. She needs to be able to easily get to her food, water, favorite resting spots, and litter boxes. In some cases, she might prefer to be undisturbed when accessing these items, even if she didn't mind having you around when she was younger.

### Water Bowls

Many of the medical problems older cats develop are accompanied by changes (increases, usually) in water intake, so providing extra water bowls can ensure that they get the water they need. Some cats love water fountains and will drink more readily from flowing water sources. (These are the cats who jump up to lick water out of the faucet.)

Although it might seem that flowing water would be every cat's choice (why else would cats keep meeting us at the sink?), cats do have individual preferences. In a study of cats in shelters by Dr. Christopher Pachel, DACVB, cats were given access to water fountains that were either on (flowing) or off (still), and researchers recorded the amount of water consumed by each cat. While some cats (22 percent) drank equally from either the still or flowing water sources, 44 percent preferred the still water. Another study, by Dr. Martha Cline and her colleagues at the University of Tennessee, produced similar results, and neither water source made a difference in the cats' hydration status or urine production.

These studies remind us that individual preferences are important. If your cat is one who waits patiently for you to turn on the faucet, a water fountain is a great way to maintain her intake of fresh water.

If your cat likes to drink running water, a fountain will help keep her hydrated.
*Andrea Y. Tu*

## Resting Spots

Vertical climbing and resting spots are important to most cats, including seniors, and many will choose to sit on windowsills, on top of cat trees, and on the back of couches and chairs.

As cats age, getting to these preferred spots can become more difficult. Many older cats prefer several small hops to one large jump, so strategically placed boxes or ottomans can help them get up to and down from those comfy spots. Pet stairs or ramps are also useful, especially for getting up on beds and couches.

Porter enjoys his new scratching post and tower, which is lower and easier to access than his previous one. *Debra F. Horwitz*

You can provide additional soft resting spots on the floor for your senior cat, including beds and pillows. In fact, one of Ursa's favorite places as she got older was a heated pet bed placed in the family room.

Keep an eye on your cat's preferred spots and make sure she still has a way to get to them.

Porter's cat bed is warmed by a nearby heating vent in the floor. *Debra F. Horwitz*

## Litter Box Challenges

When we see senior cats who are having trouble using the litter box, especially those who have been meticulous in their litter box use for years, we first look for medical causes. Many of the medical problems older cats commonly have are associated with increases in water intake and urine output, evidenced by an increase in the number and size of clumps in the litter box. Coupled with any personal preferences about litter box hygiene, this increase in the number of clumps can lead to litter box avoidance. Increasing the number of boxes or scooping more often can keep older kitties using their litter boxes.

Other adjustments may still be needed, including changing the location or shape of the box to encourage use. For some older cats, getting into and out of a high-sided box can be tough; low-sided boxes are more manageable. Others, who now have difficulty maintaining their posture while eliminating, may begin to urinate over the edge of a low box. This is what Ursa would do. She'd start out crouching, but as she eliminated, she would stand up because she couldn't stay in position.

There is a solution for these problems as well. Litter boxes that have a low entryway and a high back and sides are available commercially. For a do-it-yourself solution, get a high-sided clear plastic storage box and cut down one side to allow your cat to easily walk in, turn around, eliminate, and walk out. (See chapter 8 for ideas about modifying litter boxes to suit special situations.)

Remember that cats are more likely to use litter boxes that are within their core area (where they spend 75 percent of their time). If that area has become more limited over time, a change in box location or an additional box may be needed. Don't expect a senior cat to run down to the basement or up a flight of stairs every time she has to use the litter box — even if she did so reliably when she was younger.

## Social Changes

The longer a cat lives in a household, the more likely she is to experience social changes, such as when other pets are brought into the family or die. Cats have a wide range of reactions to social changes, and to understand how your cat may respond, you need to first look at the lifestyle and behavior of her closest genetic ancestors.

As we saw in chapter 9, domestic cats have evolved the ability to tolerate physical proximity with one another and take full advantage of the concentrated food sources that human dwellings create. Group living likely evolved from related females rearing kittens cooperatively.

Some feline behaviorists suggest that the default state for the modern cat is that of a solitary and territorial individual, like the ancestors of our modern cats, but adequate interactions with other cats during their sensitive socialization period (about two to seven weeks of age) can help them live harmoniously together. Research indicates that sociability has a genetic component as well. Some cats can become friendly despite poor early socialization, whereas others seem to be nervous or standoffish despite seemingly appropriate early social exposure.

Many of us want to bring multiple cats into our homes for various reasons. One of the most popular but ill-advised reasons is the assumption that all cats will benefit from the social companionship of another cat. Only those cats with corresponding genes, temperament, and early social exposure will enjoy the company of other cats, however. Many can learn to tolerate the presence of another cat in the home, but some cats will always feel more relaxed when they are the only cat in the household, and they may become very aggressive or extremely stressed around any cat they encounter after kittenhood.

It can be challenging to predict how a resident cat will react to a new one. Just because your older cat lived quite well with another housemate earlier on, that is no guarantee that she will be happy with a new cat or kitten. Introductions are stressful any time a new cat enters the home, but they may be even more problematic and stressful for elderly cats, who are less adaptable to change.

Taking in a new adult cat when you have an older one may be risky and unsuccessful. Taking in a new kitten is even less likely to work out, because the high energy level of the kitten is likely to be an annoyance and a torment to a more sedate senior.

Your senior cat is probably not craving a new companion, and almost certainly will not enjoy an active kitten. *Craig Zeichner*

## Nighttime Yowling

One of the most common complaints from owners of older cats is that their cat begins to wake up during the night and wander around, meowing loudly — and waking up everyone else in the house. Two related reasons contribute to the development and persistence of these behaviors.

First, physical changes, including cognitive dysfunction or loss of vision, may increase the cat's sense of disorientation and anxiety. A frequently noted feature of cognitive dysfunction is a change in the sleep-wake cycle. Many of these cats sleep more in the daytime or have other changes in their sleep pattern. When this is accompanied by some disorientation, the result can be a cat calling out during the early morning hours, just to get her bearings. Howling may give her a sense of where she is. Or she might be asking for help or need a night-light to aid her vision.

Second, our response to the behavior can encourage its persistence. What do you do when your cat begins to yowl at three a.m.? If you are like many cat owners, you do whatever is needed to get back to sleep. This may mean calling out in return as she finds her way to you, or it may mean getting up to check on, interact with, or even feed your cat. As you can imagine, this positive feedback does not change the behavior and may establish a pattern — one that you may not enjoy.

If your cat begins to yowl or wake in the night, talk to your veterinarian. She might have a medical condition that is causing her to seek more food or water, and evidence of this could show up in a physical exam or blood work. Medical conditions that have been associated with night waking and yowling include hypertension, hyperthyroidism, pain from arthritis or dental disease, sensory decline, and cognitive dysfunction. Certain medications may also affect cats differently as they age, so it is always important to tell your veterinarian about all medications and supplements your cat takes. Only after all these possible issues have been addressed can you begin to work on breaking the pattern of night waking.

To reestablish a normal sleep-wake cycle for your cat, it helps to know what her activity has been like throughout her adulthood. While it may seem that cats sleep the day away at every age, studies of activity patterns in cats have shown predictable patterns for indoor house cats (which are different from those for cats who spend time outdoors).

Historically, cats have been viewed as crepuscular, active at dawn and dusk — convenient for finding prey that are active at these times. However, indoor cats, who no longer rely on hunting for their food, appear fairly well adapted to a more diurnal pattern, with activity peaks in the morning and evening and sleep in the middle of the day. This pattern looks an awful lot like the pattern of most of our daily lives — waking up in the morning and getting ready for work or school (a tall, narrow activity peak), gone to work or school during the day (the cat sleeps), and then home in the evening, with activity stretching from dinner to bedtime (a wider peak).

When this pattern is altered, cats sleep more during periods of typically high activity and are awake more when they (and we) should be asleep. Many cats may be active to some extent during the night, changing location or going for a drink of water, but these episodes are relatively short and transient. Wandering or repeated nighttime waking is not generally part of an adult cat's activity pattern.

How you address this behavior will depend, in part, on what your cat is doing and what pattern has been established. When owners have been getting up and feeding their cats in the middle of the night, we often recommend a bedtime snack or a remote or automatic feeder. Set the feeder to deliver a meal *before* the time the cat typically wakes up. For example, a cat who is used to waking up and being fed at four a.m. will find that a meal magically appears in her automatic feeder at three thirty, so there's no need for her to remind you that it's time to eat.

You can also increase the attractiveness and comfort of resting spots by adding a heated pet bed and making sure the cat can get to the spot where she wants to rest. For some cats, it helps to give them their own room at night. Provisioned with water, a comfortable bed, food, toys, and a litter box that's easy to get into and out of, a separate room can be a good option in some situations. While no one likes the idea of closing away their cat at night, repeated night waking can cause real stress to the human-cat bond, and having such an option may preserve your close relationship.

For some cats, particularly when cognitive dysfunction is involved, veterinarians may recommend a medication or supplement that can help reset the sleep-wake cycle. Some medications act by increasing daytime wakefulness (Selegiline) and others by enhancing overnight sleep (Zylkene).

## Avoiding Pitfalls and Staying on Track

It can be difficult to watch our beloved companions age. Early signs may be subtle: a slight loss of a cat's natural grace when walking or jumping, a change in body shape, changes in mood and social interactions. You are your cat's best advocate and the one who will notice these changes first. Cats often don't display any of these signs in the veterinary exam room, so your cat is relying on you to report these early changes.

Many health problems can be treated, or at least their progress can be slowed, if they are detected and treated early in their course. For example, treating pain associated with arthritis can help cats remain active, encourage a healthy weight and muscle mass, and improve their quality of life. It is surprising what cats can continue to do well into their senior and geriatric years.

And yet, we cannot stop aging itself; many of the conditions we have discussed in this chapter are chronic and progressive. By observing our cats' behavior and being sensitive to their changing needs, however, we can allow these amazing creatures to age with grace. An eighteen-year-old cat may not be able to jump to the top of the refrigerator anymore, even with excellent pain management. But if getting to the top of the refrigerator is important to her, we can modify the environment to make sure she can still get there.

## What Did We Say?

- Behavior changes can be a sign of underlying disease in senior and geriatric cats and should prompt a veterinary visit.
- Early diagnosis and treatment of a chronic disease can enable a cat to live many more healthy years.
- Untreated pain can play a major role in behavior changes in older cats. These changes are often chalked up to "just getting old," but treating the source of the pain can make your cat more comfortable.
- Cognitive dysfunction syndrome (CDS), a degenerative disease of

the brain that is similar to Alzheimer's disease in people, is under-diagnosed in cats. Medications and supplements may help alleviate the symptoms of CDS.

- Environmental modifications are often easy to implement and can improve your cat's quality of life by preserving access to her favorite spots and activities.
- Cats' social needs vary widely, and decisions about adding a new cat to an older cat's environment should be based on each cat's history. Older cats are especially unlikely to appreciate the addition of a high-energy kitten.

# CONCLUSION

This book is only the second publication by the American College of Veterinary Behaviorists. The first, *Decoding Your Dog,* was received with rave reviews by pet owners and animal professionals alike. Not long after it was published in 2014, people began asking, "What about *Decoding Your Cat?*" Invigorated by the wonderful response to *Decoding Your Dog,* we set about creating a similar resource covering the most popular pet in the United States. Our goal was to provide a comprehensive book about the domestic cat, based on science and our collective experience of working with cats and their people. As with *Decoding Your Dog,* we wanted to set the record straight about cats, provide information that would strengthen the bond between them and their owners, and improve feline welfare.

Cats have shared people's lives for millennia, but often at a distance, in mutually beneficial coexistence. Nowadays, cats have moved out of the barn and into our homes and bedrooms, where they touch every part of our lives. This change has brought challenges to the lives of both cats and their human families. Central to this change is the recognition that cats are social and have their own ways of interacting with one another and with us. Cats also have environmental, social, emotional, and activity needs that are not always easily satisfied by life indoors. This can lead to conflict between cats and their human families, as well as among cats and dogs who share the same household. By understanding and meeting cats' various needs, we can enhance their lives and our own.

Cats can be very self-sufficient. Outdoor cats are prodigious hunters who spend many hours a day seeking out the multiple small meals they need to survive. They often live in large or small groups, sometimes ranging over vast areas, and communicate with one another by marking with their paws, faces, and urine. Outdoor life provides a plethora of opportunities for normal marking and hunting behaviors, but these cats are at great risk of harm from predators, vehicles, and even people. When cats live in the comfort of our homes, they are safer, but the desire to hunt for prey, mark their territory, and control their environment remains untamed. It is, therefore, extremely important that we find ways to satisfy those needs, as explained in this book, to prevent behaviors we would prefer not to live with.

Shepherding your cat from kittenhood into old age requires a commitment to his physical and emotional health. Now that you're at the end of this book, we hope you have learned how to listen to and read your cat, how to set up an enriching environment for him, and how to help him grow old with grace and comfort. Your partner in all of this is your veterinarian, who can advise you on health and behavior issues. At times some behavior problems may arise that are more challenging, and more hands-on behavior help will be necessary. In our resources section, we offer several options for this help, including the American College of Veterinary Behaviorists (www.dacvb.org) and the Animal Behavior Society's directory of certified applied animal behaviorists (www.animal behavior.org/ABSAppliedBehavior/caab-directory).

We appreciate the hard work of our colleagues in creating this wonderful book. We are overjoyed to be helping so many people maintain and improve their relationships with the cats in their lives. "Happy pets and happy people" is our goal, and we hope this book will help you to achieve all that you hope for with your cat.

MEGHAN E. HERRON, DVM, DACVB
DEBRA F. HORWITZ, DVM, DACVB
CARLO SIRACUSA, DVM, PhD, DACVB, DECAWBM

# APPENDIX A

## Teaching Your Cat to Like the Carrier

Lisa Radosta, DVM, DACVB

Most cats hate the carrier, and it's easy to understand why. Cats go into the carrier only when something bad is going to happen, like a long car ride or a trip to the veterinarian. It takes just one negative experience for your kitty to believe that the carrier is bad news. But you can change that perception.

The first thing is choosing the best carrier for your cat. In general, try to choose a sturdy carrier that comes apart in several places (such as a plastic carrier with a removable top section) so that your cat can be lifted out easily or examined by the veterinarian inside the carrier if necessary. Then follow these dos and don'ts to help your cat love the carrier.

Do:

- Get the carrier out of the garage, clean it up, and put it in the area where your cat usually hangs out.
- Take the carrier apart by taking the top off and removing the door for a couple of weeks to help your cat feel comfortable and perhaps rest in the bottom portion.
- Put your cat's bed in the carrier.
- Make the carrier positive and encourage discovery by placing special toys and treats inside or feeding your cat there.
- Consider placing the carrier in a safe elevated spot where your cat likes to spend time, such as a couch, a chair, or a wide windowsill.

- Teach your cat to get into the carrier with clicker training or luring.
- Use a synthetic pheromone spray inside the carrier thirty minutes before calling your cat to the carrier.
- Put something soft in the carrier before taking your cat out in it.
- When your cat is comfortable in the carrier, take him on short rides while encouraging a positive emotional state with delicious foods.
- Keep the carrier level in the car by using towels or bumpers.
- Clean the inside of the carrier with an unscented cleaner after each use.

## Don't:

- Pull the carrier out and try to force your cat inside immediately before a veterinary visit.
- Bring the carrier out only when you have to take your cat somewhere.
- Dump your cat out onto the examination table at the veterinarian's office.

If your cat already has a negative conditioned emotional response to the carrier, desensitization and classical counterconditioning may be necessary to change his emotional state. Desensitization and classical counterconditioning is a process by which the cat is slowly exposed to the stimulus (the carrier) while using a positive stimulus (food) to change his emotional state. (See chapter 6 for more information.)

Keep your cat's carrier open, available, and cozy all the time so that he can relax and sleep in it, creating a positive association. *Carlo Siracusa*

# APPENDIX B

# Medicating Your Cat

Although we hope our feline friends will always be healthy, there may come a time when it's necessary to give your cat medication. Medications are most often administered orally, as either a pill or a liquid. Given the cautious nature of cats about new and novel foods, it requires some preparation and training to make sure you can administer medication when the time comes.

## Cautions

- Never grab your cat while she is sleeping to administer a pill. This will scare her and cause her anxiety when you approach her in the future.
- Likewise, avoid catching your cat in the litter box to give a medication. This could lead to litter box avoidance and house soiling.
- Avoid adding medication to your cat's regular daily diet. Some medications are bitter-tasting and may result in her not eating at all, which of course is not healthy.
- Never medicate your cat by forcibly pushing a pill or pouring liquid into her mouth. This is an aversive procedure that will cause your cat to run away when you approach her.

## How to Begin

- It is always best to begin with kittens or young cats, but these training tools can be used with any age cat.

- Teach your cat to enthusiastically come to you instead of chasing her around.
- Offer her different treats or canned food to see which she finds most delicious. This should not be an everyday food, but rather a special high-value treat. Try to offer it at least weekly.
- If you have multiple cats, each one should have her own treat time.
- Find a quiet, elevated place and teach your cat to come to that location daily for something special. It can be a food treat, a grooming session, or just some extra petting. Use a special word cue, perhaps "treat time," to call her to the spot. Every once in a while, give her the special high-value treat as well.
- Once she is readily coming to that spot for a tasty treat, you can start giving her the medication as described in the next section.

## Administering Medication

- The easiest way to give medication is to hide it in something delicious. For many cats, Greenies Pill Pockets fit the bill. They come in several flavors; try a few to see which one your cat likes best.
- Practice giving her a Pill Pocket without medication, but be sure to close the top of the Pill Pocket so it looks similar to how it will be when a pill is inside. It may help to put something crunchy inside, such as bits of kibble, chips, or fish flakes, to prepare her for the feel of a pill when it is time to medicate her.
- Another option is crushing the pill (always ask your veterinarian or pharmacist if this will alter how the drug works) and putting it into some type of delicious food.
  * Many human foods work well — anchovy paste, salmon, chicken baby food, even ice cream.
  * Try Cheez Whiz or liver paste for nutritional supplements that are gooey.
  * Avoid adding the medication to a wet food that she usually eats, because that may put her off her regular food.
- Always reward your cat with a tasty treat after she eats the food or treat with the medication. You can also add in some playtime for an extra treat.
- A more novel idea is to teach your cat to lap up dots of food on a

plate or treats lined up in a row. For example, the first dot or treat will have no medication, the second will have medication, and the third and fourth will have none. Always change the placement of the medication in the lineup.

- Some cats are amenable to pilling syringes or swallowing a pill if it is in a gel capsule.
- Some medications are available as tasty chewable tablets or flavored liquids.
- Always discuss with your veterinarian the best way to administer a particular medication in order to achieve the best results.

# Tips for Introducing Cats and Dogs

Despite the popular cartoon images, cats and dogs can be good friends. As with cat-cat introductions, first impressions matter. You can help smooth cat-dog introductions with careful planning and an understanding of the body language in both species that indicates excitement, fear, anxiety, and aggression.

## General Safety Rules

- If the dog is known to have been aggressive toward cats in the past, schedule a visit to a veterinary behaviorist before trying to introduce the pets. Before you begin, the dog should be able to follow basic cues, including "sit," "down," and "look at me" or "watch me."
- All introductions should be done by an adult who is in control of one pet. That means a minimum of two adults.
- Identify delectable treats for the cat and equally delectable ones for the dog. These should be special, not regular daily foods.
- Before bringing a new dog home, make sure the cat has a refuge where he can retreat to whenever he feels the need. This should be a safe place that the dog cannot access, perhaps up high where the dog can't reach.
- The dog should be on a leash held by an adult.
- The cat may be free to roam around the room, or also on a harness and leash held by an adult.

- Never allow the dog to chase the cat or pick him up in his mouth.
- If at any point the dog becomes hyper-focused or agitated, salivates, stares at the cat, or tries to dart at the cat, end the introduction and contact your veterinarian for further steps.

## Introducing Your New Dog to Your Resident Cat

- When you bring the dog home, do not let him have full access to the house. Instead, confine him to one or two rooms, using baby gates and closed doors.
- Keep the dog confined until the cat is comfortable moving around the house and approaches the baby gate to investigate.
- Let the cat investigate the newcomer at his own pace.
- When the cat is comfortably approaching the gate, rubbing his cheeks and body on it and not showing any signs of fear, you can progress to controlled meetings.

## Introducing Your New Cat to Your Resident Dog

- When you bring the cat home, do not let him have full access to the entire house. Instead, confine him to a single refuge room that contains all of his basic needs, including food, water, litter box, perches, scratching posts, and hiding places. Keep the door closed at first.
- After one or two days, when the cat seems calm and acclimated, start giving the dog and cat their favorite treats on either side of the closed door.
- If the cat is not hissing or growling at the sound or smell of the dog, you can stack two baby gates in the doorway as a barrier rather than keeping the door closed.
- Feed the dog and cat treats a few feet away from each other on either side of the baby gates several times a day.
- When the cat is comfortably approaching the gate, rubbing his cheeks and body on it and not showing any signs of fear, you can progress to controlled meetings.

## Controlled Meetings

- Put the dog on a leash and walk him into the room where the cat is sitting. If the cat is the newcomer, these meetings should take place in a room other than the cat refuge.
- If the cat remains still, walk the dog around the room on a loose leash, to avoid transmitting any of your own anxiety with a tight leash.
- Do not allow the dog to act inappropriately toward the cat — barking, lunging, or chasing.
- If the dog seems distracted by the cat, ask him to "watch" or "look," or call his name to get his attention and then give him a task to do such as "sit." Reward him for compliance.
- Continue to reward calm behavior by the dog with praise and treats, to associate the cat with good things.
- Reward the cat for calm behavior as well, to associate the dog with good things.
- Maintain a distance at which the dog and the cat both remain calm.
- The cat may hiss, swat, or growl at the dog. Do not punish him (he's genuinely afraid!), so that he will not associate punishment with the presence of the dog. Move the dog farther away until the hissing or growling stops. If the cat remains fearful, go back to offering treats on either side of the baby gates for a few more days.
- Repeat these controlled meetings until both animals are calm and relaxed with each other.
- Do not allow the dog to have free run of the house when you're not home until you are sure the two animals are safe with each other. Separation when they are alone may be prudent.
- Most dogs and cats eventually learn to live peacefully with each other. But remember, a dog is a natural predator of cats, so always supervise their interactions in the beginning. Sometimes things don't go as desired, and your cat and dog may always need some degree of supervision when together, or even separation if their interactions might pose a risk to their safety.

# RECOMMENDED RESOURCES

## Professional Organizations

### American College of Veterinary Behaviorists (ACVB)
www.dacvb.org

The ACVB is a professional organization of veterinarians who have achieved board certification in the specialty of veterinary behavior. Board-certified individuals are called diplomates and have the letters "DACVB" after their names. The mission of the ACVB is to advance the behavioral health of animals by certifying veterinary behavior specialists and providing science-based education. These specialists do research and work with individual pet owners, other animal professionals, and facilities that care for animals to manage behavior problems and improve the welfare of animals.

### American Veterinary Society of Animal Behavior (AVSAB)
https://avsab.org

The AVSAB is an organization of veterinarians and research professionals who share an interest in understanding animal behavior. It is committed to improving the quality of life of all animals and strengthening the bond between animals and their owners. The website offers several expert position papers on important issues and a locator to help you find a veterinarian with an interest in behavior near you.

### Animal Behavior Society (ABS)
www.animalbehaviorsociety.org

The ABS is devoted to the scientific study of animal behavior, including applied animal behavior, which studies the behavior of companion animals and of farm, zoo, laboratory, and wild animals as it applies to their management. The website includes a list of certified applied animal behaviorists (CAABs) and associate certified applied animal behaviorists (ACAABs) who have met the society's requirements for certification. These individuals provide behavior consulting services to the public as well as to other professionals.

### Society of Veterinary Behavior Technicians (SVBT)
www.svbt.org

The SVBT promotes scientifically based techniques of animal training, management, and behavior modification. It connects veterinary technicians around the world, sharing their knowledge and experience to enhance the role of the veterinary technician in veterinary medicine and welfare.

### Academy of Veterinary Behavior Technicians (AVBT)
www.avbt.net

The AVBT certifies qualified veterinary technicians as veterinary technician specialists (VTSs) in the field of animal behavior. A VTS in behavior has demonstrated superior knowledge in scientific and humane techniques of behavior health, problem prevention, training, management, and behavior modification.

### American Association of Feline Practitioners (AAFP)
https://catfriendly.com

The AAFP supports its members in improving the health and welfare of cats through high standards of practice, continuing education, and evidence-based medicine. Among the AAFP's activities are providing its members with progressive research and valuable resources, which include peer-reviewed scientific research in the *Journal of Feline Medicine and Surgery*.

### American Animal Hospital Association (AAHA)
www.aaha.org

The AAHA accredits small animal hospitals throughout the United States and Canada that meet its standards for excellence in pet health care. The website includes pet news and informative articles written by experts, helpful videos, and activities for children.

### American Society for the Prevention of Cruelty to Animals (ASPCA)
www.aspca.org

The ASPCA website includes updates on legislative matters, animal shelter support, behavior articles, and general information about animal welfare. It also includes the Animal Poison Control Center (www.aspcapro.org/about-programs-services/aspca-animal-poison-control-center) and a searchable toxic plant database (www.aspca.org/pet-care/animal-poison-control/toxic-and-non-toxic-plants).

**American Veterinary Medical Association (AVMA)**
www.avma.org

The AVMA website includes podcasts and the latest news in veterinary medicine that may affect your pet — including pet food recalls.

## Online Resources

**DACVB Feline Body Language Tips**
https://c.ymcdn.com/sites/dacvb.site-ym.com/resource/resmgr/docs/Tip2-Feline_body_language.pdf

**AAFP Cat Friendly Homes Care Sheets**
"How to Feed a Cat": https://catfriendly.com/cat-care-at-home/how-to-feed-a-cat/
"Top 10 Tips for Your Senior Cat": https://catfriendly.com/cat-care-at-home/senior-care/10-tips/

**AAFP and ISFM Guidelines**
*AAFP and ISFM Feline Environmental Needs Guidelines:* https://journals.sagepub.com/doi/pdf/10.1177/1098612X13477537
*AAFP and ISFM Feline-Friendly Handling Guidelines:* https://journals.sagepub.com/doi/pdf/10.1016/j.jfms.2011.03.012
*AAFP and ISFM Guidelines for Diagnosing and Solving House-Soiling Behavior in Cats:* https://journals.sagepub.com/doi/pdf/10.1177/1098612X14539092
*American Association of Feline Practitioners Senior Care Guidelines:* https://journals.sagepub.com/doi/pdf/10.1016/j.jfms.2009.07.011

**Karen Pryor Clicker Training**
https://clickertraining.com/cat-training?source=navbar

**Fear Free Pets**
https://fearfreepets.com

Fear Free Pets provides online and in-person education to veterinary professionals and pet owners. The educational content offers information and tools to help owners look after their pets' physical and emotional well-being. Both complimentary and premium (for a fee) memberships are available, providing access to articles, tips, monthly deals, and fear-free veterinary visit resources. Veterinary professionals and their associated hospitals can seek Fear Free certification.

**Committed to Claws**
www.committedtoclaws.com

Committed to Claws provides cat owners with educational resources that promote understanding of the role cats' claws play in their physical and behavioral health and guide the humane management of scratching behavior. The goal is to reduce declawing through education. Solutions to scratching challenges focus on offering choices and catering to individual cats' needs.

## Additional Reading

Bradshaw, John. *Cat Sense.* New York: Basic Books, 2013.

Bradshaw, John, and Sarah Ellis. *The Trainable Cat.* New York: Basic Books, 2017.

Kirkham, Lewis. *Tell Your Cat You're Pregnant.* Melbourne, Australia: Little Creatures Publishing, 2015.

Pryor, Karen. *Clicker Training for Cats.* Waltham, MA: Sunshine Books, 2003.

## Meghan E. Herron, DVM, DACVB

Dr. Meghan Herron is an associate professor in the Department of Veterinary Clinical Sciences and the current head of the Behavioral Medicine Service at The Ohio State University Veterinary Medical Center. There she provides behavioral medicine services to dogs and cats with behavior issues, including, but not limited to, human-directed aggression, inter-pet aggression, separation anxiety, inappropriate elimination, fears, phobias, compulsive behaviors, and cognitive dys-

Penney Adams/Adler House Photography

function. When not treating patients, she has the privilege of educating future veterinarians on animal behavior, problem prevention, and treatment strategies, as well as mentoring behavioral medicine residents who will move on to become board-certified veterinary behaviorists.

Dr. Herron graduated from Arizona State University with a degree in zoology and is a graduate of The Ohio State University College of Veterinary Medicine. She started her veterinary career as a general practitioner for both dogs and cats and eventually moved on to complete a three-year residency program in behavioral medicine at the University of Pennsylvania School of Veterinary Medicine. She is board-certified by and an active member of the American College of Veterinary Behaviorists. Dr. Herron has extensive experience working with shelter and rescue animals in both the Columbus and Philadelphia areas. She has a strong interest in behavior problem prevention and improving the quality of life and adoptability of shelter animals. She has published articles in the *Journal of the American Veterinary Medical Association, Applied Animal Behaviour Science, Topics in Companion Animal Medicine, Compendium, Veterinary Clinics of North America Small Animal Practice,* and *Journal of Veterinary Behavior.*

As a frequent speaker, Dr. Herron has presented lectures around the globe, providing veterinarians, animal care personnel, and pet owners with information that is entertaining, educational, and scientifically sound. She lives in Columbus, Ohio, with her husband, Josh; daughters Rowan and Amelia; the laziest French Bulldog who ever lived, Nero; her spunky little Chihuahua, Willett; and a most playful black cat, Junebug. Sadly, her Sphynx, Mr. Girard Bigglesworth, pictured in her photo, passed away shortly before *Decoding Your Cat* was completed.

### Debra F. Horwitz, DVM, DACVB

Dr. Debra Horwitz is a graduate of Michigan State University College of Veterinary Medicine and a diplomate of the American College of Veterinary Behaviorists. She has had a referral practice for behavior problems in companion animals for over thirty years and is currently located in St. Louis, Missouri. In 2012, she received the Veterinarian of the Year award from Ceva Animal Health at the 57th Annual Purina Pro Plan Show Dogs of the Year Awards, and was voted 2012 and

*Courtesy of Debra F. Horwitz*

2014 North American Veterinary Conference Small Animal Speaker of the Year.

Dr. Horwitz is a frequent lecturer at numerous national and international veterinary meetings, including the North American Veterinary Conference, the Western Veterinary Conference, the American Animal Hospital Association annual meeting, the American Veterinary Medical Association annual convention, the Australian Veterinary Association, and the Madrid Veterinary Congress. Her articles on companion animal behavior have appeared in the *Journal of the American Veterinary Medi-*

*cal Association, Veterinary Forum, Compendium, Journal of the American Animal Hospital Association, NAVC Clinician's Brief,* and books on behavior for pet owners. She also serves on several advisory boards for corporations and publications related to animal behavior, health, and welfare. She appears locally and nationally on radio and television, as well as in local print publications and lectures.

Her most recent book for veterinarians, *Blackwell's Five-Minute Veterinary Consult Clinical Companion: Canine and Feline Behavior,* 2nd edition, was published in 2018 (the first edition, coauthored with Dr. Jacqueline Neilson, was published in 2007). She is coeditor and author of the *BSAVA Manual of Canine and Feline Behavioural Medicine,* 1st and 2nd editions. She is the behavior section editor for *Blackwell's Five-Minute Veterinary Consult,* 3rd, 4th, and 5th editions. She is coauthor of the *Lifelearn Behavior Client Handouts,* available on CD and online. Dr. Horwitz was the lead editor for *Decoding Your Dog,* a book for pet owners written by members of the American College of Veterinary Behaviorists, published by Houghton Mifflin Harcourt in 2014.

Dr. Horwitz is actively involved in organized veterinary medicine, serving on numerous committees for the American College of Veterinary Behaviorists, and is a past president of the ACVB. She has also served on the Committee for the Human-Animal Bond of the American Veterinary Medical Association. She is a member of the Greater St. Louis Veterinary Medical Association, the Missouri Veterinary Medical Association, and the American Veterinary Medical Association. Locally, she has helped train behavior helpline associates at the Humane Society of Missouri and the Nestlé Purina PetCare Office of Consumer Affairs.

## Carlo Siracusa, DVM, PhD, DACVB, DECAWBM

Born in Italy, Dr. Carlo Siracusa got his DVM from the University of Messina, Italy, and his PhD from the Autonomous University of Barcelona, Spain, defending a thesis on perioperative stress in dogs and the effect of pheromone therapy. He completed his residency in animal behavior at the School of Veterinary Medicine of the University of

John Donges/PennVet

Pennsylvania, where he is currently an associate professor of clinical animal behavior and welfare and the director of the Animal Behavior Service.

Carlo is board-certified by the American College of Veterinary Behaviorists, of which he is president, and by the European College of Animal Welfare and Behavioural Medicine. His research interests are focused on canine stress evaluation and control; canine and feline temperament evaluation; prognostic factors and treatment outcomes of behavior problems; and behavior and cognitive changes in dogs with medical disease.

Carlo was a breeder of Persians, British Shorthairs, and Scottish Folds and now shares his life with Elsa, a dilute calico domestic shorthair.

# ABOUT THE AUTHORS

### Julia Albright, MA, DVM, DACVB

Dr. Julia Albright is a diplomate of the American College of Veterinary Behaviorists and an associate professor at the University of Tennessee College of Veterinary Medicine. She obtained both a master's degree in experimental psychology and her DVM from the University of Tennessee before completing a residency and fellowship in animal behavior at Cornell University College of Veterinary Medicine. Dr. Albright's research interests include reducing stress in animal facilities, psychopharmacology, and the human-animal bond. She is also actively involved in national animal sheltering organizations. She is a consultant for the ASPCA and the current chair of the National Council on Pet Population, an organization dedicated to bringing research to the shelter community. She lives in Knoxville, Tennessee, with her two beloved black cats and various other two- and four-legged family members. She and her daughter are avid horse lovers.

### Kelly Ballantyne, DVM, DACVB

Dr. Kelly Ballantyne graduated from the University of Illinois College of Veterinary Medicine in 2005. She started her career as a primary care veterinarian and within a few years developed a strong interest in behavioral medicine. She completed a behavioral residency under the mentorship of Dr. John Ciribassi and in 2015 became board-certified in the American College of Veterinary Behaviorists. Dr. Ballantyne is a clinical assistant professor at the University of Illinois College of Veterinary Medicine.

She runs the college's behavior service at its Chicago satellite practice and also teaches veterinary students about animal behavior.

### Sara Bennett, MS, DVM, DACVB

Dr. Sara Bennett received her DVM in 2006 from Purdue University. She spent three years in general practice in southwestern Indiana before returning to Purdue to complete a residency in animal behavior with a shelter medicine focus and earn her master of science. She obtained certification as a diplomate of the American College of Veterinary Behaviorists in 2012. After board certification, she practiced veterinary behavior in the Chicago and greater Midwest area, seeing private patients and consulting with a variety of sheltering organizations for several years. Dr. Bennett is currently a clinical assistant professor of clinical sciences at the College of Veterinary Medicine of North Carolina State University. She is also a co-instructor for the University of Florida College of Veterinary Medicine online learning course Shelter Animal Behavior and Welfare, part of the Maddie's Shelter Medicine Program. She particularly enjoys addressing problem behaviors in sheltered and rescued animals — helping to protect animal welfare, making these pets more adoptable, working to strengthen the budding human-animal bond, and helping to keep these animals in their new homes.

### Sharon Crowell-Davis, DVM, PhD, DACVB

Dr. Sharon Crowell-Davis earned her DVM at Auburn University and her PhD, focusing on neurobiology and behavior, at Cornell University. She was the youngest of the founding diplomates of the American College of Veterinary Behaviorists. She has served as president of that organization and of the American Veterinary Society of Animal Behavior, as well as in multiple other offices. She is currently a professor of behavioral medicine at the University of Georgia College of Veterinary Medicine. In addition to seeing cats in the clinic, she has conducted research on domestic cats living in homes and feral cats surviving on the periphery of human existence. Her best teachers about cat behavior have always been the cats themselves. She has had many cats over the decades who have crossed the Rainbow Bridge and currently has fifteen cats, all rescues. They teach her about the complexity of cat social life and communication. Each cat has a different voice and can modify that voice based on context. Dr. Crowell-

Davis can tell who is vocalizing in another room and what is going on. The distress meow and the "another stupid squirrel has broken into the house that smells like predators" meow (that's really not a good term for it, but we haven't developed the right term yet) send her running. For everyone out there who has color biases, her tortoiseshell and calico cats are all sweet, wonderful pets.

## Terry Marie Curtis, DVM, MS, DACVB

Dr. Terry Curtis graduated with honors from the University of Florida College of Veterinary Medicine in 1997. She worked as a feline-only practitioner in Florida until the summer of 2000, when she began her residency in veterinary behavior at the University of Georgia. Concurrently, she received a master of science in psychology, investigating grooming behavior in the domestic cat. Completing her residency in June 2003, she joined the team at the UF College of Veterinary Medicine, heading up the Clinical Behavior Service. Dr. Curtis, a diplomate of the American College of Veterinary Behaviorists, does house calls in Florida and South Georgia and teaches two behavior courses at the UF College of Veterinary Medicine. She is a regular contributor to the North American Veterinary Community's VMX conference and is the coordinator of a yearly behavior symposium there. Author of a number of articles in journals such as *Veterinary Clinics of North America: Small Animal Practice* and chapters in books such as the 6th edition of *Blackwell's Five-Minute Veterinary Consult,* she is also a member of the editorial review board for *Today's Veterinary Practice* magazine and the *Journal of Feline Medicine and Surgery,* and she serves on the advisory board for Blue-Care. She was a panel contributor to the 2014 *AAFP and ISFM Guidelines for Diagnosing and Solving House Soiling Behavior in Cats.* Dr. Curtis has worked with the Hemingway House cats in Key West, discussing the subject on ABC's *Nightline* (July 2007), and appeared on NBC's *Today* show (July 2008) talking about fears and phobias in dogs.

## Leticia Mattos De Souza Dantas, DVM, MS, PhD, DACVB

Dr. Leticia Dantas earned her DVM at the Universidade Federal Fluminense in sunny Rio de Janeiro, Brazil, in 2003. She obtained a master of science in feline medicine and welfare in 2008, and a PhD in feline social and agonistic behavior and environmental enrichment for communally housed cats in 2010. Dr. Dantas has over fifteen years of experience working in academia. She has taught ethology, behavioral medicine, bioethics, and animal welfare science and has trained senior veterinary students in clinical behavioral medicine. In 2009, she started working at the Behavioral Medicine Service at the University of Georgia Veterinary Teaching Hospital, where she also did her residency. She is currently a clinical assistant professor in the Behavioral Medicine Service and its director. Dr. Dantas is the cofounder and director of ZooPsych, a consulting business in behavioral medicine and animal mental health, and a member of the advisory panel for the Fear Free Initiative. Her cat, Tiger, is a celebrity at UGA. Found very sick on the streets as a young adult, he was fostered temporarily and then adopted by Dr. Dantas's family. Besides saving another life, Dr. Dantas wanted to show veterinary students that an adult cat could learn and adapt just like a kitten. Tiger's amazing resilience and sweetness allowed him to learn to enjoy veterinary handling. For years, he went to work to teach students in low-stress handling labs and to demonstrate behavior therapy techniques. He is now eight and retired. He spends most of his days hunting in his outdoor enclosure or simply sunbathing. He is a very loud purrer and loves Christmas decorations.

### Margaret Gruen, DVM, PhD, DACVB

Dr. Margaret Gruen is a diplomate of the American College of Veterinary Behaviorists and an assistant professor of behavioral medicine at the North Carolina State University College of Veterinary Medicine. She completed her internship and residency at North Carolina State University and then obtained a PhD in comparative biomedical sciences, with a project focused on understanding pain behavior in cats with arthritis. She completed a postdoctoral program at Duke University with the Canine Cognition Center, studying cognitive development in puppies. Her research focuses on pain, cognition, and human-animal interaction, including how animals communicate with us. She lives in Raleigh, North Carolina, with her husband, children, and furry family members.

### Rachel Malamed, DVM, DACVB

Dr. Rachel Malamed is a native of Toronto, Canada. She attended the University of Guelph in Ontario, Canada, and graduated in 2001 with a bachelor of science. She then attended Ontario Veterinary College, the oldest veterinary school in Canada, and graduated in 2005 with a DVM. During her clinical behavioral medicine rotation, she realized that veterinary medicine went beyond treating animals for physical illness. She witnessed firsthand how stress could impact or exacerbate medical conditions and came to understand that addressing an animal's behavior was just as important as treating his physical health. In 2006, she moved to sunny California and did an internship, after which she did a three-year residency at UC Davis and became board-certified in clinical behavioral medicine. Dr. Malamed currently lives in Los Angeles and owns a private behavioral medicine practice. When she is not seeing patients, her two young girls keep her busy.

### Kelly Moffat, DVM, DACVB

Dr. Kelly Moffat was born and raised in Arizona. She graduated with a bachelor of science in biology from Arizona State University and attended veterinary school at Colorado State University, graduating in 1993. She completed a residency in behavior and went on to pass her certifying exam to become a diplomate of the American College of Veterinary Behaviorists in 2004. Dr. Moffat practices as a veterinary behaviorist while maintaining her general practice caseload and serving as medical director at the VCA Mesa Animal Hospital in Mesa, Arizona. She has quite the family at home, including one amazing daughter, four dogs, three cats, a horse, two guinea pigs, ten chickens, a tortoise, and a plethora of fish. She enjoys jogging and helping with local community service organizations.

### Amy L. Pike, DVM, DACVB

Dr. Amy Pike graduated from Colorado State University in 2003 and was commissioned as a captain in the US Army Veterinary Corps. Treating military working dogs spurred her initial interest in behavioral medicine. Dr. Pike did her residency program under Dr. Debra Horwitz, DACVB, and became board-certified in 2015. She is chief of the Behavior Medicine Division at the Veterinary Referral Center of Northern Virginia. She is a member of the Fear Free advisory panel and the editorial staff of the *American Veterinarian,* and she was recently named one of the Top Veterinarians of Northern Virginia by *Northern Virginia* magazine.

## Sabrina Poggiagliolmi, DVM, MS, DACVB

Dr. Sabrina Poggiagliolmi is truly a world traveler: She was born in Tuscany and grew up around the world (Canada, North Africa). She returned to Italy to attend veterinary school at the Università degli Studi di Milano, where she graduated with a doctorate in veterinary medicine in 1994. Dr. Poggiagliolmi was in private practice in Italy until she moved to the United States in 2006 to enroll in a three-year comprehensive clinical residency in veterinary behavioral medicine at the University of Georgia, where she was awarded a master of science with a major in veterinary and biomedical sciences. Dr. Poggiagliolmi is a diplomate of the American College of Veterinary Behaviorists and an integral member of the Long Island Veterinary Specialists Behavior Medicine Department. LIVS is the only facility on Long Island with a behavioral medicine department, which is committed to helping owners communicate with their pets in a more positive and productive way in order to manage behavior issues. Dr. Poggiagliolmi is an active member of both the American Veterinary Medical Association and the American Veterinary Society of Animal Behavior. When not at work, she enjoys trips to New York City, vacationing on the beach, and spending time with her two cats, Mirtillo and Patata.

## Lisa Radosta, DVM, DACVB

Dr. Lisa Radosta graduated from the University of Florida College of Veterinary Medicine in 2000. She completed a residency in behavioral medicine at the University of Pennsylvania. During her residency, she was awarded the American College of Veterinary Behaviorists resident research award two years in a row. Dr. Radosta lectures nationally and internationally to veterinarians, their staff, and laypeople. She has written book chapters for textbooks, including the *Handbook of Behavior Problems of the Dog and Cat, Blackwell's Five-Minute Veterinary Consult,* and *Canine and Feline and Small Animal Pediatrics.* She is also the coauthor of *From Fearful to Fear Free.* She has published scientific research articles in *Applied Animal Behaviour Science* and the *Veterinary Journal,* and has written review articles for *Advances in Small Animal Medicine and Surgery, Compendium, Veterinary Team Brief, NAVC Clinician's Brief,* and *NEWstat.* She is the section editor for *Advances in Small Ani-*

*mal Medicine and Surgery.* Dr. Radosta serves on the Fear Free executive council and the American Animal Hospital Association Behavior Management Guidelines Task Force. She has been interviewed for many publications, has appeared frequently on television, and has a podcast on VETgirl.

### Kersti Seksel, BVSc, MRCVS, MA, FANZCVS, DACVB, DECAWBM, FAVA

Dr. Kersti Seksel is fascinated by animals and why they do what they do. She is passionate about helping people understand animals better so that she can improve the lives of people and their pets. Dr. Seksel graduated from Sydney University, then worked in the United Kingdom, where she learned that many pets died each year because of their behavior. She has a bachelor of arts in behavioral sciences (major in psychology) and a master of arts (hons). She is a board-certified specialist in behavioral medicine in the Australian, American, and European colleges. She pioneered puppy preschool and kitten kindergarten classes, teaches the distance education course in behavioral medicine for the Centre for Veterinary Education at the University of Sydney, and is an adjunct senior lecturer at Charles Sturt University, Wagga Wagga, New South Wales. She presents at conferences nationally and internationally, runs webinars, writes textbook chapters, wrote the book *Training Your Cat,* is a regular presenter on radio and TV, and is a consultant on the Veterinary Information Network.

### Leslie Sinn, DVM, DACVB

Dr. Leslie Sinn obtained both her undergraduate degree in animal science and her DVM from the University of Georgia. She completed an internship in small animal medicine and surgery while overseeing the exotic, avian, and wildlife caseload at the teaching hospital. After five years in private practice, she joined the faculty of the Northern Virginia Community College Veterinary Technology Program. During her tenure there, she taught a variety of courses to veterinary technician students, including anesthesia and behavior. She served as dean of the program for fifteen years. Dr. Sinn is a diplomate of the American College of Veterinary Behaviorists and currently runs a behavior referral practice in the Washington, DC, area. In addition to seeing clinical cases, she consults with rescue groups, shelters, and other organizations on animal welfare and behavior issues. Dr. Sinn enjoys writing and speaking about behavior and has presented nationally and internationally on a variety of animal behavior topics, including both normal and abnormal behavior in cats.

### Beth Groetzinger Strickler, MS, DVM, DACVB, CDBC

Dr. Beth Strickler is a diplomate of the American College of Veterinary Behaviorists. She has a master's degree in psychology from Penn State University and received her DVM from the University of Tennessee. She spent several years in general practice before completing her residency in behavior, during which she completed a research project evaluating client reports of feline play. She is the owner of a specialty referral practice, Veterinary Behavior Solutions, which serves behavior patients in both Tennessee and Kentucky. She has been a visiting instructor at several veterinary colleges and enjoys lecturing regionally and nationally. She shares her life outside of work with her two active sons, two horses, and two dogs. She misses having cats in her life after the passing of her favorite kitty, Zayak, this past year.

### Karen Lynn Chieko Sueda, DVM, DACVB

Hawaii native Dr. Karen Sueda chose to pursue her veterinary education in the cooler climate of Northern California. She obtained her veterinary medical degree and completed her clinical animal behavior residency at the UC Davis School of Veterinary Medicine before moving with her cat, Tyler, to balmy Los Angeles. In addition to seeing veterinary behavior cases at VCA West Los Angeles Animal Hospital, Dr. Sueda travels throughout Southern California to work with feline patients and their owners in their homes. When time permits, she enjoys cooking, discovering new restaurants, and catching up on TV shows with Tyler on her lap.

### Wailani Sung, MS, PhD, DVM, DACVB

Dr. Wailani Sung has a passion for helping owners prevent or effectively manage behavior problems in companion animals, enabling them to maintain a high quality of life. Dr. Sung obtained her master's degree and doctorate in psychology, with a special interest in animal behavior, from the University of Georgia, and her DVM from the University of Georgia College of Veterinary Medicine. She has practiced veterinary behavioral medicine in dogs, cats, and birds in the greater Seattle area for the past ten years. She does not consider any patient or problem hopeless, and her treatment protocols are based on scientific information about animal behavior, psychopharmacology, and learning theory. Dr. Sung is a frequent contributor to *HealthyPet* magazine and the websites Vetstreet and petMD. She is a coauthor of *From Fearful to Fear Free,* in which she collaborated with Dr. Marty Becker, Dr. Lisa Radosta, DACVB, and Mikkel Becker. Dr. Sung currently works at the San Francisco SPCA. She enjoys spending her free time with her husband and their family of two dogs, a senior cat, a red-bellied parrot, and a citron-crested cockatoo.

# MEMBERS OF THE AMERICAN COLLEGE
# OF VETERINARY BEHAVIORISTS

Julia Albright (Keck)
Melissa Bain
Kelly Ballantyne
Bonnie Beaver
Sara Bennett
Jeannine Berger
Laurie Bergman
Stephanie Borns-Weil
Desireé Broach
Deb Bryant
Walter Burghardt
Christine Calder
Gabrielle Carter
E'Lise Christensen
John Ciribassi
Leslie Cooper
Sharon Crowell-Davis
Terry Marie Curtis
Leticia Dantas
Isabelle Demontigny-Bédard
Sagi Denenberg
Theresa DePorter
Marion Desmarchelier
Nicholas Dodman (Emeritus)
Margaret Duxbury
Ashley Elzerman
Ariel Fagen
Gerrard Flannigan
Diane Frank (Emeritus)
Lori Gaskins

Shana Gilbert-Gregory
Martin Godbout
Margaret Gruen
Benjamin L. Hart
Lore Haug
Meghan E. Herron
Marie Hopfensperger
Debra F. Horwitz
Katherine A. Houpt
Mami Irimajiri
Soraya Juarbe-Diaz
Mary Klinck
Colleen Koch
Gary Landsberg
Emily Levine
M. Leanne Lilly
Ellen Lindell
Scott Line
Andrew Luescher (Emeritus)
Rachel Malamed
Kenneth Martin
Patrick Melese
Petra Mertens (Emeritus)
Alexandra Moesta
Kelly Moffat
Jacqueline Neilson
Niwako Ogata
Jill Orlando
Karen Overall
Christopher Pachel

Katherine Pankratz
Amy Pike
Sabrina Poggiagliolmi
Patricia Pryor
Lisa Radosta
Eranda Rajapaksha
Marsha Reich
Ilana Reisner
Amanda Rigterink
Jill Sackman
Stephanie Schwartz
Sheila Segurson
Lynne Seibert
Kersti Seksel
Barbara Sherman (Simpson)

Elizabeth Shull
Leslie Sinn
Carlo Siracusa
Elizabeth Stelow
Meredith Stepita
Beth Strickler
Karen Sueda
Wailani Sung
Valarie Tynes
Karen Van Haaften
Vint Virga
Victoria L. Voith
Jacqueline Wilhelmy
Colleen Wilson

# INDEX

toms
definition, 75
friendliness inherited from, 39, 44,
191–92
tongues, 15, 80, 88
Tonkinese cats, 36
"touch," teaching, 137, 138
touching and tactile communication, 5
toxins, 43, 62, 247
toys. *See also* food-dispensing toys
for aging cats, 284–85
with catnip, 62
enrichment and, 61
for fearful adopted cats, 262–63
homemade, 69
for kittens, 149
for a new cat, 47
playful aggression and, 155–56
pouncing behaviors and, 244–45
rotating, 68–69, 202, 245
for training, 20, 141
training. *See also* capturing; clickers
and clicker training; learning;
punishment; reinforcement
to come when called, 269
communication and, 19–20
with conditioned reinforcers, 121,
133–35, 136–37, 140–41
dos and don'ts of, 131
to "Go to Your Spot," 136
how to begin, 133–35
luring and shaping behaviors,
135–39
routine sessions, 235–36
social behaviors and, 86–87
tool kit, 134
to "Touch," 137
to use litter box, 169
trap-neuter-return (TNR) programs
definition, 254
overview of, 255–57
semi-feral cats and, 74
trapping, 43
trauma, 43, 87
treats
for administering medications,
299–300

for distraction, 152–53, 156
for dog-cat introductions, 301, 302,
303
guests and, 159, 266
nail trimming and, 158
for newly adopted cats, 262, 264,
265
petting-intolerant cats and, 157
for training, 86–87, 134, 135–36,
138–39, 141
veterinary visits and, 159, 207
visitors and, 204
trill
as "come closer" vocalization, 11
definition, 3–4
turtles in terrariums, 63

Udell, Monique, 108
ultrasonic devices, 242
University of California, Davis, 36
University of Pennsylvania, 36
upper respiratory infections, 43, 46
urinary tract infections or problems,
171, 172, 175, 278. *See also*
feline interstitial cystitis (FIC)
urination
CKD and problems with, 278
definition, 170
fear and, 147
increased, 277, 278, 279, 287
outside of the litter box (*See* house
soiling)
process of, 166, 177
standing, 167, 177, 186
urine
blood in, 52, 98, 182, 278
cleaning items soiled with, 185
pheromones in, 4, 6
urine marking
anxiety, fear, or stress and, 50,
51–52, 167–68, 183, 194, 196,
203
cleaning after, 185
males vs. females, 40–41, 168, 177
medication for, 188
olfactory communication and, 5, 6,
51–52, 169, 177